Evgeny Sveshnikov · French Defenc

ProgressinChess

Volume 20 of the ongoing series

Founded and edited by
GM Victor Korchnoi
GM Helmut Pfleger
GM Nigel Short
GM Rudolf Teschner

2007
EDITION OLMS

Evgeny Sveshnikov

C000153014

French Defence
Advance Variation

Volume 2: Advanced Course

WHITE REPERTOIRE

With a Foreword by Anatoly Karpov

2007

EDITION OLMS

THE AUTHOR: Evgeny Sveshnikov (born 1950) is an active international player who currently represents Latvia. This Russian Grandmaster is widely recognised as a great openings expert. He has worked as a trainer for the 12th FIDE World Champion Anatoly Karpov, among others. He is especially known for having developed the system with ...e5 in the Sicilian defence which now bears his name, as well as for his work on the 2 c3 system for White against the Sicilian and the Advance Variation against the French Defence.

Bibliographic Information published by Die Deutsche Bibliothek

Die Deutsche Bibliothek lists this publication in the Deutsche Nationalbibliografie; detailed bibliographic data is available in the internet at http://dnb.ddb.de.

Copyright © 2007 Edition Olms AG
Willikonerstr. 10 · CH-8618 Oetwil a.S., Switzerland
E-mail: info@edition-olms.com
Internet: www.edition-olms.com

Printed in Germany

Editor: Ken Neat
Translator: Phil Adams
Photographic Acknowledgement: Dagobert Kohlmeyer, Russian Chess House
Typesetting and Index by: Art & Satz · Ulrich Dirr, D-80331 Munich
Printed by: Druckerei Friedr. Schmücker GmbH, D-49624 Löningen
Cover: Eva König, D-22769 Hamburg

ISBN 978-3-283-00524-5

Contents

Foreword

It gives me great pleasure, for several reasons, to introduce the author of this book. In the first place, not only are we contemporaries but we also come from the same area: he comes from Cheliabinsk and I from neighbouring Zlatoust. So "Zhenya" Sveshnikov and I have known each other from childhood. We often played together in the junior teams of the Russian Federation, and then the Soviet Union. We both had the same trainer: Leonid Aronovich Gratvol, who was fanatically devoted to developing junior chess. It is perhaps thanks to him that the future grandmaster grew to love not only the work of chess analysis but also coaching, which he started relatively young. Usually, active players prefer tournament play to spending time and energy on other chess activities. Yet Evgeny Ellinovich has managed, not only to win over seventy international tournaments during his long career, but also to bring on the talents of dozens of grandmasters and masters.

Secondly I should mention the high quality of analysis of my old comrade, his conscientiousness and his basic honesty, which I came to appreciate many times in the years when Grandmaster Sveshnikov was one of my trainers during my difficult matches against Garry Kasparov.

Thirdly, I am anxious to stress that our collaboration continues in various ways. Evgeny Ellinovich helps me prepare for important events, teaches in the Anatoly Karpov School and willingly assists when I fly with colleagues to promote the game of chess in distant regions of Russia. I should add that he often does this on his own initiative as well; it is thanks to him that chess schools have revived in the Altai and South-Urals regions.

Finally I must mention his fanatical and stubborn work in researching the openings, which eventually brought him brilliant success. I recall that thirty years ago, during a USSR championship event, I said to him pityingly: "Zhenya, why do you keep torturing yourself by playing that Sicilian with ...e7–e5? Choose something simpler and you'll play much more easily!" Today I have to admit that I was wrong: he was right not to listen to me: today everybody plays the Sveshnikov Variation! And as a fellow native of the Urals, I am pleased that this system is also known as the "Cheliabinsk Variation".

Unfortunately, his monograph on the Sveshnikov Sicilian has until now remained practically the only publication by this grandmaster in the Russian language. But now finally this new theoretical work of Evgeny Sveshnikov is available. It is devoted to the popular 3. e5 system against the French Defence. Its popularity is once more largely due to its constant adoption by Sveshnikov, who has developed a fantastic feel for its nuances. It has helped him amass a plus-score (70% from over 150 games!) against such French Defence experts as Evgeny Bareev. The author believes that Black cannot equalise against the Advance Variation and to date no-one has been able to prove the contrary.

I consider this book to be a real manual, original in its conception and excellent in its execution. It not only teaches you how to play a specific variation of the French Defence, it also helps you understand many strategic ideas and their practical application in the middlegame, which for the majority of players is even more important.

A book by such an outstanding grandmaster and theoretician should prove useful to a wide readership. Club, Internet and weekend tournament players will find that Volume 1 will quickly give them a good grounding in what is really a very unpleasant (for Black) plan of attack. Masters (and even grandmasters) will find in Volume 2 a real master-class by the world expert in this variation.

Anatoly Karpov
Many-times World Champion

* * *

Evgeny Sveshnikov and Anatoly Karpov

Introduction

I have been using the 3. e5 system against the French Defence for about thirty years. How did this weapon become part of my arsenal? In the 1970s chess information was not as readily available as it is in today's computer age; it was difficult to obtain it and process it. I got into the habit of self-reliance, trusting solely my own ideas. I understood that the move 3. e5 was not objectively the strongest, but I had no desire to compete with such experienced French-specialists as, for instance, Vaganian, in the long and complex lines that arise after the main continuation 3. ♘c3. Thus I chose the 3. e5 system against the French (and similarly 2. c3 against the Sicilian) for practical reasons, since I understood that my opponents would be focusing their attention on the moves 3. ♘c3 and 3. ♘d2 which were much more popular at that time.

By the end of the 1980s I had accumulated enough theoretical and practical material on the 3. e5 system. I prepared a talk for my pupils which I ended up giving to over a thousand people. What I found interesting was this: when I tried to teach concrete variations to players of 2nd or even 1st Category, they just looked bored and remembered nothing. On the other hand, if I explained a typical idea by means of an illustrative game, they learnt it for ever. So for learning a new pattern it is best to use well-annotated games, in which the main ideas and plans of both sides can be clearly explained. When the pupil understands the general idea he can memorise the concrete variations more easily.

At the start of the 1990s I wrote a quite extensive article on 3. e5!? for *New in Chess Year Book*. The very positive response to that article prompted me to undertake the present book project, well aware that it would require not just a lot of time …

It is well known that the choice of a plan is based on the pawn structure in the centre and the dynamic placement of the pieces. In my opinion it is not very useful to talk about a particular pawn structure without placing it in the context of a concrete opening. A student who has not reached at least the minimum level of candidate master will have difficulty in assimilating such material. My teaching experience tells me that the material can be assimilated much better if it is taught in the context of an actual opening.

I decided to begin this book with an explanation of the main ideas for each side; each plan is illustrated with games and extensive commentary. Other things being equal, I have given preference to games by the players who were the first to employ a particular plan. Incidentally, most of the annotations were made without consulting a computer, and in this lies their chief merit, since all the ideas are "human". Of course, the variations were then checked later with analysis engines, to eliminate crude oversights. The computer is a valuable assistant for the technical work but in the realm of ideas it is actually, with rare exceptions, of little use.

Further on we present the reader with a series of test positions and solutions to reinforce what has been learnt. Since one of the most common themes of the Advance Variation is to blockade the centre and play against the weakened dark squares, I have included a chapter on this topic.

I wanted to write a book that would be interesting and instructive not just to ordinary players but also to candidate masters, masters and even grandmasters. The practical strength of a player and his understanding of the opening are often at different levels. It often happens that even experienced players go astray in unfamiliar positions. That is why even for them it is useful to reflect once again upon the "why", the general bases underlying the concrete variations that they have memorised.

For advanced players who have studied the first two chapters of Volume 1, I have provided in Volume 2 some reference material in tabular "Encyclopaedia" format, plus theoretically important games with light notes only – to encourage independent analysis. I have also drawn attention to what at present appear to be the most critical positions.

Chess is not just a sport – it is also an element of culture, which is why I usually begin my opening studies with a historical review. I consider it essential to pay tribute to all those who have contributed to the development of this variation, and to trace its development.

Volume 1 (Basic Course) consists of:

1) Historical overview

2) Explanation of the plans for both sides through games annotated in detail

3) A chapter on blockade

4) Test positions

After assimilating this material you can move onto a more professional study ("one step at a time").

Volume 2 (Advanced Course) consists of:

1) Theoretically important games for independent analysis

2) Encyclopaedia

3) Conclusions: the likely future development of the 3. e5 system

4) Games for further study

5) The latest theoretical developments

Naturally I hope that this two-volume work will become not only a manual for club, Internet and weekend tournament players, but will also prove a useful reference for masters and even grandmasters.

* * *

That I have been able to bring this immensely time-consuming but equally interesting work to a successful conclusion is very much due to the efforts of International Master Vladimir Barsky, whom I should like to thank sincerely here for his collaboration in the development and completion of this book project.

Symbols

Symbol	Meaning	Symbol	Meaning
♔	King	♗	Bishop
♕	Queen	♘	Knight
♖	Rook	♙	Pawn
+	Check	#	Mate
×	captures	N	new move
0–0	short castling	0–0–0	long castling
∞	unclear position	⯅⯆	compensation for the material
±	White has a slight advantage	∓	Black has a slight advantage
±	White has a clear advantage	∓	Black has a clear advantage
+−	White has a decisive advantage	−+	Black has a decisive advantage
1–0	Black resigns	0–1	White resigns
=	equal position	½–½	Draw
→	with attack	↑	with initiative
⇄	with counterplay	□	only move
!?	interesting move	?!	dubious move
!	good move	?	bad move
!!	brilliant move	??	very bad move
ICC	Internet Chess Club	ACP	Association of Chess Professionals
PCA	Professional Chess Association		
⇧	White to move	⬇	Black to move

Chapter 1

Theoretically important games for independent analysis

In computer databases there are over 25,000 games beginning with the moves 1. e4 e6 2. d4 d5 3. e5 (C02 in the classification of the Encyclopaedia of Chess Openings). To save the reader from drowning in this sea of information, I have selected about fifty games for their instructional or theoretical value. I hope that my comments (sometimes short, sometimes quite extensive) on these games will provide a sound basis for your own investigations of this opening, since it is difficult to achieve good competitive results in modern chess without carrying out your own independent analytical work.

The first part of this chapter consists of games by great figures in chess history, by world champions and by the great chess thinker David Ionovich Bronstein. Then I present games organised into thematic sections and arranged chronologically within each section. I want to stress once again that each such classification is always relative in character.

Counterplay for Black on the queenside

Game 1
N.N. – Greco
Europe 1620

1. e4 e6 2. d4 d5 3. e5 c5 4. c3
♞c6 5. ♞f3 ♗d7 6. ♗e3 c4 7. b3 b5
8. a4 a6 9. axb5 axb5 10. ♖xa8 ♕xa8
11. bxc4 dxc4 12. ♗e2 ♞ge7 13. 0–0
♞d5 14. ♗d2 ♗e7 15. ♞g5 ♗xg5

16. ♗xg5 0–0 17. ♗f3 ♞a5 18. ♗xd5
♕xd5 19. f4 ♗c6 20. ♕d2 ♞b3 21. ♕c2

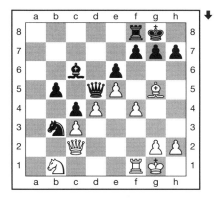

21...♞xd4 22. cxd4 ♕xd4+ 23. ♔h1 ♗e4
24. ♕c3 ♕c5 25. ♞d2 ♗d3 26. ♖c1 ♖c8
27. ♞b3 cxb3 28. ♕xc5 ♖xc5 29. ♖xc5
h6 30. ♖c3 b2 31. ♖b3 b1♕+ 32. ♖xb1
♗xb1 33. ♗e7 ♔h7 34. g4 ♗e4+ 35. ♔g1
♗f3 36. h3 h5

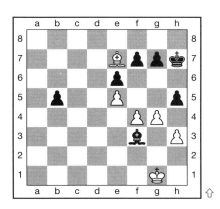

37. g5?

37. ♔f2 h×g4 38. h×g4 (38. ♔g3 g×h3
39. ♔×f3 ♔g6 40. ♗b4 ♔f5 41. ♗d2 h2
42. ♔g2 ♔e4 43. ♗×h2 ♔d3 44. ♗e1 ♔c4
45. ♔g3 b4 46. ♗d2 b3 47. ♗c1 ♔c3−+)
38...♗×g4 39. ♔e3 ♔g6 40. ♗f8 f6 41. e×f6
g×f6 42. ♔e4 ♗f5+ 43. ♔d4 ♗c2 44. ♔c3
♗d1 45. ♔d2 ♗g4 46. ♔e3 ♔f5 47. ♗d6 e5
48. f×e5 f×e5∓.

**37...♔g6 38. ♔f2 ♗d5 39. ♔e3 h4
40. ♔f2 ♔f5 41. ♔e3**

41. g6 ♔×g6 42. ♗×h4 b4 43. ♗e7 b3 44. ♗a3
♔f5 45. ♔e3 ♗g2−+.

**41...♗g2 42. ♗f8 g6 43. ♗b4 ♗×h3
44. ♗e1 ♔g4 45. ♗d2 ♗g2 46. ♔f2 h3
47. ♗c1 ♗d5 48. ♔g1 ♔g3 49. ♗e3 h2+
50. ♔f1 h1♕+**

White resigned.

Play on both wings

Cochrane – Staunton
Match, London 1841

**1. e4 e6 2. d4 d5 3. e5 c5 4. c3 ♘c6
5. f4?! ♕b6 6. ♘f3 ♘h6 7. ♗d3 ♗e7**

7...c×d4 8. c×d4 ♗d7 9. ♗c2 ♘b4 10. ♘c3
♘×c2+ 11. ♕×c2 ♘f5 12. ♕d3 h5∓.

**8. ♗c2 0–0 9. 0–0 f5 10. ♔h1 ♗d7 11. h3
♖ac8 12. a3 a5 13. ♖g1?**

13. d×c5 ♗×c5 14. b4⇄.

13...c×d4 14. c×d4 ♕c7

14...♗e8∓.

15. ♘c3 ♘a7 16. g4?!

16. ♗d3!⇄.

16...b5

(see next diagram)

16...♘b5 17. ♗d2 ♘×c3 18. b×c3 g6∓.

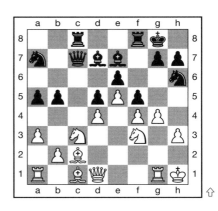

17. g×f5?

17. g5 ♘f7 18. ♗d3=.

17...b4??

17...♘×f5∓.

18. f×e6?

18. f6! ♗×f6 19. e×f6 ♖×f6 20. a×b4 a×b4
21. ♘e2+−.

18...♗×e6= 19. ♘g5?!

19. a×b4 a×b4 20. ♖a6⇄.

**19...♗×g5 20. f×g5 ♘f5∓ 21. ♗×f5 ♗×f5
22. ♘e2?**

22. a×b4.

22...♗e4+ 23. ♔h2 ♕c2

23...♖f2+ 24. ♔g3 ♕f7−+.

24. ♕e1

24. a×b4 ♖f2+ 25. ♔g3 ♖×e2 26. ♕×c2
♖e×c2 27. b×a5 ♘c6 28. ♗e3 ♖e2∓.

24...♘b5−+ 25. ♗e3 ♕d3 26. ♖g3 ♖c2

White resigned.

Development advantage for Black

Game 3
McConnell – Morphy
New Orleans 1850

Morphy provides a clear demonstration of how to play against 5. f4.

1. e4 e6 2. d4 d5 3. e5 c5 4. c3 ♘c6 5. f4?! ♛b6∓

5...c×d4 6. c×d4 ♛b6 7. ♘f3 ♘h6 8. ♘c3 ♘f5 9. ♘a4 ♛a5+ 10. ♗d2 ♗b4∓.

6. ♘f3 ♗d7 7. a3 ♘h6 8. b4 c×d4 9. c×d4 ♖c8

9...♘f5!∓ 10. ♗b2 ♖c8.

10. ♗b2

10. ♘c3! ♘×d4 11. ♛×d4 ♛×d4 12. ♘×d4 ♖×c3 13. ♗b2 ♖c8 14. ♗e2∓.

10...♘f5∓ 11. ♛d3?

11. ♛d2 ♗e7 12. ♗e2 f6!? 13. g4!? (13. 0–0 f×e5 14. f×e5 0–0±) 13...♘h6 (13...♘f×d4?!

14. ♗×d4 ♘×d4 15. ♛×d4 ♖c1+ 16. ♗d1±) 14. e×f6 g×f6 15. f5 ♘f7 16. ♘c3 ♖g8 17. f×e6 ♗×e6∞ or 12...h5! 13. 0–0 a6∓.

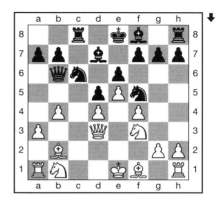

11...♗×b4+!∓ 12. a×b4?

12. ♘bd2.

12...♘×b4–+ 13. ♛d2 ♖c2 14. ♛d1 ♘e3

White resigned.

1.1 Games by World Champions

After studying the games with 3. e5 featuring World Champions, I can safely say that from the viewpoint of opening theory they contributed nothing of importance. But world champions are world champions, and it is obviously interesting to see how they handled this opening. In Volume 1 we have already seen some games by world champions; now we are going to look at a few further interesting examples.

In the following game the first World Champion did not handle the opening very well. White won only thanks to an unsound piece sacrifice by his opponent.

For and against the blockade

Game 4
Steinitz – Tinsley
London 1899

1. e4 e6 2. d4 d5 3. e5 c5 4. c3 ♘c6 5. ♘f3 f6 6. e×f6?!

Why develop the opponent's pieces for him? 6. ♗d3 or 6. ♗b5 would be better.

6...♘×f6 7. ♗d3 ♗d6 8. 0–0 0–0 9. ♖e1 ♗d7

9...♛b6⇄.

10. ♘bd2?!

10. ♘a3.

10...c×d4 11. c×d4 h6

11...♕c7∓.

12. ♘b3 ♘g4 13. ♗e3

13. h3?! ♘xf2 14. ♔xf2 ♕h4+ 15. ♔e2 (15. ♔g1 ♖xf3–+) 15...♕g3→.

13...♕f6

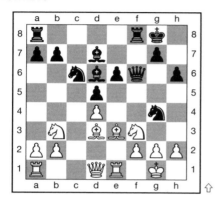

14. ♗c2

14. h3 ♘xe3 15. ♖xe3 e5 16. dxe5 ♘xe5 17. ♗b5 ♗c6 18. ♘bd4 ♘xf3+ 19. ♘xf3 (19. ♖xf3 ♕e5 20. g3 ♖xf3 21. ♘xf3 ♕xb2 22. ♗xc6 bxc6∓) 19...♕xb2 20. ♖b1 ♕f6∓ (20...♕xa2!?∞).

14...♘b4 15. ♗b1 ♖ac8 16. a3 ♗xh2+?

16...♘c6 17. ♕d3 e5!?⇄.

17. ♘xh2 ♘xe3 18. fxe3 ♕f2+ 19. ♔h1 ♘c2+

19...♗a4 20. ♕d2!±.

20. ♖e2+– ♘xe3 21. ♕d3

Black resigned.

Play on both wings

Game 5
Capablanca – Paredes
Havana (casual game) 1901

1. e4 e6 2. d4 d5 3. e5 c5 4. c3 ♘c6 5. f4?! cxd4 6. cxd4 ♕b6 7. ♘f3 ♗d7

7...♘h6! 8. ♘c3 ♘f5 9. ♘a4 ♕a5+ 10. ♔f2 b5 11. ♘c3 b4 12. ♘a4 ♗a6∓.

8. ♘c3 ♖c8 9. ♖b1 ♗b4 (9...♘h6∓) **10. ♕d3 a6** (10...♘h6) **11. a3 ♗e7 12. b4 ♘h6 13. ♗e3 ♘f5 14. ♗f2 ♘a7** (14...h5!⇄) **15. g4**

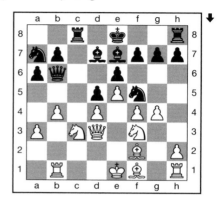

15...♘b5?

15...♘h6 16. h3 ♗b5⇄.

16. ♘a4+– ♕c7 17. gxf5 ♘xa3 18. ♕xa3 ♕c2 19. ♗d3 ♕xa4 20. ♕xa4 ♗xa4 21. ♔d2 0–0 22. f6 gxf6 23. ♗h4 ♔h8 24. ♗xf6+ ♗xf6 25. exf6 ♖g8 26. ♖hg1 h6 27. ♘e5 ♖xg1 28. ♘xf7+ ♔g8 29. ♘xh6+

Black resigned.

The future world champion played the opening very uncertainly, probably owing to his youth.

Blockading knight

Game 6
Euwe – Abdul Satar
Indonesia (simul) 1930

1. e4 e6 2. d4 d5 3. e5 c5 4. c3 ♘c6 5. ♘f3 ♗d7 6. dxc5 ♗xc5 7. ♗d3 ♕c7 8. ♕e2 ♘ge7 9. b4 ♗b6 10. 0–0 ♘g6 11. ♖e1 a5 12. b5 ♘ce7 13. a4 ♗c5 14. ♗d2 ♖d8 15. ♘a3 ♗c8 16. ♘c2 ♘f5 17. ♘cd4 ♕b6

(see next diagram)

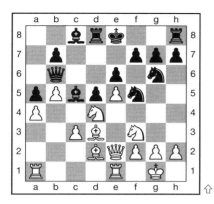

18. ♗×f5 e×f5 19. ♗g5 ♗e7 20. ♗×e7 ♘×e7 21. e6 f6 22. ♘h4 0–0 23. ♘h×f5 ♘×f5 24. ♘×f5 ♖fe8 25. ♕g4 g6 26. ♘d4 ♖d6 27. ♕f3 ♕d8 28. ♖e3 ♗×e6 29. ♖ae1 ♗f7 30. ♖×e8+ ♗×e8 31. ♕e3 ♗f7 32. ♕e7 ♕b6 33. h4 ♖d8 34. ♖e6 ♗×e6 35. ♘×e6

Black resigned.

Euwe carried out very well the idea of his predecessors – 6. d×c5 and 9. b4 followed by occupation of the d4 square. He used the same strategy in another simultaneous game: 5...h6 6. ♗d3 a6 7. d×c5 ♗×c5 8. 0–0 ♕c7 9. ♕e2 ♗d7 10. ♘bd2 ♘ge7 11. b4 ♗a7 12. ♘b3 b5 13. ♗d2 g6 14. ♘bd4 g5 15. h3 ♗b8 16. ♖fe1 ♖f8 17. a4± (Euwe–Ahmed, Indonesia (simul) 1930), although he did not succeed in converting his advantage and even went on to lose.

In the following game Alekhine failed to use this idea.

For and against the blockade

Game 7
Alekhine – A. Marshall
England (simul) 1923

1. e4 e6 2. d4 d5 3. e5 c5 4. ♘f3 ♘d7?! 5. c3 f6 6. ♗f4 ♘b6 7. ♗b5+?!

7. d×c5 ♗×c5 8. b4 ♗f8 9. ♘d4± is a strong continuation for White.

7...♗d7 8. ♗×d7+ ♕×d7 9. e×f6 ♘×f6 10. ♘e5 (10. 0–0±) **10...♕c8** (10... ♕b5!⇄) **11. a4 a5?!**

11...c×d4 12. 0–0 ♗d6 13. c×d4±.

12. ♕b3 (12.0–0±) **12...♖a6?!** (12...♘bd7±) **13. ♕b5+ ♘fd7?!**

13...♘bd7 14. ♘×d7 ♘×d7⇄.

14. 0–0 ♗d6 15. ♘g6?!

15. ♘×d7!? ♘×d7 16. ♗×d6 ♖×d6 17. ♕×a5 0–0 18. ♘d2 ♖b6⇄.

15...♗×f4 16. ♘×f4 ♘c4 17. ♖e1?

17. ♘a3 ♘×a3 18. ♖×a3 0–0 19. g3=.

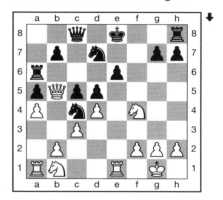

17...0–0∓ 18. ♘×e6 ♖b6 19. ♘×f8 ♖×b5 20. ♘×d7 ♖×b2–+ 21. ♘×c5 ♕f5 22. ♖f1 b6 23. ♘a6 ♕c2 24. ♘c7 ♘e3 25. ♘a3 ♕e4 26. f3 ♖×g2+ 27. ♔h1 ♕h4

White resigned. Alekhine played badly in this game and lost as a result of his mistake on move 17. On the whole he handled this variation better with the black pieces.

Play on both wings

Game 8
Nimzowitsch – Alekhine
St. Petersburg (Preliminaries) 1914

1. e4 e6 2. d4 d5 3. e5 c5 4. d×c5 ♘c6 5. ♘f3 ♗×c5 6. ♗d3 ♘ge7 7. 0–0 ♘g6

8. ♖e1 ♗d7 9. c3 ♗b6 10. ♘a3 a6
11. ♘c2 ♗c7 12. ♗xg6 hxg6 (12...fxg6!?)
13. ♗f4 ♕e7 14. ♘cd4 ♖c8 15. ♕d3 ♗b6
16. ♘xc6 ♖xc6 17. ♗e3 ♕d8 18. ♗xb6
♕xb6 19. ♘d4± ♖c4 20. b3 ♖c8 21. ♖e3
♖h5 22. ♖ae1 ♕a5 23. ♕d2 ♕a3 24. h3
♕e7 25. g4 ♖h8 26. f4 ♔d8

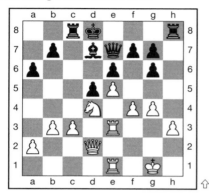

27. ♕h2

27. c4 dxc4 28. ♖c1 ♔e8 (28...g5 29. f5→)
29. ♖xc4 ♖xc4 30. bxc4 ♕c5⇄.

27...♔c7 28. f5 gxf5 29. gxf5 ♕h4
30. ♕g3 ♕h6 31. ♖f1 ♔b8 32. ♕f4
exf5 33. ♕xh6 ♖xh6 34. ♘xf5 ♖g6+
35. ♔h2 ♗xf5 36. ♖xf5 d4 37. cxd4
♖c2+= 38. ♔h1 ♖c1+

Draw.

Botvinnik only ever encountered this system
as Black and his opponents (apart from Levenfish) failed to put up serious resistance.

Counterplay by Black on the kingside

Game 9
Bondarevsky – Botvinnik
Absolute USSR Championship,
Leningrad/Moscow 1941

1. e4 e6 2. d4 d5 3. e5 c5 4. ♘f3 ♘c6
5. ♗d3 cxd4 6. 0–0 ♗c5 7. a3 ♘ge7
8. ♘bd2 ♘g6 9. ♘b3 ♗b6 10. ♖e1 ♗d7
11. g3 f6 12. ♗xg6+ hxg6 13. ♕d3 ♔f7
14. h4

Without the participation of his b-pawn – to
attack the c6-knight – White cannot establish control of the dark squares d4, e5 and
g5.

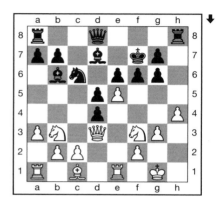

14...♕g8 15. ♗d2 ♕h7 16. ♗b4 g5!∓
17. ♕xh7 ♖xh7 18. exf6 gxf6 19. hxg5 e5
20. gxf6 ♔xf6 21. ♗d6 ♖e8 22. ♘h4 ♖g8
23. ♔h2 ♗f5 24. ♖e2 d3 25. ♖d2 dxc2
26. f4 ♗e3 27. ♗xe5+ ♘xe5 28. fxe5 ♔e7
29. ♖f1 c1♕

White resigned.

*Pawn sacrifice, Black's struggle against the
central blockade*

Game 10
Smyslov – Lisitsyn
Moscow Championship 1942

1. e4 e6 2. d4 d5 3. e5 c5 4. ♕g4

Smyslov sacrifices a pawn à la Nimzowitsch,
but does not even equalise.

4...♘c6 5. ♘f3 cxd4 6. ♗d3 ♕c7 7. 0–0
f6 8. ♗xh7 ♘xe5 9. ♘xe5 fxe5 10. ♗g6+
♔d8 11. h3 ♘f6 12. ♕d1 ♗d6

(see next diagram)

Having given up both his centre pawns and
relinquished control of the centre, White has
clearly lost the opening battle.

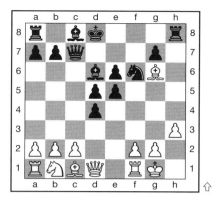

13. c3 dxc3 14. ♘xc3 ♗d7 15. a4 a6
16. ♗g5 ♗e8 17. ♗xe8 ♔xe8 18. ♖c1 ♕d7
19. f4 exf4 20. ♗xf4 ♗xf4 21. ♖xf4 ♖c8
22. ♕d3 ♔d8 23. a5 ♖e8 24. ♖ff1 ♖c6
25. b4 ♖c4 26. ♘a2 ♖xc1 27. ♘xc1 ♕d6
28. ♕b3 ♘e4 29. ♕b2 ♖f8 30. ♖xf8+
♕xf8 31. ♘d3 ♕f6 32. ♘e5 ♕f4 33. ♕d4
♕c1+ 34. ♔h2 ♕f4+ 35. ♔g1 ♕c1+
36. ♔h2 ♕c7 37. ♔g1 ♔c8 38. ♘f3 ♕c3
39. ♕xc3+ ♘xc3 40. ♔f2 ♘a2 41. ♘d4
♔d7 42. b5 axb5 43. ♘xb5 e5 44. h4
♔c6 45. ♘a7+ ♔d7 46. g4 d4 47. ♘b5
♘c3 48. ♘a3 ♔e6 49. h5 ♔d5 50. ♔e1
d3 51. g5 e4 52. h6 e3 53. ♘b1 ♘xb1
54. hxg7 d2+ 55. ♔e2 ♔d4 56. g8♕
♘c3+ 57. ♔f3 d1♕+

White resigned.

Advantage in development for Black

Game 11
Tal – Sokolsky
Vilnius 1955

1. e4 e6 2. d4 d5 3. e5 c5 4. c3 ♕b6
5. ♘f3 ♘c6 6. a3 a5 7. ♗d3 ♗d7 8. ♗c2?!

8. 0–0! cxd4 9. cxd4 ♘xd4 10. ♘xd4 ♕xd4
11. ♕e2 ⩱ (11. ♘c3 ⩱).

8...♘h6 9. 0–0

9. b3!? cxd4 10. cxd4 (10. ♗xh6 gxh6
11. cxd4 ♖g8 12. 0–0 ♖c8 13. ♕d2 ♖g4
14. ♖d1 ♘xd4 15. ♘xd4 ♖xd4 16. ♕xd4

♕xd4 17. ♖xd4 ♖xc2 18. ♖d1 ♗g7 ∓) 10...♘f5
11. ♗xf5 exf5 12. ♘c3 ♗e6 13. 0–0 ♗e7 ⇄.

9...♘f5 10. dxc5 ♗xc5 11. ♘bd2?

11. ♗xf5 exf5 12. ♘bd2 0–0 13. ♘b3 ♘xe5
14. ♘xc5 ♘xf3+ 15. ♕xf3 ♕xc5 16. ♗e3
♕b5 17. ♗d4 ⇄.

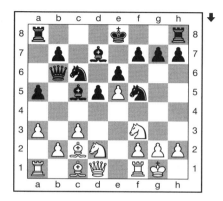

11...♗xf2+! ∓

A rare occurrence – Tal has failed to spot a
tactical shot by his opponent!

12. ♖xf2 ♘e3 13. ♕e2 ♘xc2 14. ♘c4
dxc4 15. ♕xc2 0–0–0 16. ♕e4 ♕b5
17. ♗g5 ♖df8 18. a4 ♕d5 19. ♕e3 ♘b8
20. ♖d2 ♕c6 21. ♖d6 ♕c7 22. ♘d4 h6
23. ♘b5 ♗xb5 24. axb5 ♘d7 25. b6 ♕c5
26. ♕xc5+ ♘xc5 27. ♖xa5 ♘a6 28. ♗h4
g5 29. ♗g3 ♖d8 30. ♖a4 ♖xd6 31. exd6
♔d7 32. ♖xc4 ♖c8 33. ♖xc8 ♔xc8 34. b4
♔d7 35. ♔f2 ♘b8 36. b5 f6 37. c4 e5
38. c5 ♔e6 39. ♔f3 f5 40. ♗f2 ♔d5 41. g3
e4+ 42. ♔e2 f4 43. gxf4 gxf4 44. ♗g1
♘d7 45. h3

Draw.

Petrosian played the French with Black and
inevitably came up against 3. e5. He won
three games, lost one (as a junior) and drew
seven. In his later years he preferred the
closed game resulting from ♕b6 and c4.

Pawn sacrifice by Black for the initiative

Game 12
Kholmov – Petrosian
17th USSR Championship, Moscow 1949

**1. e4 e6 2. d4 d5 3. e5 c5 4. c3 ♘c6
5. ♘f3 ♛b6 6. ♗e2 c×d4 7. c×d4 ♘ge7
8. b3 ♘f5 9. ♗b2 ♗b4+ 10. ♔f1 h5
11. ♘c3 ♗×c3 12. ♗×c3 ♗d7 13. ♛d2
a5 14. g3 h4 15. g4 ♘fe7 16. h3 f6
17. ♔g2 ♖f8 18. ♗d3 f×e5 19. ♘×e5
♘×e5 20. d×e5**

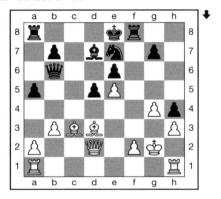

**20...d4 21. ♗×d4 ♗c6+ 22. ♔g1 ♛c7
23. ♖h2 0-0-0 24. ♗c4 ♘g6 25. ♛e3**

Draw.

Space advantage

Game 13
Tal – Petrosian
USSR Championship (Semi-final), Tbilisi 1956

**1. e4 e6 2. d4 d5 3. e5 c5 4. c3 ♘c6
5. ♘f3 ♛b6 6. a3 c4 7. ♗e2 ♗d7 8. ♘bd2
♘a5 9. 0-0 ♘e7 10. ♖b1 h6 11. ♛c2 ♛c7**
(11...♖c8⇄) **12. b3!?**

12. g3⇄ 0-0-0 13. ♖e1; 12. ♖e1⇄.

12...c×b3 13. ♘×b3 ♗a4 14. ♘fd2 ♘ec6

14...♖ac8!? 15. ♛d3 ♘×b3 16. ♘×b3 ♘f5∓.

15. ♛b2 0-0-0?! (15...♖c8) **16. ♘×a5
♘×a5**

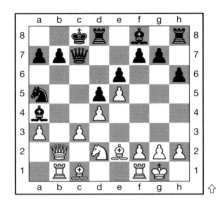

17. c4! ♗e7 18. c×d5

18. c5 ♘c6 19. ♘f3 g5 20. ♗e3±.

18...e×d5

18...♖×d5 19. ♘e4 (19.♘c4 ♘c6 20. ♗e3
♖hd8 21. ♖fc1±) 19...♗c2 20. ♘c3 ♗×b1
21. ♘×d5 e×d5 22. ♛×b1 ♔b8 23. ♗f4±.

19. ♗d1?!

19. ♗d3!? h5 20. ♘f3 (20. f4 ♖h6 21. f5
♖c6±) 20...♘c4 21. ♛e2 ♗d7 22. ♗g5±.

19...♗d7!

19...♗×d1 20. ♖×d1 ♘c4 21. ♘×c4 d×c4
22. ♗d2±.

**20. ♗c2 ♔b8 21. ♗d3 ♖c8⇄ 22. ♘b3
♘c4 23. ♛a2 ♗a4**

23...♖he8⇄.

24. ♗f5

24. ♗f4!?±.

24...♗d7 25. ♗d3 ♗a4 26. ♗f5 ♗d7

Draw. A game worthy of those two great players!

Play on both wings, counterplay by Black

Game 14
I. Zaitsev – Petrosian
37th USSR Championship, Moscow 1969

**1. e4 e6 2. d4 d5 3. e5 c5 4. c3 ♘c6
5. ♘f3 ♛b6 6. a3 c4 7. ♘bd2 ♗d7 8. ♗e2**

♘a5 9. 0–0 ♘e7 10. ♘g5 h6 11. ♘h3 0–0–0 12. ♘f4 g6 13. ♖b1 ♔b8 14. g4 ♗b5 15. ♖e1 ♘c8 16. ♗f1 ♗e7 17. h3 ♕c6 18. ♗g2 ♗a4 19. ♕e2 ♗c2

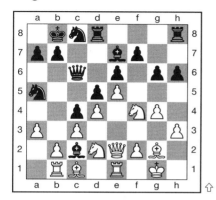

20. ♘xc4 ♗xb1 21. ♘xa5 ♕c7 22. b4 g5 23. ♘h5 ♕xc3 24. ♗d2 ♕d3 25. ♕d1 ♗c2 26. ♕c1 ♗a4 27. ♗e3 ♘b6 28. ♗f1 ♕g6 29. f4 ♖c8 30. ♕d2 ♖c2 31. ♗d3 ♖xd2 32. ♗xg6 fxg6 33. ♗xd2 gxh5

White resigned.

When the play takes place on both wings, it is quite rare for Black to win; this game is one of the exceptions.

Spassky played this variation three times against Korchnoi, but lost two games and won only one. The two final encounters in their match in St. Petersburg (1999) deserve attention, but the most interesting game played by Boris Vasilievich was with Black in Moscow 1999 against Vlastimil Hort, where in a theoretically known position he unexpectedly sacrificed the exchange.

Play on both wings

Game 15
Spassky – Korchnoi
Candidates Final, Belgrade 1977

1. d4 e6 2. e4 d5 3. e5 c5 4. c3 ♘c6 5. ♘f3 ♗d7 6. ♗e2!?

6. dxc5.

6...♘ge7 7. ♘a3 cxd4 8. cxd4 ♘f5 9. ♘c2 ♘b4

An opening tabia.

10. ♘e3

One of the possible continuations. White retains a slight advantage.

10. 0–0!? ♘xc2 11. ♕xc2 ♖c8 12. ♕d3±.

10...♘xe3 11. fxe3 ♗e7 12. a3 ♘c6 13. b4

Somewhat premature; it would be better to play 13. 0–0 0–0 14. ♗d2 f6 15. exf6 ♗xf6 16. ♗c3 ♖c8 17. ♗d3±.

13...a6

A stronger line is 13...0–0 14. 0–0 f5=.

14. ♖b1 ♘a7 15. a4 ♘c6

15...f5 16. exf6 ♗xf6 17. 0–0 0–0 18. b5 axb5 19. axb5 ♘c8 20. ♗d2±.

16. ♗d2 a5

16...0–0 17. 0–0 f5 18. exf6 ♗xf6 19. b5 axb5 20. axb5 ♘e7 21. ♗b4 ♖f7⇄.

17. b5

17. bxa5 ♘xa5 18. 0–0 ♗c6 19. ♕c2± (19. ♗b4 ♘c4 20. ♗xe7 ♕xe7 21. ♗xc4 dxc4 22. ♖a1 0–0∓).

17...♘b4 18. 0–0 0–0 19. ♕e1

19. ♖c1 ♘a2 20. ♖a1 ♘b4 21. ♕b3 ♖c8 22. ♖ac1±.

19...♔h8?!

19...♖c8 20. ♕g3 ♖c2 21. ♗d1 ♖c4 22. ♗b3 ♖c8 23. e4±.

20. ♕g3 f6 21. ♖bc1?!

Here it would better to play 21. exf6 gxf6 (21...♗xf6 22. ♘e5±) 22. ♖bc1 ♖g8 23. ♕f4 ♗e8 24. e4↑.

(see next diagram)

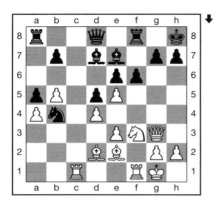

21...f5!⇄ 22. h4 ♖c8 23. h5

23. ♖xc8 ♗xc8 24. ♖c1 ♗d7 25. ♘g5⇄.

23...♖xc1 24. ♖xc1 ♘a2 25. ♖a1 ♘b4 26. ♕h3

26. ♖c1 ♘a2 27. ♖a1 ♘b4 28. ♖c1 =.

26...♗e8 27. ♔f2 (27. h6!?) **27...♕b6 28. g4**

28. ♗xb4 axb4 29. a5 ♕c7∓.

28...g5 29. hxg6 ♗xg6 30. g5= f4?! 31. exf4 ♘c2 32. ♖d1 ♗e4?!

32...♗a3 33. ♔f1 ♗e4 34. ♕h6±.

33. ♗e3

33. ♗c1!±.

33...♘xe3 34. ♔xe3 ♕c7

34...♖c8 35. ♗d3 ♖c3 36. ♔e2±;

34...♗f5 35. ♕h1 ♗e4 36. ♖g1 ♖c8 37. g6±.

35. g6! ♗xg6 36. ♕xe6 ♗a3 37. ♕xd5 ♗c1+ 38. ♔f2 ♗xf4 39. ♕c4

39. ♕c5 ♕xc5 40. dxc5 ♗xe5 41. ♖d7 h6 42. ♖xb7 ♗d4+ 43. ♔g2 ♗xc5 44. ♖c7 ♗e3 45. ♘e5±.

39...♕g7 40. ♖g1 ♕h6! 41. ♕c3

White resigned, in view of 41...♗d2 42. ♕a3 ♕h4+ 43. ♔g2 ♕f4∓.

Attack on the king

Game 16
Spassky – Korchnoi
St. Petersburg 1999

1. e4 e6 2. d4 d5 3. e5 c5 4. c3 ♘c6 5. ♘f3 ♕b6 6. a3 a5 7. ♗d3 ♗d7 8. ♗c2

Spassky repeats Paulsen's moves from one hundred and twenty years ago!

8...h5?!

This move weakens the dark squares and loses time. 8...♘h6⇄ was better.

9. 0–0 ♘h6 10. b3 ♗e7 11. ♖a2

11. dxc5?! ♗xc5 12. ♗xh6 ♖xh6 13. ♘bd2 ♗e7 14. ♕e2 g5!?↑;

11. ♗f4 cxd4 12. cxd4 ♘f5 13. ♗xf5 exf5 14. ♘c3 ♗e6 15. h4±.

11...cxd4 12. cxd4 ♖c8 13. ♗xh6?!

13. ♖e1.

13...♖xh6 14. ♕d2 ♖h8

14...h4∓.

15. h4 ♔f8 16. ♕f4 ♔g8 17. ♘bd2 g6 18. ♖d1 ♔g7 19. ♘f1 ♘a7 20. ♘g5 ♗e8 21. ♖d3 ♘b5∓

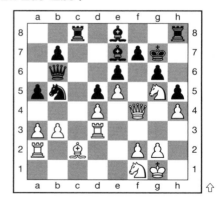

22. ♗d1 ♖c3

Untypical of Korchnoi – he declines an of-fered pawn. But 22...♘xa3!? came into con-sideration, e. g. 23. ♖f3 ♗xg5 24. hxg5 ♘b5 25. ♖d2 ♖c1∓.

23. ♖ad2 ♕c7?!

23...♖×d3 24. ♖×d3 ♞×a3∓.

24. a4! ♖×d3 25. ♖×d3 ♞c3 26. ♞g3 ♞×d1 27. ♖×d1 ♕b6

27...♕c3 28. ♖c1 ♗×g5 29. h×g5 ♕×b3 30. ♕f6+ ♔g8 31. ♞f5!+− g×f5 (31...e×f5 32. e6 ♕c4 33. ♖×c4 d×c4 34. d5+−) 32. g6 ♕×a4 33. g×f7+ ♗×f7 34. ♖c8+ ♗e8 35. ♕×e6+ ♔g7 36. ♖c7++−.

28. ♖d3 ♕c7

28...♖f8? 29. ♞×h5+! g×h5 30. ♖g3 ♔h8 31. ♞e4 ♔h7 32. ♞f6+ ♗×f6 33. e×f6 ♖g8 34. ♖×g8 ♔×g8 35. ♕g5+ ♔f8 36. ♕g7#.

29. ♖f3 ♗d8 30. ♞e2 ♕e7 31. ♕c1

31. ♞g3 b6 32. ♔h2↑.

31...♕b4 32. ♞f4 ♗×g5□ 33. h×g5 ♗c6□ 34. ♕e3 ♖c8 35. ♔h2 ♗e8 36. ♞d3 ♕×b3 37. ♕f4 ♕×a4 38. ♕f6++− ♔g8

38...♔h7 39. ♞f4! ♕b4 40. ♞×h5 ♕f8 41. ♞f4 ♕g7 42. ♕e7 ♗c6 43. ♞h5+−.

39. ♞f4 ♔h7 40. ♞×e6

Black resigned.

Pawn sacrifice to gain a blockading knight

Game 17
Spassky – Korchnoi
St. Petersburg 1999

1. e4 e6 2. d4 d5 3. e5 c5 4. c3 ♞c6 5. ♞f3 ♕b6 6. a3 a5 7. ♗d3 ♗d7 8. ♗c2 h5?! 9. 0–0 ♞h6 10. ♖a2 ♗e7 11. ♗e3 ♞f5 12. ♗×f5 e×f5 13. d×c5 ♗×c5 14. ♗×c5 ♕×c5 15. a4

15. b3!? ♗e6 16. ♖d2±.

15...♗e6 16. ♞d4 (16. ♖a3±) **16...♞×e5 17. ♞d2?!** (17. ♖e1 ⯑) **17...♞g4 18. ♖e1 ♕d6 19. ♞2f3 0–0 20. h3 ♞f6**

(see next diagram)

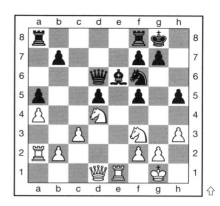

21. ♞×e6?!

With 21. ♞b5 ♕c5 22. ♞fd4 ⇄ White would gain enough compensation for the pawn.

21...f×e6 22. ♕d4 ♖ac8 23. ♞e5 ♞d7 24. ♞×d7 ♕×d7∓ 25. b3 ♕c6 26. ♖c2 ♖f6 27. ♖e5 ♕c5 28. ♕d3 ♕b6 29. c4 ♕a6 30. ♕d2

30. ♕e2!? ⇄.

30...♕d6 31. f4?!

Better was 31. ♕e2 d×c4∓.

31...♕b6+ 32. ♖e3 d×c4 33. b×c4 ♖d8 34. ♕f2 ♖d1+ 35. ♔h2 ♕b1 ∓ 36. ♖b2?!

36. g3 h4!−+.

36...♖h1+− + 37. ♔g3 ♖g6+ 38. ♔h4 ♕d1 39. ♕e2 ♕d8+ 40. ♔×h5 ♖h6#

For and against the blockade

Game 18
Hort – Spassky
Petrosian Memorial, Moscow 1999

1. e4 c5 2. c3 e6 3. d4 d5 4. e5 ♞c6 5. ♞f3 ♕b6 6. ♗e2 ♞h6 7. ♗×h6 g×h6 8. ♕d2 ♗g7 9. 0–0 ♗d7 10. ♞a3 0–0 11. ♞c2 c×d4 12. c×d4 f6 13. e×f6 ♖×f6 14. b4

(see next diagram)

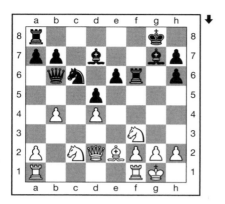

14...Ξxf3!? 15. ♗xf3 ♘xd4 16. ♘xd4 ♛xd4 17. ♛xd4 ♗xd4 18. Ξac1 ♗b6 19. g3 ♔g7 20. Ξfe1 ♔f6 21. Ξc3 Ξg8 22. ♔g2 ♗c6 23. Ξc2 a6 24. Ξce2 ♗d7 25. Ξc2 ♗c6 26. Ξce2 ♗d7±

Draw.

Kasparov played the Advance Variation with White twice in simuls against weak opponents and won both games.

Attack on the king

Game 19
Kasparov – Klimczok
Katowice (simul) 1993

1. e4 e6 2. d4 d5 3. e5 c5 4. c3 ♘c6 5. ♘f3 ♗d7 6. ♗e2 cxd4 7. cxd4 ♘ge7 8. ♘c3 ♘f5 9. 0-0 ♗e7 10. g4 ♘h4 11. ♘xh4 ♗xh4 12. ♗e3 0-0? 13. f4 h6 14. ♛d2 Ξc8 15. ♔h1 ♗e7 16. f5 ♗g5

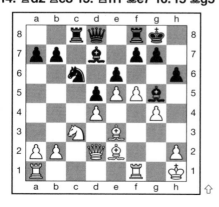

17. f6 gxf6 18. ♗xg5 fxg5 19. Ξf6+–

Blockade of a wing!

19...♔g7 20. Ξaf1 ♘e7 21. h4

Black resigned.

Play on the dark squares

Game 20
Khalifman – Dolmatov
19th EU-Cup, Rethymnon 2003

1. e4 e6 2. d4 d5 3. e5 c5 4. c3 ♘c6 5. ♘f3 ♛b6 6. a3 ♘h6 7. b4 cxd4 8. cxd4 ♘f5 9. ♗b2 ♗e7 10. ♗d3!?

One of White's best plans: to abstain from h2-h4 and instead prepare an exchange on f5, followed by play on the dark squares.

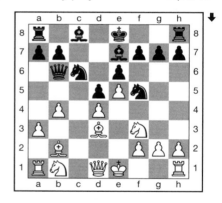

10...♗d7 11. 0-0 Ξc8 12. ♘bd2 g5

A tactically interesting moment – it is not good for Black to take the d4 pawn, since he would then lose the g7 pawn: 12...♘fxd4?! 13. ♘xd4 ♘xd4 14. ♛g4 ♘f5 15. ♗xf5 exf5 16. ♛xg7 Ξf8

A) 17. Ξac1 ♛g6 18. e6 fxe6 19. Ξxc8+ ♗xc8 20. Ξc1 ♗d7 21. ♛e5

A1) 21...f4 22. ♘f3 (22. ♛b8+ ♗d8⇄) 22...Ξg8 23. ♛b8+ ♗d8 24. g3 fxg3 25. hxg3 ♛d3 26. ♗f6 Ξxg3+ 27. ♛xg3 ♗xf6 28. Ξc7±;

A2) 21...♗f6 22. ♕b8+ ♔e7 23. ♗xf6+ ♕xf6 24. ♕xb7 ♕b2⇄;
B) 17. e6! fxe6 18. ♖ac1! ♖xc1 19. ♖xc1 a5 20. ♗d4 ♕a6 21. ♘f3 axb4 22. ♘e5!±.

13. ♘b3± h5
13...g4 14. ♘fd2 h5 (14...g3 15. hxg3 ♘fxd4 16. ♘xd4 ♘xd4 17. ♕g4 ♘f5 18. ♗xf5 exf5 19. ♕g7 ♖f8 20. e6!±) 15. ♗xf5 exf5 16. ♘c5±.

14. ♖c1 g4 15. ♘e1 a5 16. ♗xf5 exf5 17. ♘d3 axb4 18. ♘bc5

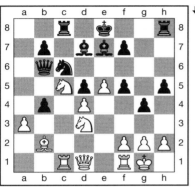

18...♗e6

18...bxa3 19. ♗xa3 ♘xd4 20. ♘f4!±.

19. axb4 ♕b5 20. ♘f4 ♖h6 21. ♗c3!± ♗g5 22. ♗d2 ♗xf4 23. ♗xf4 ♖g6 24. ♗e3 ♖g8 25. ♖e1 ♘e7 26. ♕d2 h4 27. ♗g5 h3 28. ♗xe7 ♔xe7 29. ♕h6 ♖c6 30. ♕f6+ ♔e8 31. ♖a1

Black resigned.

As we can see, the World Champions had mixed results with this system; you only have recall Steinitz and Alekhine. More deserving of attention are the games in which Euwe used the plan of giving up the white pawn centre; he played very logically and methodically to gain an advantage. The games between Spassky and Korchnoi and the Hort – Spassky game are interesting. The games in which the World Champions played Black deserve greater attention, especially those by Botvinnik and Petrosian.

1.2 Master games

David Ionovich Bronstein did not often play this system but, in contrast to the games of the World Champions, his games were brimming with new ideas. Bronstein's play was very creative, packed full of originality, whereas World Champions are concerned mainly with their competitive results. We can say that they are the champions, but Bronstein was a creator.

Generally the creators of new opening systems, the "chess researchers" are considered inferior to the champions, since the chess public is more interested in outstanding results than in theory. Theoreticians are never regarded as being on the same level as champions, even though it is precisely the former who educate the chess world.

Theory is extremely important in any field of knowledge, but chess players have never set themselves the goal of discovering the best moves in the initial position of the game.

Advantage in development,
attack on the king

Game 21
Bronstein – Kärner
Tallinn 1981

1. e4 e6 2. d4 d5 3. e5 ♗d7!? 4. ♘f3!? a6 5. ♗g5 ♕c8? 6. c4 h6 7. ♗e3 dxc4 8. ♗xc4 ♘e7 9. ♘c3 ♗c6 10. 0-0 ♕d7 11. ♖c1 a5 12. d5 exd5 13. ♗d3 ♘a6 14. a3 g6 15. e6 ♕xe6 16. ♗d4 f6

(see next diagram)

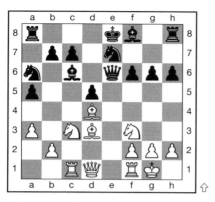

17. ♗×g6+! ♔d8 18. ♖e1 ♕d6 19. ♗f7 ♗g7 20. ♖e6 ♕d7 21. ♗×f6 ♗×f6 22. ♖×f6,

and Black resigned.

Space advantage, blockade

Game 22

Bronstein – Borges Mateos
Rubinstein Memorial,
Polanica Zdrój 1988

1. e4 e6 2. d4 d5 3. e5 c5 4. c3 ♘c6 5. ♘f3 ♕b6 6. ♗e2 c×d4 7. c×d4 ♘ge7 8. ♘a3 ♘f5 9. ♘c2 ♗b4+ 10. ♔f1 ♗e7 11. h4 f6?!

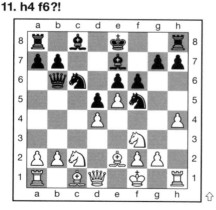

12. g4! ♘f×d4 13. ♘c×d4 f×e5 14. ♘×c6 b×c6 15. ♘×e5 0–0 16. f4 ♗d6?

16...♗f6±.

17. ♘c4!+– ♕c7 18. ♘×d6 ♕×d6 19. ♔g2

Black resigned.

For and against the blockade

Game 23

Bronstein – Roos
Hastings 1993/94

1.e4 e6 2. d4 d5 3. e5 c5 4. c3 ♘c6 5. ♘f3 ♕b6 6. a3 c4 7. ♘bd2 f6 8. b3 f×e5 9. ♘×e5 ♘×e5 10. d×e5

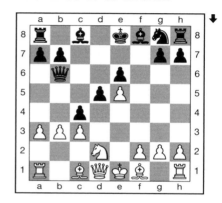

10...♗c5?!

10...♘h6!? 11. b×c4 ♗c5 12. ♕h5+ ♘f7 13. ♖b1 (13. ♕e2 0–0 14. ♖b1 ♕a5∞) 13...♗×f2+ 14. ♔d1 ♕e3 15. c×d5 0–0 (15...e×d5 16. ♘f3 ♕×c3 17. ♗d2 ♕c6 18. ♗b5 g6 19. ♖f1 g×h5 20. ♖×f2±) 16. ♕e2±.

11. ♕h5+ g6 12. ♕h4 ♕c7 13. ♘f3 ♘e7 14. b4 ♘f5 15. ♕h3 ♗e7 16. ♗e2 0–0 17. g4 ♘g7 18. ♕g3

18. 0–0±.

18...a5 19. b5 a4 20. h4 ♗d7 21. ♘d4 ♗c5 22. h5 ♗×d4 23. c×d4 g×h5 24. ♖b1 ♔h8 25. ♗g5 ♗e8 26. ♗f6 ♗g6 27. b6 ♕d7 28. ♖c1 h×g4 29. ♗×g4 ♔g8 30. ♕h3 ♖ae8 31. ♔d2 ♕b5 32. ♕c3 ♕×b6 33. ♖h3 ♕b3 34. ♕a1 ♕b6 35. ♕c3 ♖a8 36. ♖g1 ♖a5 37. ♗d1 ♖b5 38. ♖×h7 ♔×h7 39. ♖×g6 ♔×g6 40. ♕g3+ ♔f5 41. ♕g4#

* * *

Advantage in development

Game 24
I. Zaitsev – Doda
Riga 1968

**1. e4 c5 2. ♘f3 e6 3. c3 d5 4. e5 ♗d7
5. d4 ♕b6 6. ♗e2 ♗b5 7. c4!? ♗xc4
8. ♗xc4 dxc4 9. d5 exd5 10. ♕xd5 ♘e7
11. ♕e4**

11. ♕xc4.

11...♘d7

11...♕c6! 12. ♕xc4 ♘d7 13. ♘c3±.

**12. 0–0 ♕c6 13. ♕xc4 ♘b6 14. ♕e2
♘ed5?!**

14...♘g6 15. ♘c3±.

15. a4 ♗e7 16. a5 ♘d7 17. ♖d1±

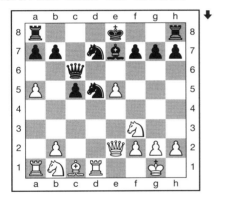

17...♘f8 18. a6 b6

18...♘e6.

19. ♗g5

19. ♘c3 ♘xc3 20. bxc3±.

19...♘g6?

19...♗xg5 20. ♘xg5 ♘f4 21. ♕f3 ♕xf3
22. ♘xf3±.

**20. ♘c3 ♘xc3 21. bxc3± 0–0 22. ♗xe7
♘xe7 23. ♖d6 ♕c8 24. ♖ad1 ♘f5
25. ♖6d2 ♕c6 26. ♕d3 g6 27. ♘g5 ♖fe8
28. f4 ♔g7 29. ♕d7 ♕xd7 30. ♖xd7+–
♖e7 31. ♖xe7 ♘xe7 32. ♖d7 h6 33. ♘e6+
fxe6 34. ♖xe7+ ♔f8 35. ♖xe6 ♔f7**

**36. ♖f6+ ♔g7 37. ♖d6 ♔f7 38. g4 b5
39. f5 gxf5 40. gxf5 b4 41. cxb4 cxb4
42. ♖d7+ ♔e8 43. e6**

Black resigned.

*Pawn sacrifice for the initiative, play on both
wings*

Game 25
I. Zaitsev – Savon
Dubna 1976

**1. e4 e6 2. d4 d5 3. e5 c5 4. c3 ♘c6
5. ♘f3 ♕b6 6. a3 c4 7. ♘bd2 ♘a5 8. g3
♗d7 9. ♗h3 ♘e7 10. 0–0 h6 11. ♘h4
0–0–0**

11...g5!? 12. ♘g2 h5

A) 13. ♘e3 g4 14. ♗g2 0–0–0 15. f4⇄ (15. f3
♗h6);

B) 13. g4 hxg4 14. ♗xg4 0–0–0 15. ♕f3 ♗e8
16. ♘e3⇄.

**12. ♘g2 ♔b8 13. ♖b1 ♕c7 14. ♘e3 ♘c8
15. f4 g6**

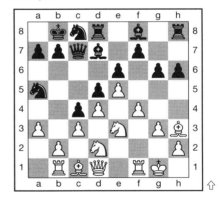

16. f5!?

16. ♘g4 ♗e7 17. ♗g2 ♘b6 18. ♕e2 ♗a4
19. ♘f3 ♘d7⇄.

**16...gxf5 17. g4 fxg4 18. ♘xg4 ♗e8
19. ♘f6± ♗c6 20. ♖f2 ♘e7 21. ♘f1 ♘b3
22. ♗e3 ♘g8 23. ♘h5 ♗e8 24. ♘fg3 ♘e7
25. ♘f6 ♗a4 26. ♕h5 ♘c8 27. ♖bf1 ♘a5
28. ♕e2 ♗e7 29. ♘fh5 ♗e8 30. ♘g7±**

♗g5 31. ♘3h5 ♕b6 32. ♗×g5 h×g5
33. ♖g2 ♘c6 34. ♖×g5 ♘8e7 35. ♗g4
♘f5 36. ♗×f5 e×f5 37. ♘f6 ♘×d4
38. c×d4 ♕×d4+ 39. ♕f2 ♕×f2+ 40. ♖×f2
♗c6 41. ♘×f5

Black resigned.

Pawn sacrifice for the initiative

Game 26
I. Zaitsev – Lempert
Moscow 1994

**1. e4 e6 2. d4 d5 3. e5 c5 4. c3 ♘c6
5. ♘f3 ♕b6 6. a3 a5!? 7. ♗d3 ♗d7 8. 0–0
c×d4 9. c×d4 ♘×d4 10. ♘×d4 ♕×d4
11. ♘c3**

11. ♕e2 ♕b6 12. ♘c3 ♗c5! 13. ♗d2 a4!
14. ♘b5 ♘e7 15. ♖ac1 ♗×b5 16. ♗×b5+ ♘c6
17. ♗×c6+ b×c6 18. ♕g4 ♗f8! 19. ♖c2 c5∓
(Halasz – Soreghy, corr. 1970).

11...♘e7

11...♖c8 12. ♕e2 ♘e7 13. ♔h1 ♕h4!? 14. f4
♘f5! 15. ♗×f5 e×f5 16. ♘×d5 ♗c5 17. ♗e3
0–0± (Velimirović – Ivkov, Titograd 1965);

11...♕b6 12. ♕g4 f5 13. e×f6?! (13. ♕g3⯑)
13...♘×f6 14. ♕g3 ♗e7! 15. ♕×g7 ♖g8
16. ♕h6 ♕d4 17. ♖d1 ♕g4 18. ♗f1 ♖g6
19. ♕f4 ♕h5 20. ♗e2 ♕h3 21. ♕f3 e5!∓
(Steinberg – Shilov, 35th USSR Championship, Kharkov 1967);

11...♘h6 12. ♘b5 ♕×e5 13. ♖e1 ♕b8 14. ♕f3
♗d6 15. ♘×d6+ ♕×d6 16. ♗f4 ♕e7 17. ♕g3
f6. Draw (I. Zaitsev – Geller, Moscow 1982).

12. ♘b5

12. ♔h1!? with the idea f2–f4; 12. ♖e1!? ♘g6
13. ♘b5 ♕b6 14. ♗e3 ♕d8 15. ♗d4 ♗e7
16. ♘d6+ ♗×d6 17. e×d6 0–0 18. ♖c1 ♖c8
19. ♖×c8 ♕×c8 20. ♕d2⯑.

**12...♕×e5 13. ♖e1 ♕b8 14. ♕f3 ♗×b5!
15. ♗×b5+ ♘c6 16. ♕×d5**

(see next diagram)

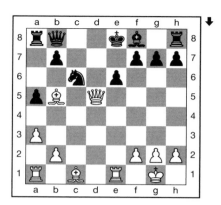

16...♕d6!

16...♗d6?! 17. ♗×c6+ b×c6 18. ♕×c6+ ♔e7
19. ♗g5+ f6 20. ♗h4 ♖e8 21. ♖ad1 ♕c7
22. ♕d5 ♗×h2+ 23. ♔h1 ♔f8 24. ♕h5 ♗e5
25. ♕×h7 ♔f7 26. ♕h5+ ♔g8 27. ♖d3±
(Reefat – Rahman, Calcutta 1994).

17. ♕c4!

17. ♕×d6? ♗×d6∓.

17...♗e7

17...♕c5 18. ♕a4.

**18. ♗f4 ♕c5 19. ♕×c5 ♗×c5 20. ♖ac1
♗d4! 21. ♖×c6! b×c6 22. ♗×c6+ ♔e7
23. ♗×a8 ♖×a8= 24. ♗e5 ♗×e5**

Draw.

This game leaves the impression that, even
with the inclusion of the moves a2–a3 and
a7–a5, Black can take the d4 pawn. (See
also Shirov – Anand, Teheran 2000, Volume
1, game 22 on page 44).

Pawn sacrifice for the initiative

Game 27
Sveshnikov – Vysochin
Yugoslav League 1998

**1. e4 e6 2. d4 d5 3. e5 c5 4. c3 ♕b6
5. ♘f3 ♗d7 6. a3 ♗b5 7. c4?! d×c4!?
8. ♘c3**

8. d5!? e×d5 9. ♕×d5 ♘e7 10. ♕e4∞.

8...♘c6 9. d5 0–0–0!

This game show that Black has a good position in this line. Hence it is possibly better

for White to play 7. b4±. Despite winning this game, after this I started playing 7. b4.

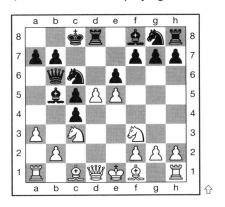

10. d6

10. ♕c2 e×d5 11. ♕f5+ ♔b8 12. ♕×f7 ♘ge7∓.

10...f6 11. ♘×b5 ♕×b5 12. ♕c2 ♘×e5 13. ♘×e5 fxe5 14. ♗×c4 ♕c6☐ 15. ♗×e6+ ♔b8 16. 0–0

16. ♗×g8? ♕×g2∓.

16...♘f6! 17. ♗e3

17. ♗g5 ♖×d6 18. ♗f5⯑.

17...♗×d6 18. b4

18. ♖ac1∞.

18...e4 19. ♗h3 ♗e5 20. ♖ac1

20. ♖ab1 ♗d4 21. b×c5 ♗×e3 22. f×e3 ♖d5! (22...♖d3 23. ♖b4 ♖hd8 24. ♖fb1 ♖d2 25. ♕b3±) 23. ♖fc1 ♖hd8∓.

20...♗d4!?

20...c×b4! 21. ♕×c6 b×c6 22. a×b4 ♘d5 23. ♖×c6 ♘×e3 24. f×e3=.

21. ♕e2 ♗×e3 22. ♕×e3 c4 23. ♕g3+ ♔a8 24. ♕×g7 ♘d5?!

(see next diagram)

24...♖hg8 25. ♕f7±.

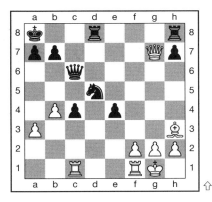

25. ♕g4! e3?!

25...♖hf8 26. ♕×e4 ♘f4 27. ♕×c6 ♘×h3+ 28. g×h3 b×c6 29. ♖×c4±;

25...♖he8 26. ♖fe1 e3 27. ♕×c4 e×f2+ 28. ♔×f2 ♕f6+ 29. ♔g1 ♖×e1+ 30. ♖×e1 ♘f4⯑ 31. ♗d7!± (31. ♗g4? ♘d3∓).

26. ♕×c4 ♕×c4 27. ♖×c4 e2 28. ♖e1± ♖he8

28...♘f4 29. ♗g4!± h5 30. ♖×f4 h×g4 31. ♖e4 ♖d3 32. ♖e3+−.

29. f3 b5 30. ♖d4 ♘c3 31. ♗d7!

31. ♖×d8+ ♖×d8 32. ♗f5 h5 33. g4±.

31...♔b8 32. ♖d3 a6 33. ♖×c3 ♖×d7 34. ♔f2 ♖d2 35. g4+− ♔b7 36. g5 ♔b6 37. h4 a5 38. b×a5+ ♔×a5 39. ♖c7 ♔a4 40. ♖×h7 ♔×a3 41. g6 b4 42. ♖a7+ ♔b2 43. g7 b3 44. h5 ♔c3 45. ♖c7+ ♔b4 46. h6 b2 47. ♖b7+

Black resigned.

Pawn sacrifice for the initiative

Game 28
Circenis – Katishonok
Latvia 2001

1. e4 e6 2. d4 d5 3. e5 c5 4. c3 ♕b6 5. ♘f3 ♘c6 6. a3 c4 7. ♘bd2 ♘a5 8. b4!? (Keres) 8...c×b3 9. ♗b2 ♗d7 10. c4 ♗a4 11. ♖c1 ♘e7 12. c5 ♕d8 13. ♗d3 ♘g6 14. g3 ♗e7 15. ♕e2 a6 16. h4 h6 17. h5 ♘f8 18. ♘h4 ♕d7 19. f4 ♘h7 20. ♕g4 0–0–0 21. ♗c3 ♕c7 22. ♕e2 ♔b8

(see next diagram)

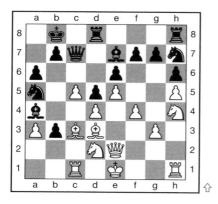

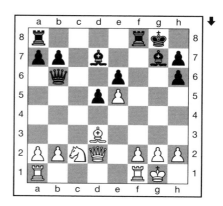

23. ♗×a6 ♗×h4 24. ♖×h4 f6 25. ♗b5 ♗×b5□ 26. ♕×b5 ♘c6 27. ♘×b3‡ f×e5 28. d×e5 d4 29. ♗a5 ♘×a5 30. ♘×a5 ♖d5 31. ♖h2 d3 32. ♖b2 d2+ 33. ♖×d2 ♖×d2 34. ♔×d2 ♖d8+ 35. ♔e3 ♖d5 36. ♘b3+– ♘g5 37. ♕e8+ ♖d8 38. ♕g6 ♕c6 39. f×g5 ♕d5 40. ♕c2

Black resigned. That is how chess is played in Latvia!

Pawn sacrifice for the initiative, blockading knight

Game 29
Sveshnikov – Filipenko
Cheliabinsk 1975

By means of a pawn sacrifice I succeeded in taking the initiative and starting an attack on the kingside. An important role was played by the blockading knight on d4. Black never had time to dislodge the knight from its blockading square.

1. e4 c5 2. c3 e6 3. d4 d5 4. e5 ♘c6 5. ♘f3 ♕b6 6. ♗e2 ♘h6 7. ♗×h6 g×h6

7...♕×b2 8. ♗c1 ♕×a1 9. ♕c2 c×d4 10. ♘fd2 d×c3 11. ♘b3 ♘b4 12. ♘×a1 ♘c2+ 13. ♘×c2 ♗d7 14. ♘×c3 ♖c8 15. ♔d2∞.

8. ♕d2 ♗d7 (8...♗g7 9. ♘a3) **9. 0–0 ♗g7 10. ♘a3 0–0 11. ♘c2 c×d4 12. c×d4 f6 13. ♗d3 f×e5 14. ♘×e5 ♘×e5 15. d×e5**

15...♕×b2?!

15...♗×e5! 16. ♕×h6 ♖f7 17. ♖ae1 ♕×b2 18. ♕g5+ ♗g7 19. ♕h5 h6‡; 15...♖f7‡.

16. f4 ♖ac8 17. ♖ab1 ♕c3 18. ♕e3 b6

18...b5 19. ♖f3.

19. ♘d4 ♕c5

19...♖c4? 20. ♘e2±.

20. ♗a6 ♕c3 21. ♗d3 ♕c5 22. g4!?→ (22. ♗b5±) **22...♕e7 23. ♖f3 ♔h8?!**

23...h5!? 24. g5 h6 25. ♖g3⇄.

24. ♔h1 ♖g8? (24...♖c3) **25. ♖e1 ♖ce8 26. ♖h3 ♗f8 27. ♖g1 ♕b4**

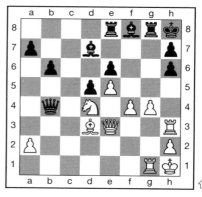

Black has an extra pawn but when you look at the position, it seems that White is the one with more pawns! This is not entirely an optical illusion - White controls a lot more squares.

28. g5!?

28. f5 exf5 29. gxf5 Rxg1+ 30. Kxg1 Bc5
31. Rh4 Bxd4 32. Rxd4 Qb2 33. e6 Rg8+
34. Kf1 Qxh2 35. exd7 Qh1+ 36. Ke2 Rg2+
37. Qf2 Rxf2+ 38. Kxf2 Qh2+ 39. Kf3 Qh1+
(39...Qd6 40. Bb5 Kg7 41. Bc6±) 40. Ke3
Qg1+ 41. Kf3 Qh1+=.

28...Bc5 29. Rxh6 Rg7 30. Qh3+– Ree7

30...Qxd4 31. Rxh7+ Kg8 32. Rxg7+ Kxg7
33. Qh7+ Kf8 34. Qh8+ Kf7 35. g6+ Ke7
36. Qf6#.

31. Bxh7! Rxh7 32. g6

Black resigned.

Pawn sacrifice to establish a blockade

Game 30
Dür – Damjanović
Graz 1979

This variation is one of White's most serious
tries for advantage.

**1. e4 c5 2. c3 e6 3. d4 d5 4. e5 Nc6
5. Nf3 Qb6 6. a3 Bd7 7. b4 cxd4
8. cxd4 Rc8 9. Bb2 Nh6 10. Nc3 Na5
11. Na4 Qc6 12. Rc1 Nc4 13. Bxc4 dxc4
14. Nc3**

The critical position. It is not easy for Black
to equalise.

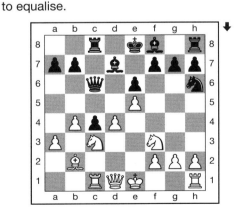

**14...Be7 15. 0–0 0–0 16. d5 exd5
17. Nd4 Qg6 18. Nxd5 Bg5 19. f4± Bd8
20. Qe2**

20. Ne3!? Nf5 21. Ndxf5 Bxf5 22. Bd4
Bd3⇄.

**20...Bf5 21. Nxf5 Nxf5 22. Kh1 b5
23. Rcd1 h5 24. Bc3 Re8 25. Qf3**

Draw.

Pawn sacrifice to establish a blockade

Game 31
Olesen – Whiteley
Newcastle upon Tyne 1995

**1. e4 e6 2. d4 d5 3. e5 c5 4. c3 Nc6
5. Nf3 Qb6 6. a3 cxd4 7. cxd4 Bd7
8. b4 Rc8 9. Bb2 Nh6 10. Nc3 Na5
11. Na4 Qc6 12. Rc1 Nc4 13. Bxc4 dxc4
14. Nc3 b5 15. 0–0 Qb7**

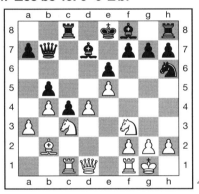

**16. d5 exd5 17. Nd4⯐ Be7 18. Qf3 Bc6
19. Nxc6 Qxc6 20. Nxd5 Bg5 21. Rcd1
0–0 22. Qg3 Qg6 23. Nc3**

23. f4 Bd8 24. Qh3 Nf5 25. Kh1±
(25. Bd4±).

23...Nf5 24. Qh3

Draw.

For and against the blockade

Game 32
I. Zaitsev – Laine
Heart of Finland Open, Jyväskylä 1994

**1. e4 e6 2. d4 d5 3. e5 c5 4. c3 Nc6
5. Nf3 Qb6 6. a3 Bd7 7. b4 cxd4 8. cxd4
Rc8 9. Be3 Nh6 10. Bd3 Ng4 11. 0–0**

♘xe3 12. fxe3 g6 13. ♕e1 ♗g7 14. ♘c3 ♘b8 15. ♔h1 (15. ♖c1±) 15...0–0 16. e4!±

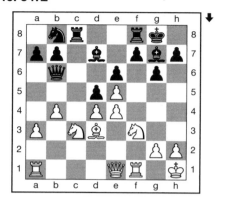

16...f6 17. exd5 fxe5 18. dxe5+– exd5 19. ♘xd5 ♕e6 20. ♕e4 ♔h8 21. b5! ♖c5 22. ♘f4 ♕g4 23. ♘h4! ♗f5 24. ♘xf5 (24. ♕b4+–) 24...gxf5 25. ♕xb7 ♖xe5 26. ♖ac1 ♕h4 27. g3 ♕d8 28. ♖c7

Black resigned.

For and against the blockade

Game 33
Cherniaev – Korniukhin
Vladivostok 1995

This game is interesting in that it shows that this variation does not bring White any advantage.

1. e4 e6 2. d4 d5 3. e5 c5 4. c3 ♘c6 5. ♘f3 ♕b6 6. a3 c4 7. ♘bd2 f6 8. b3 fxe5 9. bxc4?!

According to Bronstein it is better to play 9. ♘xe5.

9...e4 10. ♘g5 ♘f6 11. f3?!

11. ♖b1 ♕c7 12. g3 h6 13. ♘h3 g5↑;

11. ♗e2 ♕a5 12. ♗b2 ♗d6 13. ♗h5+ ♔e7!±.

11...♕a5?! (11...e3∓) **12. ♕c2!?**

(see next diagram)

12. ♘b3 ♕xc3+ 13. ♗d2 ♕b2 14. ♗c1 ♕c3+ 15. ♗d2=.

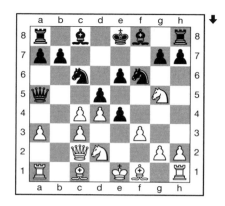

12...♘xd4?!

12...h6!? 13. ♘h3 ♗d6 14. fxe4 0–0!? (14...♘xe4 15. c5 ♗c7 16. ♘xe4 dxe4 17. ♗d2±) 15. e5 ♘xe5! 16. dxe5 ♗xe5⩱

17. ♗b2 ♗d7 18. ♘f3 ♗a4 19. ♕d3 ♗d6 20. ♗e2 e5⇄.

13. cxd4+– e3 14. c5 ♗d7 15. ♗d3 exd2+ 16. ♗xd2 ♕a4 17. ♕b2

Black resigned.

For and against the blockade

Game 34
McShane – Gdański
4th IECC, Istanbul 2003

1. e4 e6 2. d4 d5 3. e5 c5 4. c3 ♘c6 5. ♘f3 ♕b6 6. ♗e2 ♘h6 7. ♗xh6 gxh6 8. ♕d2 ♗g7 9. 0–0 0–0 10. ♘a3 cxd4 11. cxd4 f6 12. exf6 ♖xf6 13. ♘c2 ♗d7 14. b4

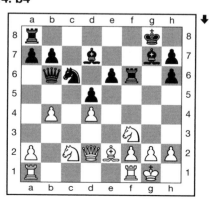

14...a6

14...♖xf3!?, Hort – Spassky, Moscow 1999 (see game 18 on page 21);

14...♖af8!? 15. b5 ♘e7 16. ♘e5 ♗e8 17. a4 ♘g6 (17...♘f5 18. a5 ♕c7∞; G. Kislov – Vysochin, Voronezh 2001) 18. ♘g4 ♖6f7 (18...♖f4!? 19. g3 h5 20. g×f4 h×g4 21. ♗×g4 ♘×f4 ⯑).

A) 19. ♘×h6+ ♗×h6 20. ♕×h6 ♘f4 21. ♗g4 (21. ♗h5 ♖f6 22. ♕g5+ ♗g6 ⯑) 21...♖f6 ⯑;

B) 19. g3 h5 20. ♘h6+ ♗×h6 21. ♕×h6 ♘f4!!↑, Kun – Szűk, Budapest 2000.

15. a4 ♖ff8 16. ♖a3 ♗e8 17. ♖e1

17. ♖e3 ♘e7 18. a5 ♕d6 19. ♗d3 ♘f5 (19...♘c6 20. ♖fe1 ♕f4 21. g3 ♕f7 22. ♗f1 ♗d7 23. ♗g2±, Savić – Antić, Banja Koviljača 2002) 20. ♗×f5 ♖×f5 21. ♖fe1 ♖f6 22. ♘e5 ♗a4 23. ♖g3 ♖af8 24. ♘d3 ♔h8 25. ♘e3 h5↑ (Antonio – Lputian, Shenzhen 1992).

17...♘e7?!

17...♗g6 18. ♗d3 ♗h5⇄.

18. a5 ♕d6 19. ♘e5

19. ♗d3!?.

19...♘g6

19...♖c8 20. ♖h3 ♘g6 21. ♗d3±;

19...♘f5 20. ♗d3± (20. ♖h3 ♘×d4).

20. ♖g3± ♔h8

20...♘×e5 21. d×e5 ♕×e5? 22. ♗g4±.

21. ♗d3 ♘f4 22. ♖f3 ♘×d3 23. ♖×f8+ ♕×f8 24. ♘×d3±

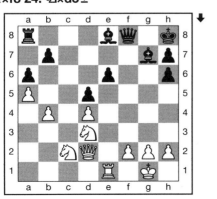

24...♗g6?!

24...♗a4!? 25. ♖×e6 (25. ♘c5 ♗×c2 26. ♕×c2 ♗×d4 27. ♘×e6 ♖e8 28. ♕d2 ♕f6 29. ♘×d4 ♖×e1+ 30. ♕×e1 ♕×d4 ⇌) 25...♖c8
A) 26. ♘e3 ♗d7 27. ♖b6 ♗×d4 28. ♘c5 (28...♖×b7? ♗c6) 28...♗×c5 29. b×c5 ♕×c5=;
B) 26. ♘c5 ♗×c2 27. ♕×c2 ♗×d4 28. h4 ♗×c5 29. b×c5± ♖×c5 30. ♕b2+ ♔g8 31. ♕e5 d4 32. ♕×d4 ♖c1+ 33. ♔h2 ♖c6 34. ♖e3 (34. ♖×c6 b×c6 35. ♕c4+ ♔g7 36. ♕×c6 ♕×f2 37. ♕b7+ ♔g8 38. ♕b3+ ♕f7 39. ♕×f7+ ♔×f7 40. ♔g3 ♔f6 41. ♔g4 ♔e5 42. ♔h5 ♔f4 43. ♔×h6 ♔g4 44. h5 ♔h4=) 34...♖f6 35. f4± (35. ♕d7).

25. ♖×e6 ♕f5 26. ♖e3

26. ♘f4!± ♖c8 27. ♘e1.

26...♖c8 27. ♘de1! ♖c4

27...♖c2? 28. ♘×c2 ♕×c2 29. ♕×c2 ♗×c2 30. ♖e8++−.

28. ♖e2 ♕g5 29. ♕d1 ♗h5 30. f3 ♔g8 31. ♖d2 ♗f7

31...♗g6!? 32. ♕e2 ♖c3 ⯑.

32. ♕e2 h5 33. ♕f2 ♗g6 34. h4

White has stabilised the position and fortified the d4 pawn; now he takes the offensive.

34...♕f4 35. g3 ♕c7 36. ♔h2 ♖c3 37. ♘e3 ♕d6 38. ♘1g2 ♗h6 39. ♕e2 ♖b3 40. ♖b2 ♖d3

40...♕×b4 41. ♖×b3 ♕×b3 42. f4±.

41. ♖d2 ♖b3 42. ♖b2 ♖d3 43. b5 a×b5 44. f4

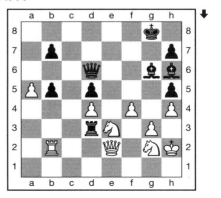

44...♗e4?!

44...♕d7 45. ♘e1 ♖a3 46. ♘f3 ♗g7 (46...♖xa5 47. ♘e5 ♕e6 48. ♕f3 ♗e4 49. ♕xh5±) 47. ♘e5 ♗xe5 48. fxe5 ♖xa5 49. ♕f3 b4 50. ♖f2 ♕f7 51. ♕g2 ♕d7 52. g4!? ♗e4⇄.

45. ♕xh5 b4 46. ♘f5 ♗xf5 47. ♕xf5 ♖c3

Better was 47...♖xd4 48. ♘e3 ♗f8 49. h5±.

48. ♖e2 ♖c6 49. ♖e5

49. ♖e8+ ♗f8 50. ♘e3+−.

49...♗g7 50. ♖xd5 ♕f8 51. ♕d7 ♖c8 52. ♖b5 ♖c2 53. ♖xb7 ♕f6 54. ♕d5+ ♔h8 55. ♖xb4

55. ♖f7+−.

55...♗f8 56. ♖b8 ♕g7 57. ♖b7

Black resigned.

Space advantage, typical endgame

Sveshnikov – Donchev
Lvov 1983

1. e4 c5 2. c3 e6 3. d4 d5 4. e5 ♘c6 5. ♘f3 ♕b6 6. a3 c4 7. ♗e2 ♗d7 8. 0–0 ♘ge7 9. ♘bd2 ♘a5 10. ♖b1 ♘ec6 11. ♖e1 ♗e7 12. ♕c2 ♖c8 13. ♘f1 ♕b3 14. ♗d1 ♕xc2 15. ♗xc2 ♘b3 16. ♗f4 ♘ca5 17. ♘g3 ♗a4 18. ♖e2 b5 19. ♘h5 ♔f8 20. ♗g5 ♘c6 21. ♗xe7+ ♘xe7 22. ♖f1 ♘a5 23. ♗b1 ♘ac6 24. g4 ♖c7 25. ♘h4 g6 26. ♘g3 a5 27. f4 ♘d8 28. f5 ♔e8 29. ♘f3 b4 30. axb4 axb4 31. ♖ef2 ♖a7 32. ♘g5 ♗b3 33. h4 ♗a2

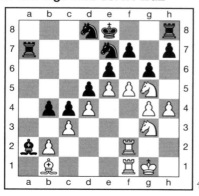

34. fxe6 fxe6 35. ♗c2 ♗b3 36. ♗b1 ♗a2 37. ♗c2 ♗b3 38. ♗xb3 cxb3 39. cxb4 ♘ec6 40. ♘e2 h6 41. ♘h3 ♖b7 42. ♘hf4 g5 43. ♘d3 gxh4 44. ♔h2 ♖g8 45. ♔h3 ♘xb4 46. ♘df4 ♔d7 47. ♔xh4 ♔c8 48. ♖f3 ♘c2 49. ♘h5 ♖b4 50. ♘f6 ♖f8 51. ♖d1 ♘c6 52. ♖fd3 ♖f7 53. ♔h5 ♖a7 54. ♔xh6 ♖aa4 55. g5 ♘2xd4 56. ♘xd4 ♖xd4 57. ♖xd4 ♘xd4 58. ♖xd4 ♖xd4 59. g6 ♖h4+ 60. ♔g5

Black resigned.

Typical endgame

Hába – Faragó
Wattens 1996

1. e4 e6 2. d4 d5 3. e5 c5 4. c3 ♕b6 5. ♘f3 ♘c6 6. a3 c4 7. ♘bd2 ♘a5 8. ♖b1 ♗d7 9. ♗e2 ♘e7 10. ♘f1 ♕b3 11. ♗f4 ♗a4 12. ♕xb3 ♗xb3 13. ♘e3 ♘g6 14. ♗g3 f5 15. exf6 gxf6 16. ♘h4 ♗h6 17. 0–0 ♗xe3?!

17...♘f4 18. ♗xf4 ♗xf4 19. g3 ♗c7 20. f4±.

18. fxe3 0–0 19. ♖bc1 ♗a4 20. ♗g4 ♗d7 21. ♖f2 ♘c6 22. ♖cf1 ♔g7

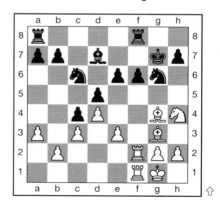

23. e4!? dxe4 24. d5 ♘ce7

24...♘ce5 25. ♘xg6 ♘xg6 (25...hxg6 26. ♗xe5 fxe5 27. dxe6±) 26. dxe6±.

25. dxe6 &c6 26. &d6 &ae8 27. ♘f5+ ♘xf5 28. &xf8+ ♘xf8 29. &xf5 ♘xe6 30. &xe6 &xe6 31. &d1 &g6

31...e3!? 32. &e2 f5⯑.

32. &f4 f5 33. g3 &a4 34. &d5 e3 35. &f1 &c2 36. &fd4 &d3+ 37. &e1 &g5 38. h4+ &h5?!

38...&f6 39. &d6±.

39. g4+

Black resigned.

Space advantage

Game 37

Korchnoi – Iruzubieta Villaluenga
Oviedo (Rapidplay) 1992

1. e4 e6 2. d4 d5 3. e5 c5 4. c3 ♘c6 5. ♘f3 &d7 6. a3 ♕b6 7. b4 cxd4 8. cxd4 &c8 9. &b2 ♘h6 10. ♘c3 ♘a5 11. ♘a4 ♕c6 12. ♘c5?!

I think that White has no opening advantage after this move. In fact he must play very carefully to hold the balance. Instead, 12. &c1± is better.

12...♘c4 13. &xc4?!

13. &c1⇄.

13...dxc4 14. 0–0 ♕d5 15. ♕e2

15. ♘xd7 ♕xd7⯑.

15...&c6⯑

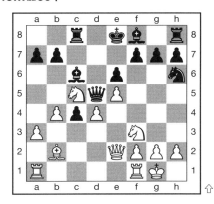

16. &fe1 &e7 17. &ac1 0–0 18. ♘e4 ♘f5

18...♕xe4 19. ♕xe4 &xe4 20. &xe4 b5⯑.

19. &cd1

19. ♕xc4 ♕xc4 20. &xc4 &xe4 21. &xc8 &xc8 22. &xe4 &c2 23. &a1 &a2 24. &c3 &xa3 25. &d2 &b3⯑.

19...♕xe4 20. ♕xe4 &xe4 21. &xe4 c3 22. &c1 h5⯑ 23. h3 &fd8 24. &f1 &c4

24...a5!?⯑.

25. &e2 b5 26. g4 hxg4 27. hxg4 ♘h6

27...c2!? 28. &d2 ♘h4 29. ♘e1 &dc8 30. ♘d3 g5⯑.

28. ♘e1 a5 29. bxa5 &a8 30. ♘c2 &xa5 31. &d3 b4

Draw. 32. axb4 &a2 33. &d1 &xc2+ 34. &d3 &xc1 35. &xc1 &xb4 36. &xc3 &h7⇄.

Advantage in development going into the endgame; play on the c-file

Game 38

Sveshnikov – Luther
Nova Gorica 2000

This game illustrates just how dangerous it is for Black to part with his dark-squared bishop.

1. e4 e6 2. d4 d5 3. e5 c5 4. c3 ♘c6 5. ♘f3 &d7 6. &e2 ♘h6 7. 0–0 cxd4 8. cxd4 ♘f5 9. ♘a3 &xa3 10. bxa3 ♕b6 11. &e3 ♘xe3 12. fxe3 ♕d8 13. &b1

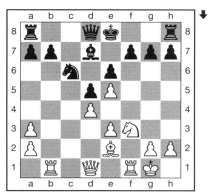

13...b6

Now the Black position deteriorates. Instead 13...♞a5! leads to an interesting game: 14. ♛e1 0–0 15. ♝d3 ♜c8 16. ♛g3 (16. e4 ♝c6=) 16...h6 17. ♞e1 (17. h4 ♜c3 18. ♞e1 ♛e7 19. ♜f6 ♛xa3∓) 17...♛g5 18. ♛h3 b6 (18...f6 19. ♝b5±; 18...♜c3 19. ♜f3 ♛e7 20. ♜g3 ♚h8 21. ♛g4 f5!) 19. ♜f3 ♚h8∞.

14. ♝b5 ♜c8 15. ♛a4 0–0 16. ♝xc6 ♜xc6 17. ♛xa7 ♝e8 18. ♜fc1 ♜xc1+ 19. ♜xc1 f6 20. ♛c7± ♝a4!

Making use of his lead in development, White heads for the endgame. This is a typical method. However, Black finds a good defensive resource.

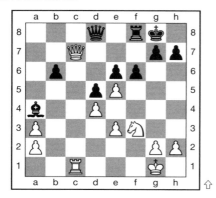

21. h3?!

This gives away a large part of White's advantage. It was much better to play 21. ♚f2!?± ♛xc7 22. ♜xc7 fxe5 23. dxe5 ♜f7 24. ♜c8+ ♜f8 25. ♜xf8+ ♚xf8 26. ♞g5+−. Also good is 21. ♛a7±.

21...♛xc7 22. ♜xc7 ♜f7 23. ♜c8+ ♜f8 24. ♜c1

24. ♜c3±.

24...♜a8 25. ♜c3 ♝d1 26. ♚f2?!

26. ♞e1 ♝e2 27. ♞c2±.

26...♝xf3 27. gxf3 fxe5 28. dxe5 b5 29. ♚g3 ♚f7 30. f4 ♜a4 31. ♚g4 d4 32. exd4 ♜xd4 33. h4 ♜d2 34. ♜c7+ ♚f8 35. f5 ♜d4+ 36. ♚g3

Here the game was agreed drawn in view of 36...h6+ 37. ♚g6 (37. ♚h5 exf5 38. ♚g6 ♜xh4 39. ♚xf5 ♜a4=) 37...♜g4+ 38. ♚h7 exf5 39. h5 or 36...exf5 37. e6= ♜e4.

Space advantage; typical endgame

Game 39
Grischuk – Radjabov
FIDE Grand Prix, Dubai 2002

1. e4 e6 2. d4 d5 3. e5 c5 4. c3 ♞c6 5. ♞f3 ♝d7 6. ♝e2 ♜c8 7. 0–0 a6 8. ♚h1!? cxd4!? 9. cxd4 ♞ge7 10. ♞c3 ♞g6 11. ♝d3 ♝e7 12. ♝e3 0–0 13. ♜e1 ♞a5 14. ♜c1 ♞c4 15. ♜c2 ♞xe3 16. fxe3 b5 17. a3 ♛b6 18. h4 ♝xh4 19. ♞xh4 ♞xh4 20. ♝xh7+ ♚xh7 21. ♛h5+ ♚g8 22. ♛xh4 ♛d8 23. ♛xd8 ♜fxd8 24. ♜ec1 f6 25. ♞e2 ♜c4 26. b3 ♜xc2 27. ♜xc2 ♜c8 28. ♜xc8+ ♝xc8 29. b4 ♚f7 30. ♚h2 ♚g6 31. g4 f5 32. ♚g3 ♚g5 33. gxf5 ♚xf5 34. ♚f3 ♝d7 35. ♞c1 ♚g5 36. ♚g3 ♚f5 37. ♞b3 ♚g5 (37...♚e4 38. ♞c5+) **38. ♞c5 ♝c8**

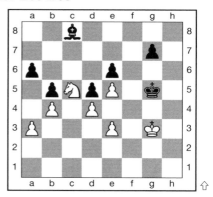

39. e4! dxe4 40. ♞xe4+ ♚h5

40...♚f5 41. ♞d6+.

41. ♞c5 ♚g5 42. ♞e4+ ♚h5 43. ♚f4 ♚h4 44. ♞g5 ♝d7 45. d5! exd5 46. e6 ♝e8 47. ♞f7 d4 48. ♚e4 g5 49. ♞d6 g4

49...♝c6+?! 50. ♚xd4 g4 51. ♚c5+−; 49...♝g6+! 50. ♚xd4 g4= 51. ♚e3 g3 52. e7 ♚h3 53. ♞e4 g2 54. ♞g5+ ♚g4 55. ♞f3 ♚f5

56. ♘h4+ ♔f6 57. ♘×g2 ♔×e7 58. ♔d4 ♔d6 59. ♘e3 ♗h7 =.

50. ♘×e8 g3 51. ♘d6 g2 52. e7 g1♕ 53. e8♕ ♕e3+ 54. ♔d5 ♕×e8 55. ♘×e8 d3 56. ♘d6 d2 57. ♘f5+ ♔g4 58. ♘e3+ ♔f3 59. ♘d1

Black resigned.

Counterplay by Black against the e5 pawn with f7–f6

Game 40
Keres – Ståhlberg
6th Olympiad, Warsaw 1935

1. e4 e6 2. d4 d5 3. e5 c5 4. ♘f3 ♕b6 5. ♗d3 c×d4 6. 0–0 ♘d7 7. ♘bd2 ♘e7 8. ♘b3 ♘c6 9. ♖e1 g6 10. ♗f4 ♗g7 11. ♕d2 0–0 12. h4 ♕c7?!

12…a5!? ⇄.

13. ♕e2 f6 14. e×f6 ♕×f4 15. ♕×e6+ ♖f7 16. f×g7 ♘de5 17. ♕e8+ ♔×g7 18. ♖×e5 ♗h3 19. ♕×a8 ♘×e5

19…♗×g2 20. ♖f5!+−.

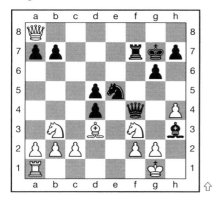

20. ♕e8!+− ♘c6 21. ♕×f7+ ♔×f7 22. ♘g5+ ♔f6 23. ♘×h3 ♕×h4 24. ♖e1 g5 25. ♘d2 ♕h6 26. ♘f3 g4 27. ♘fg5 ♕h5 28. ♘×h7+ ♔g7 29. ♘f4 ♕h6 30. ♘g5 ♕d6 31. ♘h5+ ♔f8 32. ♖e6 ♕b4 33. ♗g6 ♘e7 34. ♖f6+ ♔g8 35. ♗h7+

Black resigned.

Counterplay by Black against the e5 pawn with f7–f6

Game 41
Enders – Uhlmann
27th GDR Championship, Eggesin 1978

1. e4 e6 2. d4 d5 3. e5 c5 4. c3 ♘c6 5. ♘f3 ♕b6 6. a3 c4 7. ♘bd2 f6?! 8. b3!?

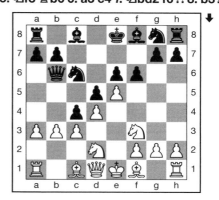

8…f×e5

8…c×b3 9. ♘×b3

A) 9…f×e5 10. ♘×e5 (10. d×e5±) 10…♘×e5 (10…♘f6 11. c4±) 11. d×e5 ♕c7 12. ♗b5+ ♗d7 13. ♗×d7+ ♔×d7 14. 0–0→;

B) 9…♕c7 10. c4!?± f×e5 11. c×d5 e×d5 12. d×e5 ♗g4

B1) 13. ♕×d5 ♖d8 14. ♕e4 ♗×f3

B1a) 15. g×f3 ♕×e5 16. ♗b2 ♕×e4+ (16…♕e7 17. ♕×e7+ ♘g×e7 18. ♘c5±) 17. f×e4 ♘f6 18. f3± (18. ♗g2±);

B1b) 15. ♕×f3 ♕×e5+ 16. ♕e2 ♗d6 17. ♗b2 ♕×e2+ 18. ♗×e2 ♘f6 (18…♗e5 19. ♗×e5 ♘×e5 20. ♘c5±) 19. 0–0–0 0–0 20. ♖he1!?±;

B2) 13. ♗b2!± ♘ge7 14. ♖c1 ♖d8 15. h3 ♗×f3 (15…♗h5 16. ♘bd4±) 16. ♕×f3 d4 (16…♘g6 17. e6 ♗d6 18. ♖c2!?±) 17. ♕e4 (17. e6 ♕e5+ 18. ♗e2 ♕×e6 19. ♘c5 ♕d5 20. 0–0 d3 21. ♖fd1 d2 22. ♖c2±)

B2a) 17…♕×e5 18. ♕×e5 ♘×e5 19. ♘×d4 ♘7c6 20. ♘×c6 (20. ♘e6 ♘d3+ 21. ♗×d3 ♖×d3 22. ♔e2 ♖b3 ⇄) 20…♘×c6 21. ♗c4±;

B2b) 17...♘g6 18. f4 ♕b6 19. ♗c4 d3

B2b1) 20. ♔d1 ♕f2 21. ♘d2 ♘xf4 22. ♖f1 ♕e2+ 23. ♕xe2 dxe2+ 24. ♗xe2 ♘xg2! (24...♘xe2 25. ♔xe2±) 25. ♖f3 g6 26. ♖cc3 ♗h6 27. ♖cd3 ♘f4⇄;

B2b2) 20. ♖b1!? ♗e7 (20...♘a5 21. ♘xa5 ♕xa5+ 22. ♔f2!?±) 21. g3±.

9. bxc4

9. ♘xe5!? (Bronstein) 9...♘xe5 10. dxe5 ♘h6 11. bxc4 ♗c5 12. ♕h5+ ♘f7 13. cxd5 ♗xf2+ 14. ♔d1↑.

9...e4

In this position White has no advantage, so he should follow Bronstein's suggestion on move 9.

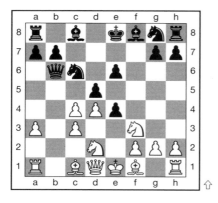

10. ♘h4?

10. ♘g5 ♗e7 11. ♖b1

A) 11...♕c7 12. cxd5 exd5 13. c4!± ♗f5 14. cxd5 e3 15. dxc6 ♗xb1 16. ♘e6! exd2+ 17. ♗xd2 ♕b6 (17...♕xc6? 18. ♗b5+−) 18. ♗c4!⇄;

B) 11...♕d8 12. ♖xb7!? (12. h4 ♘f6 13. ♗e2⇄) 12...♗xg5 (12...e3 13. ♖xe7+ ♕xe7 14. ♘df3±) 13. ♖xg7 ♔f8□ 14. ♖xg5 ♕xg5 15. ♘xe4∞;

10. ♖b1

A) 10...♕d8 11. ♘e5 ♘xe5 12. dxe5

A1) 12...♘e7 13. cxd5 exd5 14. ♗b5+ ♘c6 (14...♗d7 15. ♕b3±) 15. ♘b3±;

A2) 12...a6 13. cxd5 exd5 14. c4±;

B) 10...♕a5 11. ♘b3 ♕c7 (11...♕a4 12. ♘e5 ♘f6⇄) 12. ♘g5 ♘f6 13. cxd5 exd5 14. c4 ♗f5∓.

10...♘f6 11. g3 ♗e7 12. ♖b1 ♕c7 13. ♗e2 0–0 14. 0–0 ♘a5!∓ 15. c5 b6 16. ♘b3 ♘xb3 17. cxb6 axb6 18. ♕xb3 ♗a6 19. ♖e1 ♘d7 20. ♘g2 ♖fc8 21. ♗g4 ♘f8 22. ♕xb6 ♕d7 23. ♘f4 ♗d6 24. ♕b2 ♕f7 25. ♕d2 ♖c6 26. ♔g2 ♖ac8 27. ♗e2 ♗xf4 28. ♕xf4 ♗xe2 29. ♕xf7+ ♔xf7 30. ♖xe2 ♖xc3 31. ♗f4 ♘g6 32. ♗d6 ♖8c4 33. ♖a2 ♖xd4 34. a4 ♖c6 35. a5

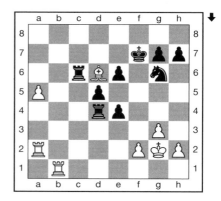

35...♖xd6 36. a6 ♖d2 37. ♖xd2 ♖xa6 38. ♖b4 ♘e5 39. ♖c2 ♔f6 40. ♖c8 ♘d3 41. ♖b7 ♖a2 42. ♖f8+ ♔e5 43. ♔f1 ♖a1+ 44. ♔e2 ♘e1 45. ♖xg7 ♘f3 46. ♖xf3 ♖a2+ 47. ♔e1 exf3 48. ♖f7 ♖a3 49. ♖xh7 ♔e4 50. ♖f7 e5 51. h4 ♖a1+ 52. ♔d2 ♖f1

White resigned.

Counterplay by Black against the e5 pawn with f7–f6

Game 42
Morozevich – Bareev
11th Amber (blindfold), Monaco 2002

1. e4 e6 2. d4 d5 3. e5 c5 4. c3 ♘c6 5. ♘f3 ♕b6 6. a3 ♘h6 7. b4 cxd4 8. cxd4 ♘f5 9. ♗e3 f6

The right move; now White has no advantage.

10. exf6 gxf6 11. ♗d3 ♘xe3 12. fxe3 ♗h6

12...e5.

13. ♕e2 ♗d7 14. ♘c3 ♘e7 15. 0–0 0–0–0

15...e5 16. e4! exd4 17. ♘xd5 ♘xd5 18. exd5+ ♗e3+ 19. ♔h1 ±.

16. ♔h1 ♖ac8 17. ♘d1 ♗g7 ⇄

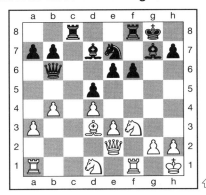

18. ♘f2 e5 19. dxe5 fxe5 20. e4 d4 21. ♖ac1 ♘g6 22. ♖xc8 ♗xc8 23. g3 ♗h6 24. ♘d2 ♗g7 25. ♘c4 ♕e6 26. b5 ♕e7 27. ♘d1 ♗d7 28. ♖xf8 ♕xf8 29. a4 ♕b4? 30. h4 ♕c5 31. ♘f2 ♘h8?!

31...♔g8 32. h5 ♘e7 33. ♘g4 ♗g7 34. h6 ♗h8 35. ♕f3 ♘g6 36. ♘f6+ ♗xf6 37. ♕xf6 ♕f8 38. ♕xf8+ ♔xf8 ⇄.

32. ♘g4 ♘f7 33. ♕f3↑ ♕e7 34. ♘a5?! ♗c8

34...♗d2 35. ♘c4 ♗b4 ∓.

35. ♘c4 ♗c1 36. ♔h2 h6 37. ♕d1 ♗a3 38. ♗f1 ♗b4 39. ♗h3 ♕c5 40. ♘b2 ♕c3 41. ♘d3 ♗d6 42. ♘gf2 ♗xh3 43. ♔xh3 ♕c4 44. ♕g4+ ♔f8 45. ♕d7 ♕xa4 46. ♕xb7 ♕a1

46...♕a5 47. ♔g4 ♔g7 48. ♔f5 h5 49. g4 ♕d8 50. gxh5 ♕xh4 51. ♔e6 ♕f6+ 52. ♔d5 ♕d8 ⇄.

47. ♔g2 ♔g7 48. ♕d7 ♕a2 49. ♔h3 ±

Black exceeded the time limit.

Counterplay by Black on the kingside

Game 43

Zhuravliov – Sveshnikov

Moscow 1975

1. e4 c5 2. ♘f3 e6 3. c3 d5 4. e5 ♘h6 5. d4 ♘f5 6. ♗d3 ♘c6 7. 0–0 cxd4 8. ♗xf5 exf5 9. cxd4 ♗e7 10. ♘c3 ♗e6 11. ♘e2 g5 12. ♕b3 ♖b8 13. ♗d2 f4!

13...0–0? 14. ♘xg5! ±.

14. ♖ac1 ♕d7 15. ♔h1 ♗f5 16. ♘e1 0–0 17. ♘d3 f6! 18. ♘c5 ♗xc5 19. ♖xc5 fxe5 20. dxe5!

20. ♕xd5+? ♕xd5 21. ♖xd5 ♗e4 ∓.

20...♗e6 21. ♖e1! d4 22. ♕d3 ♖bd8 23. ♘g1 ♖f5 24. ♕b5? g4?!

24...♖df8.

25. ♖e4! ♖df8

25...d3 26. ♖xf4 ♖xf4 27. ♗xf4 d2 28. ♗xd2 ♕xd2 29. ♕xb7 ♗d5 30. e6!.

26. ♘e2 f3

26...d3 27. ♘xf4 ♖xf4 28. ♖xf4 ♖xf4 29. ♗xf4 d2 30. ♗xd2 ♕xd2 31. ♕f1 ∞.

27. ♖xg4+ ♔h8 28. ♘f4 ♖5f7 29. ♖h4 fxg2+ 30. ♔g1 ♖g8 31. ♖h6

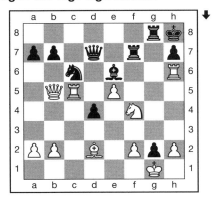

31...♖xf4! ∓ 32. ♗xf4 d3 33. ♖c1 d2?

33...a6!.

34. ♖d1 ♘d4 35. ♕d3 ♗f5 36. ♕e3 ♕d5 37. e6! ♖g7 !? 38. ♖xd2?

38. e7? ♖xe7! 39. ♕xe7 ♘f3+ 40. ♔xg2 ♘h4+− +;

38. ♖f6! h5 39. e7!±.

38...♕c4! 39. ♖d1 ♘e2+ 40. ♕xe2 ♕xe2 41. ♖c1 ♗d3 42. ♖c8+

White resigned.

Black counterplay on the c-file

Game 44
Benjamin – Gulko
US Championship, Key West 1994

A theoretically important game. So far no way for White to gain an advantage has been found.

1. e4 e6 2. d4 d5 3. e5 c5 4. c3 ♘c6 5. ♘f3 ♗d7 6. ♗e2 ♘ge7!? 7. ♘a3 cxd4 8. cxd4 ♘f5 9. ♘c2 ♕b6 10. 0-0 ♖c8 11. ♗d3 ♘b4 12. ♘xb4 ♗xb4 13. a3 ♗e7

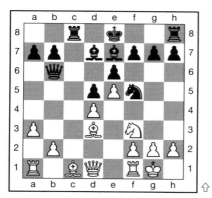

14. ♗xf5

What else can White do? Now he plans to exchange the dark-squared bishops. In fact there is another move – 14. ♔h1 !?.

14...exf5 15. ♗g5 ♗xg5 16. ♘xg5 0-0 17. ♕d2 ♖c4 18. ♘f3 ♖fc8 19. ♖ac1 ♕c7 20. ♖xc4

Draw. 20...♕xc4 (20...dxc4? 21. ♖c1 ±) 21. ♖e1 ⇄ or 21. ♕g5⇄.

Development advantage for Black; counter-attack on the king

Game 45
Svidler – Shirov
León (Rapidplay) 2004

This game is of interest mainly for its length: even in rapidplay it is extremely rare for a player of Svidler's class to lose in just 13 moves.

1. e4 e6 2. d4 d5 3. e5 c5 4. c3 ♕b6 5. ♘f3 ♗d7 6. ♗e2

6. a3.

6...♗b5 7. dxc5!?

A relatively uncommon move; the main alternatives are 7. 0-0 ♗xe2 8. ♕xe2 ♕a6!? or 7. c4!? ♗xc4 8. ♗xc4 dxc4 9. d5 exd5 10. ♕xd5 ♘e7 11. ♕xc4 (11. ♕e4, I. Zaitsev–Doda, Riga 1968, game 24 on page 25) 11...♕a6 12. ♘a3 ♕xc4 13. ♘xc4 ♘d5 14. ♗g5 ♘d7 15. 0-0-0 ♘7b6= (McShane–Thórhallsson, 35th Olympiad, Bled 2002).

7...♗xc5 8. b4?

8. 0-0 ♗xe2 9. ♕xe2 ♕a6! (9...a5?! 10. c4 ♘e7 11. ♘c3±, Movsesian–Volkov, Panormo (Blitz) 2002) 10. ♕xa6 (10. ♕c2 ♘d7 11. a4 ♖c8⇄, Kupreichik–V. Molnar, Rimavska Sobota 1990) 10...♘xa6 11. b4 ♗b6 12. a4±. The worth of the move 6. ♗e2 depends very much on the evaluation of this endgame.

8...♗xf2+ 9. ♔f1

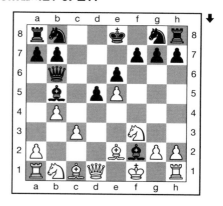

White is a pawn down and unable to castle, but the f2 bishop has problems getting back into its own camp.

9…♗d7

An earlier game had gone 9…♗c6!? 10. ♕d3 a6 11. a4 ♘e7 12. ♖a2 ♘f5 13. g4 ♘h4 14. a5 ♕a7 15. ♘xh4 ♗xh4 16. ♗e3 b6 17. ♗xb6 ♕b7 18. ♗d4 f6⇄ (Kristjánsson – Thorsson, Reykjavík 1998). Obviously 9…♗xe2+? 10. ♕xe2 is bad.

10. ♕d2

White protects the e3 square and threatens to win the bishop with 11. ♗d3. An earlier try was 10. c4!, which seems more consistent, e. g. 10…dxc4?! (grandmaster M. Golubev suggests 10…♘a6!? 11. c5 ♘xc5 12. bxc5 ♗xc5 with an unclear position) 11. ♘a3!± a6? 12. ♘xc4 ♕a7 13. ♘d6+ ♔f8 (13…♔e7 14. ♗g5+ f6 15. exf6 gxf6 16. ♘e4+−) 14. ♘c8!, and Black resigned (Rogers – Sribar, Wijk aan Zee 1977).

10…♘h6 11. ♗d3?

This leads to a lost position. The computer suggests 11. a4!? a5 (11…♘g4? 12. a5+−) 12. ♗d3 ♘g4 13. ♕g5 h5⇄.

11…♘g4∓ 12. ♕g5?!

The difference between this and the variation above is that here the b5 square is not defended. However, Black is clearly better in any case, e. g. 12. h3 ♗e3 13. ♕c2 ♘f2!? or 12. ♕f4 ♗e3!? 13. ♕xg4 ♗xc1 14. ♕xg7 ♖f8.

12…♗b5! 13. c4

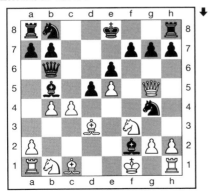

13…♗g3!

White resigned, in view of 14. ♕d2 dxc4.

Play on both wings

Game 46
Portisch – Milić
12th Olympiad, Moscow 1956

1. e4 e6 2. d4 d5 3. e5 c5 4. c3 ♘c6 5. ♘f3 ♗d7 6. a3 ♕b6 7. b4 cxd4 8. cxd4 ♖c8 9. ♗b2 ♘h6 10. ♘c3 ♘f5 11. ♘a4 ♕d8 12. ♗d3 (12. ♖c1; 12. ♘c5) **12…b6 13. 0–0 ♗e7 14. ♘c3 g6 15. ♗a6 ♖b8 16. ♖c1** (16. ♕d3±) **16…0–0 17. ♗b5 ♕e8 18. ♕a4 ♖c8 19. ♘e2?! ♖c7!**

19…♘xe5!? 20. ♖xc8 ♘xf3+ 21. gxf3 ♗xb5 22. ♖xe8 ♘xa4 23. ♖xf8+ ♔xf8 24. ♖c1 ♗b5⯑.

20. ♖c3

20. ♘g3 ♘xe5∓;

20. ♖fe1 ♘xe5 21. ♖xc7 ♘xf3+ 22. gxf3 ♗xb5 23. ♕xa7 ♗d6∓.

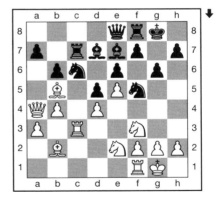

20…♘xe5∓ 21. ♖xc7 ♘xf3+ 22. gxf3 ♗xb5 23. ♕c2 ♗d6 24. ♖xa7 ♕b8−+ 25. ♖a4 ♖c8 26. ♕d1 ♗xh2+ 27. ♔h1 ♗d6 28. ♖g1 ♕b7 29. ♘c3 ♗xa4 30. ♘xa4 ♖c4 31. ♘c3 ♖xd4 32. ♕a4 ♖h4+ 33. ♔g2 ♕c8

33…d4 34. ♕e8+ ♔g7 35. ♘e4 ♖xe4 36. fxe4 ♕xe4+−+.

34. ♖c1 ♕d8 35. ♘e2 ♖h2+ 36. ♔g1

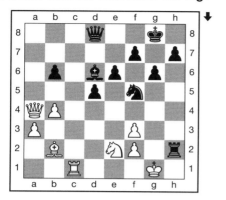

36...♖h5

36...♘e3!–+.

37. ♕a6 ♗f8

37...♕g5+ 38. ♘g3 d4–+.

38. ♖c8 ♕e7

38...♕g5+ 39. ♘g3 ♘xg3 40. ♖xf8+ ♔xf8
41. ♕c8+=.

39. ♕xb6 d4?!

39...♘d6 40. ♖c7 ♕h4 41. ♘g3 ♕h2+
42. ♔f1 ♖h4∓.

40. ♗xd4

40. ♕d8!? e5 41. ♘g3⇄.

40...♕g5+

40...♘xd4 41. ♕xd4 ♖d5±.

**41. ♘g3 ♘xg3 42. ♖xf8+= ♔xf8
43. ♕d6+ ♔e8 44. ♕c6+**

Draw.

Play on both wings

Game 47
Kupreichik – Timoshchenko
Odessa 1968

**1. e4 e6 2. d4 d5 3. e5 c5 4. c3 ♕b6
5. ♘f3 ♗d7 6. ♘a3 cxd4 7. cxd4**

(see next diagram)

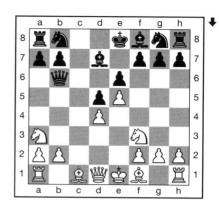

7...♘c6

7...♗b4+ 8. ♗d2 ♘e7 9. ♗d3 (9. ♗e2 ♗xa3
10. bxa3 ♗b5 11. ♗xb5+ ♕xb5 12. ♖b1 ♕d7
13. ♕b3 b6⇄ 14. a4) 9...♗xd2+ 10. ♕xd2
♘bc6 11. ♘c2 ♕xb2 12. 0–0 ♕b6 13. ♖ab1
♕c7 14. ♖fc1

A) 14...h6 15. ♘e3 (15. ♖b3) 15...♖c8
16. ♕b2 b6 17. ♖c1 ⯮;

B) 14...0–0 15. ♕g5⯮ f6 16. exf6 ♖xf6
17. ♘e3 h6 (17. ... ♖xf3 18. gxf3 ♗e8 19. ♕g3
♕xg3+ 20. fxg3 b6 21. ♘c2 ±) 18. ♕h4

B1) 18...♖b8 19. ♘e5 ♕d8 20. ♘3g4 ♖f8
21. ♘xh6+ gxh6 22. ♕xh6 ♖f7 23. ♕h8+
(23. ♘xf7 ♔xf7 24. ♕h7+ ♔f6 25. ♖c3 ♕g8
26. ♕h6+ ♔f7 27. ♕h5+ ♔f8⇄ 28. ♗h7?!
♕h8∓) 23...♔xh8 24. ♘xf7+ ♔g7 25. ♘xd8
♖xd8 26. ♖xb7 ♔f6 27. f4±;

B2) 18...♖af8 19. ♘e5 ♗c8.

**8. ♗e2 ♗b4+ 9. ♔f1 ♗e7 10. h4 f6
11. ♖h3 ♘h6 12. ♗xh6 gxh6 13. ♕d2
0–0–0 14. exf6 ♗xf6 15. ♘b5 e5
16. dxe5 ♗xh3 17. exf6 ♗g4 18. a4 ♗xf3
19. ♗xf3 a6 20. ♕f4 axb5 21. ♗g4+ ♖d7
22. axb5 ♘a5 23. ♕b4 ♕c7 24. b6 ♕h2
25. ♖xa5 ♕h1+ 26. ♔e2 ♖e8+ 27. ♕e7**

Black resigned.

Play on both wings; play on the dark squares

Game 48
Kupreichik – Lautier
GMA Open, Belgrade 1988

**1. e4 e6 2. d4 d5 3. e5 c5 4. c3 ♞c6
5. ♞f3 ♛b6 6. ♗e2 ♞h6 7. ♗×h6!? g×h6**

7...♛×b2 8. ♗c1 ♛×a1 9. ♛c2 c×d4±.

8. ♛d2 ♗g7 9. 0–0 0–0

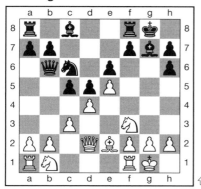

10. ♞a3! c×d4 11. c×d4 ♗d7

11...f6!? 12. e×f6 ♖×f6 13. ♞c2⇄.

**12. ♞c2 f6 13. e×f6 ♖×f6 14. b4 ♖af8
15. b5 ♞e7 16. ♞e5± ♗e8 17. g3 h5
18. a4 ♞f5 19. a5 ♛c7 20. ♖ac1± ♞d6
21. ♞e3 ♛e7 22. ♛b2 h4 23. ♗d3**

Better is 23. b6 a6 (23...a×b6 24. ♛×b6+−)
24. ♖c7 ♛d8 25. ♗d3±.

**23...h×g3 24. h×g3 ♞e4 25. ♗×e4 d×e4
26. b6 a×b6 27. ♛×b6 ♛a3 28. ♞3g4
♖×f2**

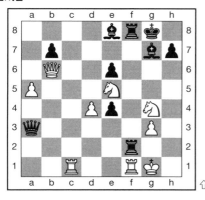

29. ♖×f2?!

29. ♞×f2 ♛×g3+ 30. ♔h1 ♗c6! 31. ♖×c6
(31. ♞fg4 ♖×f1+ 32. ♖×f1 ♛h4+ 33. ♔g1
♛g3+ 34. ♔h1 ♛h4+ 35. ♔g2 e3+
36. ♞×c6 ♛×g4+=) 31...♛h4+□ 32. ♔g2
♗×e5 33. d×e5 ♛g5+ 34. ♔h2 ♛f4+ 35. ♔g2
♛f3+ 36. ♔g1 ♛g3+ 37. ♔h1 ♛f3+ 38. ♔h2
♛f4+=.

**29...♛×c1+= 30. ♔g2 ♖×f2+ 31. ♞×f2
♛c8⇄ 32. ♞fg4 ♗h5 33. ♞e3 ♗h6
34. ♞3c4 e3± 35. ♛d6?**

35. ♛b3!.

35...e2 36. ♔f2

36. ♛b4 ♛d8−+.

36...♗f8 37. ♛b6

37. ♛d7 ♛×d7 38. ♞×d7 ♗b4−+.

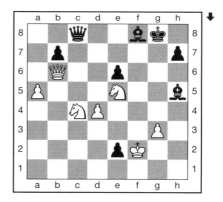

37...♗g7?

37...♗e7!−+ 38. ♞d2 e1♛+ 39. ♔×e1
♛c1+−+.

**38. g4□= ♗×g4 39. ♞×g4 ♛×c4
40. ♛d8+ ♔f7 41. ♛d7+ ♔g6 42. ♛e8+
♔g5 43. ♛e7+ ♔g6 44. ♛e8+ ♔g5
45. ♛e7+ ♔×g4 46. ♛×g7+ ♔f5
47. ♛×h7+ ♔f6 48. ♛h4+ ♔f7 49. ♛h7+
♔f6**

Draw.

Play on both wings

Game 49
Sveshnikov – Naumkin
Moscow 1989

1. e4 e6 2. d4 d5 3. e5 c5 4. c3 ♘c6
5. ♘f3 ♗d7 6. dxc5 ♗xc5 7. ♗d3 ♘ge7
(7...a5!?) 8. b4 ♗b6 9. b5 ♘a5 10. 0-0
(10. h4!?) 10...♖c8! 11. a4 ♘g6 12. ♖e1
f6 13. ♖a2 0-0

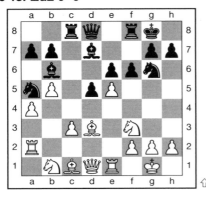

14. ♗xg6 hxg6 15. ♕d3 ♔f7 16. ♗e3 ♖h8
17. ♖ae2 ♘c4 18. ♗d4 ♖h6 (18...g5!?)
19. h4 a6 20. bxa6 bxa6 21. ♘bd2 ♗xd4
22. cxd4 ♖h8 23. ♘b3 fxe5 24. dxe5
♗xa4 25. ♘bd4 ♗d7 26. g3 ♕e8 27. ♖b1
♖f8 28. ♖b7 ♔g8 29. ♘g5 ♖d8 30. f4
a5 31. h5 a4 32. ♖h2 a3 33. hxg6 ♖b8
34. ♖xb8 (better is 34. ♕c2!) 34...♕xb8
35. ♕d1 ♖e8□ 36. ♕h5 ♔f8

36...♕b1+ 37. ♔f2 ♕b2+ (37...♔f8 38. ♘h7+!
♔g8 39. ♘f6++−) 38. ♔f3+−.

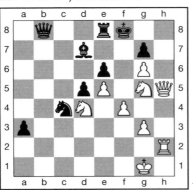

37. ♕h8+?

Better 37. ♘h7+ ♔g8 38. ♘f6+!+−.

**37...♔e7 38. ♕xg7+ ♔d8 39. ♘gxe6+
♔c8□ 40. ♖h7 ♘b6**

More stubborn was 40...♕b1+ 41. ♔h2
♕b2+ 42. ♔h3 ♖d8 43. ♕xd7+! (43. f5
♕f2⇄) 43...♖xd7 44. ♖xd7 ♔xd7 45. g7
♕b8 46. ♘f8+ ♔e7 47. g8♕ ♕xf8 48. ♘c6+
♔e8 49. ♕e6+ ♕e7 50. ♕xe7#.

**41. ♘c5 a2 42. ♘xd7 a1♕+ 43. ♔h2
♕b2+ 44. ♔h3 ♕c7□ 45. ♘xb6+**

Black resigned.

Play on both wings

Game 50
Sveshnikov – Piskov
Bled 1990

1. e4 e6 2. d4 d5 3. e5 c5 4. c3 ♘c6
5. ♘f3 ♕b6 6. a3 ♗d7 7. b4 cxd4 8. cxd4
♖c8 9. ♗e3 ♘h6 10. ♗d3 ♘g4 11. 0-0
♘xe3 12. fxe3 g6 13. ♘c3 ♗h6 14. ♕e1
0-0

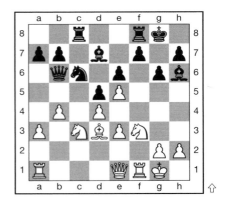

15. ♘a4

15. ♘d1! f6 (15...♗g7 16. ♘f2 f5 17. exf6
♖xf6 18. ♘g4 ♖ff8 19. ♕h4 ♕d8 20. ♘g5+−)
16. exf6 ♖xf6 17. ♘f2 (17. ♕h4 ♗g7 18. ♘f2
e5 19. b5 ♘xd4 20. exd4 e4 21. ♘e5 ♗f5∓)
17...e5 (17...♗g7 18. ♘g4 ♖xf3 19. ♖xf3

♘xd4 20. ♘f6+ ♔h8 21. ♖f4±) 18. b5 ♘xd4
19. ♘xe5 ♗xb5 20. exd4±.

**15...♕d8 16. ♘c5 ♖c7 17. h4 b6 18. ♘xd7
♕xd7 19. ♗b5 ♕c8 20. g4 ♘e7 21. g5
♗g7 22. ♖c1 ♖xc1 23. ♕xc1 ♕xc1
24. ♖xc1 ♖c8 25. ♖xc8+ ♘xc8**

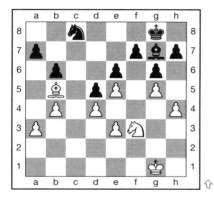

It might appear that there is no point in playing on in this ending; there are bishops of
opposite colour and Black has no weak-
nesses. But in reality White has practically
an extra piece – his king! His plan is first to
achieve the e3–e4 break, followed by d4–d5
to make use of his more active king. Black
lacks counterplay, his pieces have only the
e7 and f8 squares at their disposal, and the
f7 pawn needs to be defended by the king.

26. ♗a6!

This move prevents Black's only possibility
of counterplay with a7–a5, after which the g7
bishop would be "resurrected".

**26...♘e7 27. ♔f2 h6 28. ♔g3 ♗f8
29. ♔f4 ♘f5 30. e4 dxe4 31. ♔xe4 ♘g3+
32. ♔d3 ♗e7 33. d5! exd5 34. ♔d4 hxg5
35. hxg5 ♘e4 36. ♔xd5 ♘xg5 37. ♘d4!**

Centralisation!

**37...♘e6 38. ♘b5 ♗d8 39. ♔c6 g5
40. ♘xa7 g4 41. ♗f1 ♘d4+ 42. ♔b7 f5
43. exf6 ♔f7 44. a4 ♔xf6 45. ♗g2 ♔e5
46. ♗h1 b5 47. axb5 ♘xb5 48. ♘c6+**

48. ♘xb5 ♗e7 =.

48...♔f4 49. ♘xd8 ♔e3 50. ♔c6 ♘c3

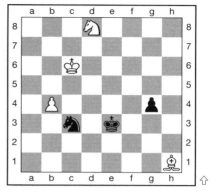

51. b5?

White misses the win: 51. ♘e6! g3 52. ♘g5
♔f2 53. ♘e4+ ♔g1 54. ♘xg3 ♔h2
55. ♘e4+– ♘e2 56. ♗f3 ♘d4+ 57. ♔d5 ♘xf3
58. b5+–.

**51...♘xb5 52. ♔xb5 g3 53. ♘e6 ♔f2
54. ♘f4 g2!**

I had overlooked this neat resource and the
game finished in a draw.

Play on both wings

Game 51
Sveshnikov – Portisch
Interzonal, Biel 1993

This game was very important in a competitive sense, since it was played in the penulti-
mate round of the Interzonal and winning it
would practically guarantee my qualification
for the Candidates.

**1. e4 c5 2. c3 e6 3. d4 d5 4. e5 ♘c6
5. ♘f3 ♕b6 6. ♗e2?!**

Better is 6. a3!.

6...cxd4!

6...♘h6?! 7. ♗xh6! gxh6 (7...♕xb2 8. ♗e3!±)
8. ♕d2±.

7. cxd4 ♘h6 8. b3

8. ♘c3 ♘f5 9. ♘a4 ♗b4+ 10. ♗d2 ♕a5= is
preferable.

8...♘f5 9. ♗b2 ♗b4+ 10. ♔f1□

10. ♘c3 ♘cxd4.

43

10...♗e7

10...0–0.

11. ♘c3 ♕d8

11...♘cxd4? 12. ♘a4.

12. g3 f6!?

12...0–0 13. ♔g2 ♗d7⇄.

13. ♔g2 fxe5 14. dxe5 0–0

Portisch has played the opening very well indeed. At a later stage I managed to win a pawn but then played poorly and failed to convert.

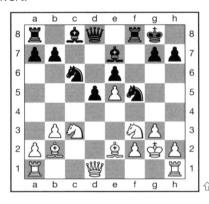

15. ♖c1 ♗d7 16. ♗d3 ♕e8

Here 16...♗e8!∓ is stronger, e.g. 17. ♘e2 ♗h5 18. ♗xf5 ♖xf5 (18...♗xf3+ 19. ♔xf3 ♖xf5+ 20. ♔g2 ♕a5 21. ♘d4 ♘xd4 22. ♗xd4⇄) 19. ♘f4 ♗xf3+ 20. ♕xf3 ♕d7∓.

17. ♘e2 ♕f7 18. ♖f1 ♖ad8 19. a3 g5?!

19...a6 20. b4 b5∓.

20. h3 ♗e8?!

Inconsistent; 20...h5 is better.

21. b4!

Now White is able to finish his development and assume the initiative.

21...a6 22. ♕d2 h6

22...♕h5.

23. ♖ce1

23. g4!? ♘d6 24. ♕e3 ♘c4⇄.

23...d4?

After the correct 23...♘d6! 24. ♘ed4 ♘c4 the position offers chances to both sides.

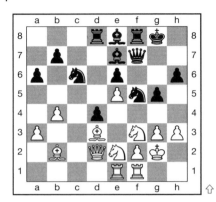

24. ♗e4± d3 25. ♘c1 ♘fd4 26. ♖e3 a5! 27. ♘xd4

27. ♘xd3!? axb4 28. ♘xd4 ♘xd4 29. axb4 (29. ♘xb4 ♘f5 30. ♖d3 ♗b5=) 29...♗b5.

27...♘xd4 28. ♖xd3 ♘f5□ 29. ♖xd8 ♗xd8 30. ♗d4?!

30. ♕xd8? ♘e3+!∓; 30. ♘d3! ♗b5 31. ♖c1 and ♘c5±; 30. ♘b3!±.

30...♗b5 31. ♖e1 ♗c7 32. ♗c5 ♖d8 33. ♕c3 b6! 34. ♗e3 axb4 35. ♕xb4 ♕d7! 36. ♕b3?!

36. ♘b3 ♘xe3+ 37. ♖xe3 ♗xe5 38. a4=.

36...♗c6 37. ♕c4 ♗d5! 38. ♗xd5 ♕xd5+ 39. ♕xd5 ♖xd5∓ 40. f4 ♖a5 41. ♗f2 gxf4 42. gxf4 ♖xa3 43. ♘e2 ♖a2

43...♘e3+ 44. ♗xe3 ♖xe3 45. ♔f2 ♖xh3 46. ♖c1=.

44. ♔f3 ♔f7 45. ♖c1 ♖a3+ 46. ♔g2 ♖a7 47. ♘c3 ♗d8 48. ♖d1 ♖a8 49. ♖d7+ ♔g6 50. ♘e4 b5 51. ♗c5 ♖a2+ 52. ♔f3 ♘h4+ 53. ♔e3 ♘f5+ 54. ♔f3 ♗h4 55. ♖b7 ♖b2 56. ♖b6 ♖b3+ 57. ♔e2 ♘g7 58. ♗f8 ♘h5 59. ♖xe6+ ♔f5 60. ♖xh6 ♘xf4+ 61. ♔d2

Draw.

Play on both wings

Game 52
Sveshnikov – Kiriakov
Russian Championship, Elista 1994

**1. e4 e6 2. d4 d5 3. e5 c5 4. c3 ♘c6
5. ♘f3 ♗d7 6. ♗e2 ♘ge7 7. ♘a3 c×d4
8. c×d4 ♘f5 9. ♘c2 ♕b6 10. 0–0 ♘a5!?**

I think that this is one of Black's most important resources.

11. g4

11. ♘e3 ♘×e3 (11...♘e7 12. b3 ♗b5
13. ♗a3±) 12. f×e3 ♗e7 ⇄.

11...♘e7

11...♘h6

A) 12. b4 ♘c4 (12...♗×b4 13. ♖b1+−)
13. ♗×h6 g×h6 14. ♗×c4 d×c4 15. ♘d2±;

B) 12. ♗×h6 g×h6 13. b4 ♘c6 (13...♘c4±)
14. b5 ♘a5 ⇄.

**12. ♘fe1 ♗b5 13. ♘d3 h5 14. g×h5 ♘f5
15. ♗e3 ♖c8**

15...♘c4 16. a4 ♘c×e3 17. f×e3 ♗c4 18. ♘f4
♗b3 19. ♗b5+ ♔d8 20. ♕e2 ♗×c2 21. a5
♕c7 22. ♖fc1 ♖c8 23. a6 b6 24. ♗a4±,
Sveshnikov – Dolmatov, Naberezhnye Chelny
1988 (Volume 1, page 27).

16. b4 ♘c6 17. a4 ♗c4 18. ♖b1 ♕d8

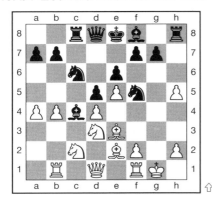

**19. ♘f4 ♗×e2 20. ♕×e2 ♕h4 21. h3 ♗e7
22. ♕g4 ♘×e5 23. d×e5 ♖×c2 24. ♖bc1**

♕×g4+ 25. h×g4 ♘×e3 26. f×e3 ♖×c1
27. ♖×c1 ♔d7 28. ♔f2 b6 29. b5 ♗d8
30. e4 ♗g5 31. ♔f3 d×e4+ 32. ♔×e4 ♖a8
33. ♖f1 ♔e8 34. ♘h3 ♗e7 35. g5 ♖c8
36. ♔d3 ♖d8+ 37. ♔e4 ♖c8 38. ♔d4
♖d8+ 39. ♔c4 ♖c8+ 40. ♔d3 ♖d8+
41. ♔e4 ♖c8

Draw. Black played well, equalising the position step by step.

Play on both wings

Game 53
Guido – Foisor
Montecatini Terme 1994

**1. e4 e6 2. d4 d5 3. e5 c5 4. c3 ♘c6
5. ♘f3 ♗d7 6. ♗e2 ♘ge7 7. ♘a3 c×d4
8. c×d4 ♘f5 9. ♘c2 ♕b6 10. 0–0 ♖c8**

10...♗e7.

11. ♗d3!

11. g4.

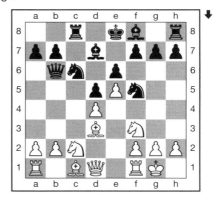

11...a5

Preparing to capture on d4, which does not work yet: 11...♘f×d4? 12. ♘f×d4 ♘×d4
13. ♗e3 ♗c5 14. b4+−.

11...♘b4 12. ♘×b4±;

11...♗e7 12. g4±.

12. a3 a4 13. ♗×f5 e×f5 14. ♘e3 ♕b5

14...♘e7!? 15. g3!? ⇄.

15. b3! a×b3

15...♕×b3 16. ♕×b3 a×b3 17. ♘×d5! (17. ♖b1
♗e6 18. ♖×b3 ♖c7 19. ♖b5 ♖d7) 17...♗e6
18. ♘b6 ♖d8 19. ♗b2 (19. ♖d1? ♗c5)
19...♘e7 20. ♖fd1 ♘d5 21. ♘×d5 ♗×d5
22. ♖d3 and ♘d2±.

16. ♖b1

16. a4? b2!−+.

16...♗e6?!

16...♘a5! 17. a4 ♕c6 18. ♗d2 f4 19. ♗×a5
f×e3 20. ♕×b3 e2 21. ♖fe1 ♕×a4 22. ♕×a4
♗×a4 23. ♖×e2=.

17. ♖×b3

17. ♕×b3 ♕×b3 18. ♖×b3 ♖c7.

17...♕a6 18. ♗d2! g5?

18...♗×a3? 19. ♕b1 g6 20. ♘c2! (20. ♖b5!?
0−0 21. ♘×d5 ♗×d5 22. ♖×d5 ♖fd8
23. ♖×d8+ ♖×d8 24. ♗g5 ♖d7 25. ♖d1±)
20...♗e7 21. ♕b2! (threatens ♖a1 with an attack on the queen a6 and pawn b7) 21...0−0
(21...♘d8!? 22. ♘b4 ♕a4 23. ♖a1 ♕d7
24. ♗h6⯑) 22. ♖a1 ♕e2 23. ♖e3 ♕c4
24. ♖c3 ♕e2 25. ♕×b7+−;

18...♗e7 19. ♕b1±;

18...g6 19. ♕b1 ♖c7 20. ♖b5 ♖d7 21. ♘c2
followed by ♕b3 and ♖b1±.

19. ♘×g5! ♘×d4 20. ♘×e6! f×e6

20...♘×b3 21. ♘×d5! ♕×e6 22. ♗g5!+− with
the threat of ♘c7+.

21. ♕h5+ ♔d7

21...♔d8 22. ♕h4++−.

22. ♕f7+ ♗e7

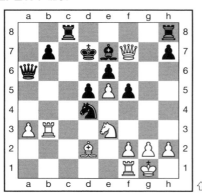

23. ♘×d5!! ♘e2+

23...♘×b3 24. ♕×e7+ ♔c6 25. ♘b4+.

24. ♔h1 e×d5

24...♘g3+ 25. h×g3 ♕×f1+ 26. ♔h2 e×d5
27. ♖×b7+ ♖c7 28. e6+! ♔c8 29. ♖×c7+ ♔×c7
30. ♕×e7+ ♔b8 31. ♕d6++−.

25. ♗g5! ♖ce8

25...♖he8 26. ♕×d5+ ♔c7 27. ♗×e7 ♖×e7
28. ♖×b7+! ♕×b7 29. ♕d6#;

25...♘g3+ 26. h×g3 ♕×f1+ 27. ♔h2 ♖ce8
28. ♕×d5+ ♔c8 29. ♖×b7+−.

26. ♖fb1

Black resigned.

Play on both wings

Game 54
Sveshnikov – Matveeva
Capelle la Grande 1995

**1. e4 e6 2. d4 d5 3. e5 c5 4. c3 ♕b6
5. ♘f3 ♗d7 6. a3 ♗b5 7. c4 ♗×c4
8. ♗×c4 d×c4 9. ♘bd2 ♕a6 10. ♕e2 ♘e7
11. ♘×c4 ♘d5 12. 0−0 ♘c6 13. d×c5
♗×c5 14. b4 b5**

14...♗×b4⇄.

**15. ♘d6+ ♗×d6 16. e×d6 ♖d8 17. ♗b2
♖×d6 18. a4 ♘c7 19. ♖fc1 0−0 20. ♘e5
♖c8**

20...♕b7 21. ♘×c6 ♖×c6 22. ♖×c6 ♕×c6
23. ♖c1 ♕d7 (23...♕d6 24. ♗e5+−) 24. ♕e5
♘e8 25. a×b5±.

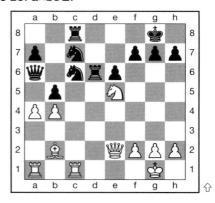

21. ♖×c6!+– ♖×c6 22. ♕f3 f6 23. ♘×c6 ♘d5 24. a×b5

Black resigned.

Play on both wings

Game 55
I. Zaitsev – Naumkin
Moscow 1995

1. e4 e6 2. d4 d5 3. e5 c5 4. c3 ♘c6 5. ♘f3 ♕b6 6. a3 c4 7. ♘bd2 ♘a5 8. ♗e2 ♗d7 9. 0–0 ♘e7 10. ♖b1 (Zaitsev) **10...h6**

10...♕c7 11. ♘g5 h6 12. ♘h3 0–0–0 13. ♘f4 ♔b8 14. ♘h5 ♔a8 15. g4 ♘c8 16. f4 ♘b6 17. ♕e1 (I. Zaitsev–Vasyukov, 37th USSR Championship, Moscow 1969);

10...♗b5 11. ♘e1 ♘b3 12. ♘×b3 ♗a4 13. ♗e3 ♗×b3 14. ♕d2 ♘c6 15. g3 ♘a5 16. ♘g2 ♗a4 17. ♗h5± (Sveshnikov–Ivkov, Chigorin Memorial, Sochi 1983);

10...♖c8 11. g3 h6 12. ♘h4 ♗b5 13. ♖a1 ♘b3 14. ♘×b3 ♗a4 15. ♗e3 ♕×b3 16. ♕d2 ♖c6! 17. ♗d1 ♕b5 18. ♗g4± (Sveshnikov–Gofshtein, Rostov on Don 1976; see also Volume 1, Test position 50 on page 142, Solution on page 153).

11. ♕c2!?

11. g3 0–0–0 12. ♘h4 f5 13. e×f6 g×f6 14. ♗g4, I. Zaitsev–Faragó, Szolnok 1975 (Volume 1, game 53 on page 105); 11. ♖e1!?.

11...0–0–0

11...♘b3 12. ♘×b3 ♗a4 13. ♘fd2 (13. ♗e3 ♗×b3 14. ♕d2±) 13...♗×b3 14. ♘×b3 c×b3 15. ♕d3 ♖c8 16. ♕f3±.

12. b3 c×b3 13. ♘×b3 ♗a4 14. ♘fd2 ♘ec6

14...♕c7!? 15. ♕a2 (15. ♕d3!?±) 15...♘×b3 16. ♘×b3 ♘f5±.

15. ♕a2 ♘×b3

15...♕c7 16. ♘×a5 ♘×a5 17. ♗b2±.

16. ♘×b3 ♕c7 17. ♗e3 ♔b8

17...♘a5?! 18. ♘×a5 ♕×a5 19. c4±; 17...♗e7 18. c4 d×c4 19. ♗×c4±.

18. ♘d2

18. ♗a6!? ♗×b3 19. ♕×b3 ♘a5 20. ♕a4 ♔a8 21. ♖b5!+–.

18...f6

18...♘a5 19. c4 d×c4 20. ♘×c4 ♘×c4 21. ♗×c4 ♗c6 22. ♖fc1±.

19. f4 ♗e7 20. e×f6 g×f6?!

20...♗×f6 21. ♘f3 ♖hf8±.

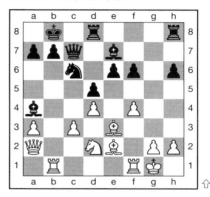

21. c4!± ♔a8

21...d×c4 22. ♕×c4 ♕a5 23. ♗f3 ♔a8 24. ♕×e6±.

22. ♗f3 ♗d6

22...d×c4 23. ♕×c4 ♕a5 24. ♕×e6 ♖he8 25. ♘c4 ♕c7 26. ♕f7±.

23. c×d5 e×d5 24. ♗×d5 ♖he8 25. ♘c4 ♖b8 26. ♖fc1?

26. ♕d2±.

26...♗×f4 27. ♗×f4 ♕×f4⇄ 28. ♔h1?!

28. ♕f2.

28...♖ed8?!

28...♘e7 29. ♘a5 (29. ♗f3 ♗c6) 29...♘×d5 30. ♕×d5 ♖ed8 31. ♕e6 ♕×d4∞; 28...♕×d4!?∓.

29. ♘b2 ♕×d4?!

29...♗b5! 30. a4 ♘b4 31. ♕b3 ♘×d5 32. a×b5 ♖bc8∓.

30. ♗c4⯑ ♘e5

30...b5 31. ♗f1 ♘e5 32. ♘×a4 b×a4 33. g3 a5 34. ♗g2+ ♔a7 35. ♖c7++−.

31. ♘×a4 ♘g4?

31...♘×c4 32. ♕×c4 ♕×c4 33. ♖×c4 b5 34. ♖h4 b×a4 35. ♖×b8+ ♔×b8 36. h3=.

32. h3!±

32. ♖f1 ♕e5 33. g3 ♕e4+ 34. ♔g1 (34. ♕g2 ♕×g2+ 35. ♔×g2 ♘e3+=) 34...♕d4+ (34...♕e3+ 35. ♖f2) 35. ♔h1 ♕e4+=.

32...♘f2+ 33. ♔h2 ♕f4+ 34. g3

34. ♔g1 ♘×h3+ 35. ♔h1 (35. g×h3 ♖d2 36. ♕×d2 ♕×d2 37. ♗f1 ♖g8+ 38. ♔h1 ♕d5+ 39. ♔h2 ♕e5+ 40. ♔h1 ♕e4+− +) 35...♘f2+ 36. ♔g1 ♘h3+=.

34...♘g4+!? 35. h×g4

35. ♔h1! ♕e4+ 36. ♕g2 ♘f2+ 37. ♔h2+−.

35...♖d2+ 36. ♔h3! ♕f2 37. ♕×d2□ ♕×d2 38. ♖d1 ♕a5 39. ♗d5!+− a6

39...♕×a4 40. ♗×b7+ ♖×b7 41. ♖d8+ ♖b8 42. ♖b×b8#.

40. ♘b6+ ♔a7 41. ♘c8+ ♔a8

41...♖×c8 42. ♖×b7+ ♔a8 43. ♖b5++−.

42. ♘b6+ ♔a7 43. ♘d7 b5

43...♖d8 44. ♖×b7+ ♔a8 45. ♘b6++−.

44. ♘×b8 ♔×b8 45. ♖bc1 ♕×a3 46. ♖c6! ♕a4 47. ♖e1 ♕d4 48. ♖e8+ ♔a7 49. ♖e7+ ♔b8 50. ♖d6

Black resigned.

Play on both wings

Game 56
Sveshnikov – Brumen
Bled Open 2000

1. e4 e6 2. d4 d5 3. e5 c5 4. c3 ♘c6 5. ♘f3 ♗d7 6. ♗e2 ♘ge7 7. ♘a3 c×d4 8. c×d4 ♘f5 9. ♘c2 ♘b4 10. 0–0 ♘×c2 11. ♕×c2 ♕b6 12. ♕d3 h6 13. b3 a6 14. a4 ♗b4 15. ♗b2

(see next diagram)

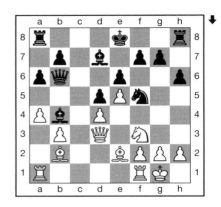

15...g5?!

15...0–0; 15...♖c8.

16. ♖ac1 ♖c8 17. ♖×c8+ ♗×c8 18. ♘e1! ♗d7 19. ♘c2 ♗e7 20. ♘e3 ♕b4 21. ♗d1! ♘×e3 22. ♗c3! ♕b6 23. f×e3 h5 24. ♕d2! g4 25. ♗a5! ♕a7 26. ♗b4 ♗g5 27. ♗c2

27. ♗c5!± b6 28. ♗d6.

27...♖g8 28. ♕f2 ♖g7

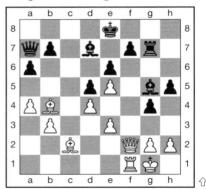

29. ♗g6

29. ♗c5! b6 30. ♗d6±.

29...♕b6 30. ♗×f7+ ♔d8 31. ♗d2

31. ♗d6 ♕×b3 32. ♔h1 ♕×e3 33. ♕c2 ♗c6;
31. ♕e1! ♗×e3+ 32. ♕×e3 ♕×b4 33. ♗×h5+−;

31. ♗f8! ♕×b3 32. ♔h1 ♖h7 33. ♗g6 ♖h8 34. ♗g7 ♖g8 35. ♕f7 ♖×g7 36. ♕×g7+−.

31...♗e7! 32. ♗×h5 ♕×b3 33. ♕f4 g3! 34. h×g3 ♕×a4 35. ♖c1 ♕a2 36. ♕f2 ♗b5 37. ♕e1 b6 38. ♗b4 ♗g5 39. ♕c3

♗c4 40. ♗d1 a5 41. ♗a3 ♖f7 42. ♗c2 ♗a6

42...♔c8!∓.

43. ♗g6! ♕f2+ 44. ♔h2 ♗c4 45. ♖c2 ♕f1 46. ♕b2 b5 47. ♖c1 ♕f2 48. ♖c2 ♕f1 49. ♖c1 ♕f2 50. ♖c2

50. ♖xc4!? ♕xb2 51. ♗xb2 ♖f2 (51...dxc4 52. ♗xf7 ♔e7±; 51...♖g7 52. ♖c5 ♖xg6 53. ♖xb5 ♗xe3 54. ♔h3 ♗f2 55. ♖b3±) 52. ♖c2±.

50...♕f1 =

Draw, since 51. ♖xc4 ♖f2 loses.

Play on both wings

Game 57
Sveshnikov – Dizdar
Slovenian League, Bled 2002

1. e4 e6 2. d4 d5 3. e5 c5 4. c3 ♘c6 5. ♘f3 ♗d7 6. ♗e2 ♘ge7 7. ♘a3 cxd4 8. cxd4 ♘f5 9. ♘c2 ♘b4 10. 0–0 ♘xc2 11. ♕xc2 ♕b6 12. ♕d3 ♖c8 13. g4!? ♘e7 14. ♗d2 h5 15. h3 a6

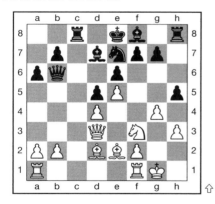

16. ♖fc1?!

16. a4!? hxg4 17. hxg4 ♘c6 (17...♘g6 18. b4!?) 18. a5 ♕c7!? 19. ♖fc1 ♕d8!? 20. ♔g2 ♘b4! 21. ♖xc8 ♗xc8 22. ♕b3 ♘c6 23. ♗d3 ♗e7 24. ♖c1 ♕c7 25. g5 f5 26. g6±.

16...hxg4 17. hxg4 ♖xc1+ 18. ♗xc1

18. ♖xc1 ♗b5 19. ♕e3 ♗xe2 20. ♕xe2 ♕xb2∓.

18...♗b5 19. ♕c2

19. ♕b3?? ♗xe2 20. ♕xb6 ♗xf3–+.

19...♗xe2 20. ♕xe2 ♘c6 21. ♗e3 ♗e7 22. ♔g2 ♔d7 23. ♕c2?!

23. ♖c1 =.

23...♘b4 24. ♕b3 ♕b5 25. a3 ♘d3

25...♕d3 26. ♕xd3 ♘xd3 27. ♖d1 ♘xb2 28. ♖b1 ♗xa3 29. ♗c1 ♘c4 (29...♘d3 30. ♗xa3 ♘f4+ 31. ♔f1 b5 32. ♖b3±) 30. ♗xa3 ♘xa3 (30...b6!?±) 31. ♖xb7+ ♔c6 32. ♖xf7 a5 33. ♖e7!?.

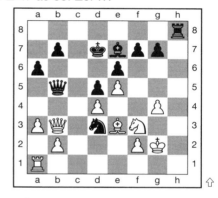

26. ♕a2

26. ♕xb5+ axb5 27. b3 ♖c8∓ (27...♖a8 28. ♖d1 ♘b2 29. ♖b1 ♗xa3 30. ♘g5 f6 31. ♘f3 ♘d3 32. ♖d1 ♘b4 33. ♖h1 ⩱) 28. ♔f1 ♖c3 29. b4 ♘b2 30. ♔e2 ♘c4 31. ♗c1 ♖c2+ 32. ♔f1 f6∓.

26...♖c8 27. b3

27. b4 ♕a4 28. ♕d2 ♘xb4 29. ♗g5 f6! (29...♘c2 30. ♖b1 b5 31. ♗xe7 ♔xe7 32. ♕g5+ ⇄) 30. exf6 gxf6 31. ♗xf6 ♗xf6 32. ♕xb4 ♕xb4 33. axb4 ♖c4 34. b5 axb5 35. ♖d1 b4 36. g5 ♗g7 37. ♔g3 ♔d6 38. g6 ♔e7 39. ♔f4 b3 40. ♘e5 ♖b4–+.

27...♖c3 28. ♖b1 ♕c6 29. ♖d1 ♕b5

29...♖c2? 30. ♕b1 ♕c3 31. ♖d2+–.

30. ♖b1 ♕c6 31. ♖d1 ♘c1 32. ♕b1

32. ♗xc1 ♖xc1 33. ♖d2 (33. ♖xc1 ♕xc1∓) 33...♕b5∓.

32...♘xb3 33. ♕h7 ♕c8

33...♗×a3 34. ♖h1 ♕c8 35. ♕×g7 ♕f8
36. ♕×f8 ♗×f8 37. ♖h7 ♔e8 38. ♘g5 ♖c8
39. ♖×f7 ♗e7 40. ♖g7⇄.

34. a4 ♕f8 35. ♖b1 b5

35...♗b4 36. ♘g1!?=.

36. a×b5 a×b5

36...a5 37. ♘d2 a4 38. ♘×b3 a×b3 39. ♗d2
♖c2 40. ♕d3±.

37. ♘d2?!

37. ♘g1! g6 38. ♘e2 ♖d3 39. ♘f4 ♖c3
40. ♘e2=.

37...♖×e3□ 38. ♘×b3 ♖c3 39. ♘d2?!∓

39. ♖a1! ♗a3 40. ♘d2 b4 41. ♘b1∓.

Draw.

Play on both wings

Game 58
Timman – Cu. Hansen
Malmö 2003

1. e4 e6 2. d4 d5 3. e5 c5 4. c3 ♘c6
5. ♘f3 ♕b6 6. a3 ♘h6 7. b4 c×d4 8. c×d4

8. ♗×h6 g×h6 9. c×d4 ♗d7 10. ♗e2 ♖c8
11. 0–0 ♗g7 12. ♕d2 0–0 13. ♖a2 f6 14. b5
♘a5 15. e×f5 ♖×f6 16. ♘e5 ♗e8 17. ♕e3
♖f5⇄ (Bosch–Lputian, Wijk aan Zee 1999).

8...♘f5 9. ♗b2 ♗d7

9...♗e7 10. ♗d3 a5 11. ♕a4 0–0 12. b5
♘h4 (Kiik–Korchnoi, Rilton Cup, Stockholm
2003; Volume 1, page 95) or 12...f6 (Lastin–
S. Ivanov, Aeroflot Open, Moscow 2004; Volume 1, game 25 on page 51).

10. g4 ♘h6

10...♘fe7!? 11. ♘c3 ♘a5 12. ♘d2
(12. ♕c2, Sveshnikov–Radjabov, Tallinn
2004, game 61 on page 53) 12...♖c8
13. ♖c1 ♘g6 14. h4 ♗e7 15. g5 h6 16. g×h6
♖×h6 17. h5 ♘h4 18. ♕g4 ♘f5 19. ♗d3±,
Grischuk–Radjabov, Wijk aan Zee 2003.

11. h3

11. ♖g1! f6 12. e×f6 g×f6 13. ♘c3 ♘f7
14. ♘a4! (14. ♖c1 ♗h6 15. ♖c2 ♘e7 16. h4
♗f4 17. ♗d3 h6 18. ♖e2 ♕c7 19. ♕b3
♘d6⇄, Lautier–Bauer, French Championship, Val d'Isère 2002) 14...♕d8 15. ♘c5±
b6 16. ♘×d7 ♕×d7 17. ♖c1, Vasyukov–
Bukhman, St. Petersburg 1994.

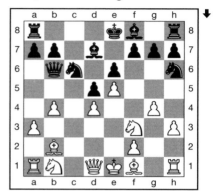

11...♗e7

11...f6 12. ♗d3 ♘f7 13. ♘bd2 (13. 0–0 ♖c8
14. ♘bd2 a5 15. b5 ♘e7 16. a4 ♘g6 17. ♗×g6
h×g6 18. ♔g2 g5∞, Belkhodja–Morovic Fer-
nandez, 35th Olympiad, Bled 2002) 13...f×e5
14. d×e5 ♗e7 15. ♖c1 ♘g5 16. h4 ♘×f3+
17. ♕×f3 ♘d4 18. ♕e3 ♘b5 19. ♘f3 ♕×e3+
20. f×e3 a5 21. ♗×b5 ♗×b5 22. ♘d4 ♗d7
23. b5 ♗d8 24. a4±, Sveshnikov–Lputian,
Tilburg 1992;

11...♖c8 12. ♘c3 ♘a5 13. ♘a4 ♕c6 14. ♖c1
♘c4 15. ♖×c4!? d×c4 16. ♘c3 ♕b6 17. ♗g2
a5 18. b5 ♗×b5 19. d5 ♗c5 20. 0–0 ♖d8
21. d6 ♗c6 22. ♕e2⩱, Shirov–Sadvakasov,
Astana 2001.

12. ♗d3

12. ♘c3!? 0–0 13. ♘a4 ♕d8 14. ♘c5 ♖b8
15. ♗d3 ♗e8 16. ♕b1 g6 17. ♕c1↑, Hába–
Koutsin, Wattens 1999.

12...♖c8 13. ♘bd2

13. ♕d2 ♘g8 14. 0–0 f6 15. ♖e1 f×e5
16. d×e5 ♘h6 17. ♘d4 ♘f7 18. ♘×c6 ♗×c6=,
Merenkov–Podlesny, Moravia 1996.

13...♘b8

A typical 'French' idea: Black prepares to exchange light-squared bishops on b5. Timman hinders this.

14. ♕e2 a6

Renewing the threat.

15. ♘b1!?

A purely prophylactic move: if Black insists on exchanging bishops, White will exchange on b5 and then the knight will come to c3 to attack the doubled pawn, which cannot be defended.

15. ♘b3±.

15...♘c6

15...♗b5 16. ♗xb5+ axb5 17. ♘c3 ♖c4 18. ♘d2!? ♕xd4 (18...♖xd4? 19. ♕e3 ♘d7 20. ♘xb5+−) 19. ♘xc4 bxc4 20. ♘b5±.

16. 0–0 0–0 17. ♘c3

The knight heads for c5. Black cannot reply with ♘a5 since the b2 bishop is protected by the queen.

17...♘xd4?

Black underestimates White's attacking chances. It was better to withdraw the queen to d8 and then prepare the f7–f6 break.

18. ♘xd4 ♕xd4 19. ♘e4 ♕b6 20. ♘f6+!

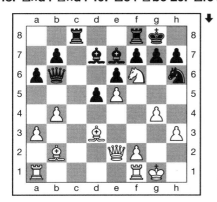

20...♗xf6

20...gxf6 21. exf6 ♗d6 22. ♕d2+−.

21. exf6 ♗b5

Here 21...e5!? would have been more stubborn: 22. ♕xe5 (22. ♗xe5!?) 22...♕xf6 23. ♕xf6 gxf6 24. ♗xf6±.

22. ♗xb5 ♕xb5 23. ♕e3+−

Black can no longer defend the dark squares, and his h6 knight is completely useless.

23...d4 24. ♗xd4 ♖fd8 25. ♖fd1?!

After 25. fxg7 e5 26. ♗b2 ♖c6 Black would still have had some defensive chances. In my opinion the most precise course was 25. a4! ♕d5 26. ♗b6 ♖d7 27. ♖ad1 ♕xd1 28. ♕g5+−.

25...♖d5

Black has parried the most dangerous threat – the incursion of the queen to g5 – and at the same time he sets a trap.

26. ♗b2!

After 26. fxg7 Black had the surprising riposte 26...♘xg4! (Notkin) 27. hxg4 ♕d7!, and Black regains the piece, e. g. 28. ♖d2 e5 29. ♗c3 ♖xc3!.

26...♖g5 27. ♖ac1 ♖e8 28. ♕f4

28. ♖d3!?±.

28...♖g6 29. ♖c5 ♕e2 30. ♖d2 ♕e1+ 31. ♔h2 ♕f1

The threat was 32. ♖c1 trapping the queen, and if 31...e5 White could win with 32. ♖xe5 ♖xe5 33. ♗xe5 gxf6 34. ♖d8+ ♔g7 35. ♗d4 ♕e7 36. ♕d6+−.

32. ♖h5?!

32. fxg7 f5!? 33. g5 ♘f7 34. h4 h6 35. ♖c1 ♕b5 36. ♗f6+−.

32...♘f5?!

32...♕b1! (Psakhis) 33. fxg7 ♘f5±.

33. ♕f3 ♘h6

33...♕b1 34. ♕e2 with the threat of ♖d1.

34. fxg7 f5 35. g5 ♘f7

(see next diagram)

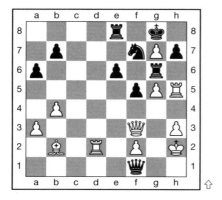

36. ♗f6

Here 36. ♖xh7! would have finished matters: 36...♔xh7 37. ♕h5+ ♘h6 38. g8♕+ ♖exg8 39. ♖d7+.

36...♘xg5 37. ♗xg5 h6 38. ♖d1 ♕b5 39. ♗xh6 ♕e5+ 40. ♔h1 ♕f6 41. ♗e3

Black resigned.

Play on both wings

Game 59
Sveshnikov – Dvoiris
Cheliabinsk 2004

1. e4 c5 2. c3 e6 3. d4 d5 4. e5

Semion had certainly not expected that a Sicilian would turn into an Advance French!

4...♘c6 5. ♘f3 ♕b6 6. a3 ♘h6 7. b4 cxd4 8. cxd4 ♘f5 9. ♗b2 ♗d7

Another possibility is 9...♗e7.

10. g4 ♘h6?!

Dvoiris is again unlucky! In 1993 I played a thematic match against Lputian to investigate this position, so I was very familiar with the ideas. At the moment theory considers 10...♘fe7 to be the best continuation.

11. ♖g1! f6 12. exf6 gxf6 13. ♘c3 ♘f7 14. ♘a4 ♕c7 15. ♖c1! ♕d6

After lengthy reflection, Semion Isaakovich comes up with a new move. The stem game

of this variation was Short–Lputian, Batumi 1999 (Volume 1, game 52 on page 103), in which 15...♕f4 was played. Although Smbat managed to draw the game, the variation is considered dubious for Black. Dvoiris's new move does nothing to change this assessment.

16. ♘c5 ♗c8

16...♕f4 17. ♘xb7 ♘g5 18. ♘xg5 fxg5 19. ♖g3±.

17. h4 ♗e7

White is better. If 17...e5, then 18. dxe5 fxe5 19. g5 with an attack.

18. g5 fxg5?!

This weakens the e5 square even more.

19. hxg5 (19. ♘xg5±) **19...♖g8**

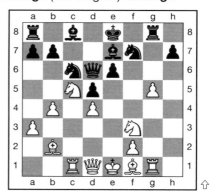

White has seized the key square e5 and prevented Black from castling. Strategically the game is already decided – it just remains for White to wrap it up with an attack on the king.

20. ♘d3!?

White refines his plan: the knight is headed for e5. Now the black king will have no safe haven. Instead 20. b5 ♘cd8 21. ♗d3± was also good.

20...♗d8

20...♕d8 21. ♘fe5 ♘fxe5 22. ♘xe5 ♘xe5 23. dxe5 ♖xg5 24. ♖xg5 ♗xg5 25. ♕h5+ ♔f8 26. ♖c3+−.

21. ♘de5 ♖g7 22. ♗d3+−

22. ♗b5±; 22. ♘×f7±.

22...♘c×e5 23. ♘×e5 ♘×e5 24. d×e5 ♕e7 25. ♕h5+ ♔f8 26. g6 h×g6 27. ♗×g6 ♗d7 28. ♖c3 ♔g8 29. ♖h3

Black resigned.

Play on both wings

Game 60
Sveshnikov – Golovanov
Cheliabinsk 2004

1. e4 e6 2. d4 d5 3. e5 c5 4. c3 ♘c6 5. ♘f3 ♕b6 6. a3 c4 7. ♘bd2 ♘a5 8. g3 ♗d7 9. h4 ♘e7?!

9...h5! 10. ♗h3 ♘h6!⇄.

10. ♗h3± ♕c7 11. 0−0 ♘c8 12. ♘e1

12. h5±.

12...h5?! 13. ♖b1 ♘b6 14. ♘df3 0−0−0 15. ♗g5 ♖e8 16. ♘g2 ♗a4 17. ♕e2 ♘d7 18. ♘e3 ♔b8 19. ♗f4 ♘c6 20. ♖be1 ♘b6 21. ♘g5 ♘d8 22. ♘g2 ♗e7 23. ♘f3 ♘c8 24. ♗g5 ♗f8 25. ♘f4

25. ♗×d8 ♖×d8 26. ♘g5 ♗e8±.

25...♕b6 26. ♘h2

26. ♗×d8!? ♖×d8 27. ♘g5 ♗e8 28. ♘×h5 f6 (28...♗e7 29. ♗g4 ♗×g5 30. h×g5 ♗a4 30. ♔g2±) 29. ♘×f6! g×f6 30. e×f6±.

26...g6 27. ♘f3

27. ♗f6 ♖g8 28. ♘f3±.

27...♗g7 28. ♕d2

28. ♗f6 ♗×f6 29. e×f6 ♘d6 30. ♘g5 (30. ♘e5 ♕c7 31. ♗g2±) 30...♘c6 (30...♕c7 31. ♕d2±) 31. ♗×e6±.

28...♘c6 29. ♖e2 ♕c7 30. ♘g2 b5 31. ♖fe1 a5 32. ♗f6 ♗×f6 33. e×f6± ♘d6 34. ♘g5 b4 35. a×b4 a×b4 36. ♘f4 ♖hf8?!

(see next diagram)

36...♗b5 37. ♗×e6 f×e6 38. ♘f×e6+−.

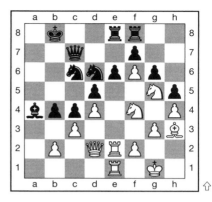

37. ♗×e6 f×e6 38. ♘f×e6 ♕d7 39. ♘c5+− ♕a7?!

39...♕f5 40. ♘×a4 ♖×e2 41. ♕×e2 ♖×f6 42. ♘c5±.

40. ♕f4 ♖d8 41. ♖e6

Black resigned.

Attack on the king

Game 61
Sveshnikov – Radjabov
Tallinn (Rapidplay) 2004

1. e4 e6 2. d4 d5 3. e5 c5 4. c3 ♘c6 5. ♘f3 ♕b6 6. a3 ♘h6 7. b4 c×d4 8. c×d4 ♘f5 9. ♗b2 ♗d7

9...♗e7!?.

10. g4 ♘fe7 11. ♘c3 ♘a5 12. ♕c2!? ♘c4 13. ♗×c4 d×c4 14. ♘d2 ♕c6

14...♕×d4? 15. ♘ce4+−.

15. ♘ce4 c3!?

15...♘d5 16. ♘×c4 ♘b6 17. ♘cd6+ ♗×d6 18. ♘×d6+ ♔e7 19. ♕×c6 ♗×c6 20. 0−0± (20. ♖g1 ♘c8=, Sveshnikov – Potkin, Russian Championship, Krasnoyarsk 2003; Volume 1, page 95).

16. ♘d6+

16. ♕×c3 ♘d5 17. ♕×c6 ♗×c6 18. ♖g1 (18. f3 ♘f4∞) 18...♖d8∞ (18...h5!? 19. g5 ♘f4 20. ♖g3 h4 21. ♖f3 ♘g2+ 22. ♔f1 h3∞).

16...♔d8 17. ♘×f7+ ♔e8 18. ♘d6+ ♔d8

(see next diagram)

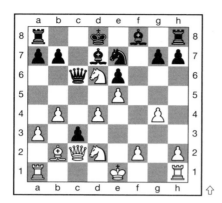

19. ♘f7+

19. ♘2e4!? c×b2 20. ♛×b2 ⯑ ♘g6 21. ♖c1 ♗×d6 22. ♖×c6 ♗×c6 23. ♘×d6 (23. e×d6 ♗×e4 24. 0–0 ♖c8 25. d5 e5±) 23...♗×h1 24. ♘f7+ ♔d7 25. ♘×h8 ♖×h8 26. ♛b3 b5 27. a4 a6±;

19. ♛×c3 ♛×h1+ 20. ♔e2 ♛g2 21. ♘f7+ ♔e8 22. ♘d6+ ♔d8 23. ♘f7+=.

19...♔e8 20. ♘d6+ ♔d8

Draw.

Chapter 2

Encyclopaedia

Table 1

1. e4 e6 2. d4 d5 3. e5

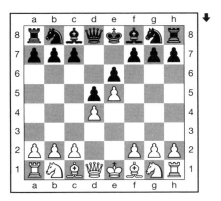

	3	4	5	6	7	8	9	10	
1	...	♘f3[1]	c4[2]	♘c3	cxd5[5]	♗c4	bxc3	0-0	
	♘e7	b6	♗b7[3]	♘bc6[4]	♘xd5	♘xc3[6]	♗e7	0-0[7]	⇄
2	...	♘f3!?[8]	♗g5![9]	c4	♗e3	♗xc4	♘c3	0-0	
	♗d7	a6	♕c8?[10]	h6[11]	dxc4	♘e7	♗c6	♕d7[12]	±
3	...	c3[13]	♘f3[14]	a4	♘a3	♗xa6	0-0 [18]	♕d3	
	b6	♕d7	a5[15]	♘e7[16]	♗a6[17]	♘xa6	c6[19]	♘c7[20]	±
4	...	dxc5	♘f3[22]	♗d3	0-0[24]	♖e1	c3	♘a3	
	c5	♘c6[21]	♗xc5	♘ge7[23]	♘g6	♗d7	♗b6[25]	a6[26]	⇄
5	...	♕g4?!	♘f3	♗d3	0-0	♖e1	c3[30]	♘xc3	
	...	cxd4![27]	♘c6	♘ge7![28]	♘g6	♗e7[29]	dxc3[31]	♗d7![32]	∓
6	...	♘f3!?	♗d3!?[34]	0-0	♗f4[36]	♗g3	♘bd2[38]	exf6[40]	
	...	♘c6[33]	cxd4	♘ge7[35]	♘g6	♗e7[37]	f5[39]	gxf6[41]	⇄
7	...	c3	♘f3[43]	♗e2[44]	c4!?[46]	♗xc4	♘bd2	a3[49]	
	...	♕b6[42]	♗d7	♗b5[45]	♗xc4[47]	♕b4+[48]	dxc4	♕b5[50]	⇄

Note: the author has included many games in the encyclopaedia tables more than once, to take account of possible transpositions.

1   4. c3 b6 5. ♘d2 ♕d7 6. ♘df3 c5 7. ♘h3 ♗a6 8. ♗×a6 ♘×a6 9. ♕e2 ♘c7 10. ♘f4 ♕b5! 11. ♕×b5+ ♘×b5 12. a4 ♘c7 13. a5 ♘c6 14. a×b6 a×b6 15. ♖×a8+ ♘×a8 16. ♗e3 c4!= Hennings – Bednarski, Polanica Zdrój 1969.

2   **5. c3** ♕d7 See 3…b6;

5. b4!? ♘f5 6. c3 c5 (6…a5 7. b5±) 7. a3 ♗e7 8. ♗d3 (8. g4 ♘h4 9. ♘×h4 ♗×h4 10. ♗e3 0–0!?⇄) 8…c4 9. ♗c2 ♘d7 10. h4 h5 11. ♗g5 f6?! (⌓ 11…♘f8±) 12. ♗f4?! (⌓ 12. e×f6 g×f6 13. ♗×f5 e×f5 14. ♗f4±) 12…♘f8 13. ♘bd2 ♘g6 14. ♗h2 ♔f7⇄ Vysochin – Alekseev, Kiev 1999.

3   5…d×c4 6. ♗×c4 ♗b7 7. ♘c3 ♘bc6 8. 0–0 ♕d7 9. ♕e2 ♘b4 10. a3 ♘bd5 11. ♗a6 ♗c6 12. ♗e3 ♘f5 13. ♖ac1 ♗e7 14. ♘×d5 ♗×d5 15. g4 ♘h6 16. ♘d2 ♘g8 17. ♘b1!?± I. Zaitsev – Lupu, Bucharest 1993.

4   6…♕d7 7. c×d5 ♘×d5 8. ♗d3 c5 9. 0–0 ♘×c3 10. b×c3 c×d4 11. ♘×d4 ♘c6 12. ♖b1 ♗c5 13. ♗e3 0–0–0?! 14. ♗b5 ♗×d4 15. ♗×d4 ♕d5 16. ♗×c6 ♗×c6 17. f3 h5 18. a4↑ Kupreichik – Vaganian, USSR 1980.

5   7. a3 ♕d7 8. ♗e3 d×c4 9. ♗×c4 ♘a5 10. ♗b5 ♗c6 11. ♗d3 ♘d5 12. ♘e4 ♗b5 13. 0–0 ♗e7 14. ♖e1± Krason – Dobosz, Poland 1980.

6   8…♗b4.

7   11. ♗d3 ♘a5 12. ♕e2 (12. ♗e3 c5 13. ♘d2 c×d4 14. c×d4 ♘c6 15. ♗e4±; 12. ♕c2!? h6 13. ♖d1!? ♗×f3 14. g×f3±) 12…a6 13. ♗f4 ♗d5 14. ♖fe1 (14. ♗×a6 ♖×a6 15. ♕×a6 ♗c4 16. ♕a7 ♕d7∞; 14. c4!? ♗×f3 15. ♕×f3 ♕×d4 16. ♖ad1 ♕c5 17. ♕e4 g6 18. ♗h6 ♖fd8 19. ♖fe1 ⁝; 14. a4 ♕d7 15. ♕c2! h6 16. ♘d2 c5 17. c4 ♗b7 18. d×c5 ♗×c5 19. ♖fd1±) 14…b5 15. ♘d2 c5 16. ♕g4 g6 17. ♘e4 [⌓ 17. ♗h6 ♖e8 18. d×c5! ♕c7 (18…♗×g2?! 19. ♗e4! ♗×e4 20. ♘×e4±) 19. a4±] 17…c×d4 18. c×d4 ♘c6⇄ Kupreichik – Petrosian, Moscow 1979.

8   4. c3 a6

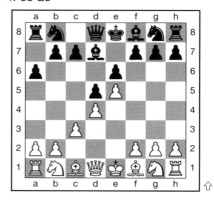

a) 5. ♗e3 ♘e7 6. ♘f3 ♗b5 7. ♘bd2 ♘f5 8. ♗g5 ♕d7 9. g4 ♘e7 10. a4 ♗×f1 11. ♘×f1 h5!? 12. g×h5 ♖×h5 13. ♘g3 ♖h8 14. h4± Boe Olsen – Alekseev, Tula 2000;

b) 5. ♗d3!? c5 [5…♗b5 6. ♗c2 a5 7. ♘e2± (7. a4 ♗a6 8. ♘e2 c5 9. ♘d2 ♘c6 10. ♘f3 ♕b6!?⇄) 7…c5 8. d×c5 ♕c7 9. ♘a3 ♗a6 10. ♗a4+ ♘d7 11. ♗e3 ♘e7 12. ♗×d7+ ♕×d7 13. ♘d4±] 6. ♘f3 c×d4 7. c×d4 ♗b5 8. ♗×b5+ a×b5 9. 0–0±;

c) 5. ♘d2 ♗b5 (5…c5!? 6. ♘df3 c×d4 7. c×d4 ♕b6 8. ♘h3 ♘c6 9. a3 ♘ge7 10. b4 ♘f5 11. ♗e3 h6 12. ♗d3 g5 13. g4 ♘×e3 14. f×e3 ♗g7⇄ Najer – Bauer, ACP Blitz 2004) 6. ♗×b5+ a×b5 7. ♘e2 ♘d7 8. 0–0 h5?! 9. ♘f4 g6 10. ♘f3 ♘b6 11. h4 ♘h6 12. ♘d3 ♘f5 13. g3 ♗e7 14. ♗g5 ♖a7 15. ♕c1 ♔f8 16. ♔g2 ♔g7 17. ♖h1 ♘c4 18. ♕f4± Motylev – Rustemov, Tomsk 2004.

9   **5. c4** d×c4 6. ♗×c4 ♗c6 7. 0–0 ♘e7 8. ♘c3 h6 9. ♕e2 ♘d7 10. ♖d1± Lau – Benjamin, New York 1985;

5. ♘c3 ♗b4 6. ♗e2 ♘e7 7. 0–0 c5 8. a3 ♗×c3 9. b×c3 ♗a4 10. d×c5 ♘bc6 11. ♖b1 ♕c7 12. ♗f4 0–0 13. ♗d3± Prié – Bauer, French Championship, Nantes 1993;

5. c3 ♗b5 6. ♘bd2 ♘c6 7. a4 ♗×f1 8. ♘×f1 f6 9. ♘g3 ♕d7 10. h4 f×e5 11. d×e5 ♘d8⇄ Ginzburg – Firman, Hengelo 2001.

10 5...♘e7 6. h4!? [6. ♘c3!? c5 (6...h6 7. ♗h4 g5 8. ♗g3 ♘f5 9. ♗d3 ♘×g3 10. h×g3 c5 11. d×c5 ♗×c5 12. ♕d2⇄) 7. ♗d3 c×d4 8. ♘×d4 ♕b6 9. ♘b3 ♘bc6 10. ♕e2 ♘g6 11. 0-0-0?! (11. ♗×g6 h×g6 12. 0-0-0⇄) 11...d4 (11...♘g×e5! 12. ♘×d5 e×d5 13. f4 ♗g4−+) 12. ♗×g6 h×g6 13. ♘e4∞ Kavalek – Benjamin, US Championship, Estes Park 1985] 6...♗b5 7. ♗×b5+ a×b5 8. h5 h6 9. ♗f4 ♘d7 10. c3 ♘b6 11. ♘bd2 ♘c4 12. b3 ♘×d2 13. ♕×d2 c6 14. ♖h3 ♘c8 15. ♔f1± Kiik – Kärner, Helsinki 1995.

11 6...d×c4 7. ♗×c4 ♗c6 8. ♘c3 h6 9. ♗h4 ♗e7 10. d5 e×d5 11. ♘×d5 ♕d7 12. 0-0 ♗×d5 13. ♗×d5 ♗×h4 14. e6! f×e6 15. ♘e5 ♕×d5 16. ♕h5+ ♔e7 17. ♖ad1+− Grosar – Sulava, Pula 1992.

12 11. ♖c1! ♗×f3 (11...a5? 12. d5 e×d5 13. ♗d3!!+− Bronstein – Kärner, Tallinn 1981) 12. ♕×f3 c6 13. ♘e4±.

13

a) 4. ♗b5+ c6 (4...♗d7?! 5. ♗d3 c5 6. c3 ♘c6 7. ♘f3 f6 8. 0-0 f×e5 9. d×e5 ♕c7 10. ♖e1 ♘h6 11. c4! d4 12. ♘a3± Anand – Rogers, Interzonal, Manila 1990) 5. ♗a4 (5. ♗d3 ♗a6 6. ♘f3 ♗×d3 7. ♕×d3±) 5...b5 (5...a5 6. c3 ♗a6 7. ♘e2 ♘e7 8. 0-0 ♘d7 9. ♖e1 ♖c8 10. ♘g3± Erenburg – Deutsch, Tel Aviv 2002) 6. ♗b3 c5 7. c3 ♘e7 8. ♘f3 ♘ec6 9. 0-0 h6 10. ♗e3 ♘d7 11. ♘bd2 c4 12. ♗c2 b4⇄ Shabalov – Seirawan, US Championship, Chandler 1997;

b) 4. ♘h3!? ♗a6 5. ♗×a6 ♘×a6 6. 0-0 ♕d7 7. ♗e3 ♘e7 8. a4 ♘b8 9. a5 ♘bc6 10. a×b6 c×b6 11. c3 ♘a5 12. ♘a3± Velimirović – Marić, Yugoslavia 1966;

c) 4. ♘f3 ♘e7!? [4...♕d7 5. c4!? ♘e7 (5...♗b4+!? 6. ♘c3 ♘e7 7. a3 ♗×c3+ 8. b×c3 ♗a6 9. c×d5 ♕×d5 10. ♗×a6 ♘×a6 11. 0-0 ♘b8= Kupreichik – Vaganian, Berlin 1991) 6. ♘c3 ♗b7 7. ♗e2 (7. ♗e3! h6 8. ♖c1 ♘bc6 9. a3± Volkov – Vaganian, Aeroflot Open, Moscow 2005) ♘bc6 8. 0-0 d×c4 9. ♗×c4 ♘a5 10. ♗b5 ♗c6 11. ♗d3 ♘d5 12. ♗d2± Sax – Short, London 1980] 5. ♘c3 ♗a6 6. ♗×a6 ♘×a6 7. 0-0 ♕d7 8. ♘e2 (8. ♕e2 ♘b8 9. a4 ♘bc6 10. ♖d1±) 8...♘b8 (8...c5 9. d×c5 b×c5 10. ♘g3 ♕b5 11. b3 h6 12. c4! ♕b7 13. ♕e2± Svidler – Rustemov, German League 2003/04) 9. ♘g3 ♘bc6 10. b3 0-0-0 11. ♗b2 ♔b7 12. c4 ♘f5 13. ♕e2 ♗e7 14. ♖ad1 g5⇄ Ulibin – Rustemov, Tomsk 2004; 4. f4?!;

d) 4. c4!? d×c4 5. ♗×c4 ♗b7 6. ♘f3 ♘e7 7. ♘c3 ♕d7 8. 0-0 h6 9. ♕e2 ♘bc6 10. a3 ♘a5 11. ♗a2 ♘d5 12. ♗d2± I. Zaitsev – Kärner, Sochi 1977;

e) 4. f4?!.

14 a) 5. a4 a5 (5...♗a6 6. ♗×a6 ♘×a6 7. ♕d3 ♕c8 8. b4 ♘e7 9. b5 ♘b8 10. ♘d2 a6 11. ♖b1 a×b5 12. a×b5 c6⇄ Ye Jiangchuan – Ivanchuk, FIDE World Championship, Moscow 2001) 6. ♘d2 (6. ♘f3±; 6. f4?! ♘e7 7. ♘d2 h5 8. ♘df3 ♗a6 9. ♗×a6 ♘×a6 10. ♗e3 ♘f5 11. ♗f2 ♗e7= Kupreichik – Korchnoi, Sochi 1970) 6...♘e7 7. ♘df3 c5 8. ♗d3 ♗a6 9. ♘e2 ♗×d3 10. ♕×d3 ♘bc6 11. 0-0 c×d4 12. ♘e×d4 ♘×d4 13. ♘×d4 ♘c6 14. ♘b5 ♗c5⇄ Ehlvest – Vaganian, 34th Olympiad, Istanbul 2000;

b) 5. h4 ♗a6 6. ♗×a6 ♘×a6 7. h5 c5 8. ♘e2 f6 9. ♗f4 ♘e7 10. ♘d2 ♘c6 11. ♘f3 ♖c8 12. 0-0 ♘ab8 13. ♖e1± Movsesian – Tibenský, Kaskády 2002;

c) 5. ♗e3 ♘e7 6. f4 h5 7. ♘d2 ♘f5 8. ♗f2 ♗a6 9. ♗×a6 ♘×a6 10. ♘e2 g6 11. ♘f3 ♗e7

12. ♕d3 ♘b8 13. 0–0 c5 14. c4± Kupre-ichik–Vaganian, 44th USSR Championship, Moscow 1976.

15   5...♘e7 6. h4 c5 7. h5 h6 8. b3?! ♗a6 9. ♗×a6 ♘×a6 10. ♕e2 ♘c7 11. d×c5 b×c5 12. c4 ♘c6 13. ♖h4?! d4 14. ♘bd2 0-0-0⇄ Schmitt–Short, Montpellier 2004; **5...c5** 6. a4 (6. h4!? ♗a6 7. ♗×a6 ♘×a6 8. ♕e2 ♘c7 9. h5 ♘h6?! 10. ♗g5 ♘f5 11. g4± Blatný–Gonzalez Rodriguez, Bern 1995) 6...♗a6 7. ♗×a6 ♘×a6 8. ♕e2 ♘c7 9. a5±.

16   6...h5 7. ♘a3 ♗×a3 8. ♖×a3 ♘e7 9. g3 ♗a6 10. h3 c5 11. ♗×a6 ♘×a6 12. ♔f1 c×d4 13. c×d4 0-0-0 14. ♔g2 ♔b7 15. ♖c3 ♖c8 16. ♘g5± Dvoiris–Vaganian, Istanbul 2003.

17   7...h5 8. ♘c2 ♗a6 9. ♗×a6 ♘×a6 10. 0-0 ♘f5 11. ♗g5 c5 12. ♘e3 ♘×e3 13. f×e3 b5 14. ♘h4 b4 15. ♘g6! f×g6 16. ♕d3→ Hába–Mészáros, Kecskemét 1993.

18   9. h4!?.

19   ⌒ 9...♘b8.

20   11. ♘c2 (11. b3 c5 12. c4) 11...c5 12. h4! c4? (⌒ 12...♘c6 13. h5 h6±) 13. ♕e2 h5 14. ♗g5± Sveshnikov–Vaganian, Moscow 1985.

21   4...♗×c5 5. ♕g4 (5. ♗d3 ♕b6 6. ♕e2 ♘c6 7. ♘f3 f6 8. 0-0 f×e5 9. ♘×e5 ♘×e5 10. ♕×e5 ♘f6 11. ♘c3 0-0⇄ Bron-stein–Korchnoi, Herceg-Novi 1970) 5...♘e7 (5...♔f8 6. ♘f3 ♘e7 7. ♗d3 ♘bc6 8. 0-0 ♘g6 9. ♕g3 ♕c7 10. ♖e1 a6 11. c3± Karlovich–Alvarez Vila, Oropesa del Mar 2000) 6. b4 (6. ♕×g7 ♘g6∞) 6...♗b6 7. ♕×g7± (Keres) 7...♖g8 8. ♕×h7 ♕c7 9. ♘f3 ♘bc6 10. ♗f4 ♘d4 11. c3 ♘×f3+ 12. g×f3 ♗d7 13. a4 a5 14. b5 d4 15. c4±.

22   5. ♗f4?! ♗×c5 6. ♗d3 ♕b6! [6...♘ge7?! 7. ♘f3 ♘g6 8. ♗g3 0-0 9. 0-0 f5 10. e×f6 ♕×f6 11. c4!? ♕×b2 12. ♗×g6! (12...♕×a1? 13. ♗×h7+ ♔×h7 14. ♕c2+ ♔g8 (14...g6 15. ♘g5+ ♔g7 16. ♘c3±) 15. ♘c3±) 12...h×g6 13. c×d5!∞ Velimirović–Kholmov, Yugoslavia–USSR, Odessa 1975] 7. ♗g3 ♕×b2 8. ♘d2 ♘×e5∓.

23

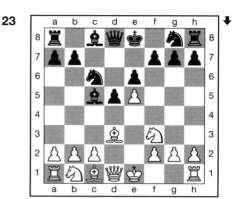

a) 6...f5!? 7. c3 [7. 0-0 ♘ge7 8. c3 0-0 9. b4 ♗b6 10. b5 ♘a5 11. ♘bd2 ♗d7 12. ♗a3 ♖c8 13. ♖c1 ♗c5 14. ♗b4⇄ (Keres–van Does-burgh, Unofficial Olympiad, Munich 1936) 14...♘g6! 15. ♕a4 b6∞] 7...a6 8. ♘bd2 ♘ge7 9. ♘b3 ♗a7 10. 0-0 0-0 11. ♖e1 ♘g6⇄ Tarrasch–Lasker, St. Petersburg 1914;

b) 6...♕c7 7. ♗f4 ♘ge7 8. ♕e2 ♘g6 9. ♗g3 a6 10. c3 b5 (10...♗d7 11. ♘bd2 0-0 12. h4 h6⇄) 11. ♘bd2 ♗b7 12. h4± Hankipohja–Sorri, Finland 1967;

c) 6...f6 7. ♕e2 (7. ♗f4? f×e5 8. ♘×e5 ♕f6-+) 7...f×e5 [7...♕c7!? 8. ♗b5 (8. ♗f4 g5! 9. ♗g3 g4 10. ♘fd2 ♘×e5∓; 8. e×f6 ♘×f6∓) 8...f×e5 (8...♔f7!?⇄) 9. ♕×e5 ♕×e5+ 10. ♘×e5 ♘ge7∓] 8. ♘×e5 ♘f6 9. ♗f4 [9. 0-0 ♘×e5 10. ♕×e5 0-0 11. c4 ♕b6 12. ♕e2 ♗d7 (12...e5!∓) 13. ♘d2 ♖ac8⇄ Makropoulos–Hug, 21st Olympiad, Nice 1974] 9...0-0 10. 0-0 ♘e4 (10...♕e8! ⌂ ♘h5= Glek) 11. ♘×c6 b×c6 12. ♗e3 ♗×e3 13. ♕×e3⇄ Becker–Maróczy, Carls-bad 1929.

24   7. ♗f4 ♕b6 (7...♘g6 8. ♗g3 f5 9. e×f6 ♕×f6 10. ♗×g6+ ♕×g6 11. 0-0 0-0= Polu-gaevsky–Antoshin, Tbilisi 1956) 8. 0-0 ♕×b2 9. ♘bd2 ♕b6 (⌂ 9...♘g6!) 10. ♖b1 ♕a3 11. ♗g3 0-0∓) 10. ♘b3 (10. c4!? h6 11. ♕c1 ♘b4 12. ♗e2 ♗d7 13. a3 ♘a6 14. ♖b1↑ Keres–Alexandrescu, Unofficial Olympiad, Munich 1936) 10...♘g6 11. ♗g3 ♗e7 12. h4⇗ Nimzowitsch–Spielmann, San Sebastian 1912.

25 9…a5 10. a4 ♕b8?! (10…♕b6!?) 11. ♕e2 ♗b6 12. ♘a3 0–0 13. ♘b5± ♘a7?! 14. ♗e3 ♗×e3 15. ♕×e3 ♘×b5 16. a×b5 b6 17. ♘d4 f5 18. f4± Steinitz–Showalter, Vienna 1898.

26 11. ♘c2 ♗c7 12. ♗×g6 h×g6 (12…f×g6!?) 13. ♗f4 ♕e7 14. ♘cd4 ♖c8 15. ♕d3 ♗b6⇄ Nimzowitsch–Alekhine, St. Petersburg 1914.

27 a) 4…♘c6 5. ♘f3 (5. c3 c×d4 6. c×d4 ♕b6 7. ♘f3 ♘h6∓ Atalik) 5…♕a5+ 6. c3 [6. ♗d2?! ♘h6! 7. ♕g5 ♕b6 8. b3 ♘f5 9. ♗d3 ♘f×d4 10. ♘×d4 ♘×d4 (10…c×d4 11. 0–0 ♕c7 12. f4∓ Atalik) 11. 0–0 ♗d7 12. ♘c3 h6 13. ♕h5 ♗e7 14. ♖fe1 g6 15. ♕d1 h5 16. a4 ♗c6 17. ♕c1 h4 18. h3 ♖h5∓ Popadić–Atalik, Budva 2003] 6…c×d4 7. ♘×d4 [△ 7. ♗e2 d×c3 (7…h5!?) 8. ♘×c3 ♘ge7 9. ♗d2∓] 7…f5 (7…♘×e5!∓) 8. ♕d1 ♘×d4 9. ♕×d4 ♘e7 10. ♗f4 ♘c6 11. ♕d2 ♗e7∓ Hector–Dokhoian, Copenhagen 1991;

b) 4…♕a5+!? 5. c3 (5. ♘d2 ♘c6 6. ♘gf3? ♘h6 7. ♕f4 ♘b4 8. ♔d1 c4∓ Nei–Gleizerov, Österskär 1995; 5. ♗d2 ♕b6 6. b3 c×d4 7. ♘f3 ♘c6 8. ♗d3 ♘b4 9. 0–0 ♘×d3 10. c×d3 ♘e7 11. ♘a3 ♗d7⇄ Pinski–Zontakh, Kazimierz Dolny 2001) 5…c×d4 6. ♕×d4 (6. ♘f3 ♘c6 7. ♗d3 d×c3 8. ♘×c3 d4 9. ♘×d4 ♕×e5+ 10. ♗e3 ♘f6 11. ♕h4 ♘×d4 12. ♕×d4 ♕×d4 13. ♗×d4 ♗d7∓) 6…♘c6 7. ♕f4 ♘ge7 8. ♗d3 ♘g6 9. ♗×g6 h×g6 10. ♘f3 ♕a6 11. ♘g5 ♘d8 12. ♘d2 ♕d3 13. ♘b3 b6 14. ♗d2 (14. ♘d4 ♗a6 15. ♕f3 ♕×f3 16. ♘g×f3 f6 17. ♗e3 g5 18. g4 ♗d3∓) 14…♗d7 15. 0–0–0 ♖c8 16. ♗e1 ♕a6∓ I. Rabinovich–Botvinnik, Moscow 1937.

28 6…♕c7!? 7. 0–0 ♘×e5 (7…f6 8. ♗×h7 ♘×e5 9. ♘×e5 f×e5 10. ♗g6+ ♔d8 11. h3 ♘f6 12. ♕d1 ♗d6 13. c3 d×c3 14. ♘×c3 ♗d7∓ Smyslov–Lisitsyn, Moscow 1942) 8. ♘×e5 ♕×e5 9. ♗f4 ♘f6 10. ♕g3 (10. ♗b5+ ♗d7 11. ♗×d7+ ♔×d7 12. ♕g3 ♕f5∓) 10…♕h5∞; **6…f6** 7. ♗×h7 ♘×e5 8. ♘×e5 f×e5 9. ♕g6+ ♔e7 10. ♗×g8 ♖×g8∞ Baranov–Yakhin, USSR 1974.

29 8…♕c7 9. ♕g3 [9. ♕h5∞; 9. ♗g5?! ♘g×e5 (9…a6) 10. ♘×e5 ♘×e5∓]

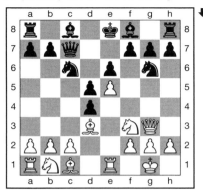

9…♗d7 10. h4 ♖c8 11. h5 ♘ge7 12. ♘bd2 f6 13. ♘b3 f×e5 14. ♘×e5 ♘×e5 15. ♖×e5 ♘c6 16. ♗f4→; **9…♗c5?!** 10. h4 ♔f8 (10…0–0 11. h5 ♘h8 12. ♗g5 g6 13. ♘f3±) 11. h5 ♘ge7± Nimzowitsch–Székely, Kecskemét 1927; **9…f5**; **9…♗d7⇄** ; **9…f6** 10. ♗×g6+ h×g6 11. c3 d3 12. ♕×g6+ ♕f7 13. ♕×d3 f×e5∓ Yukhtman–Matulović, USSR–Yugoslavia, Kiev 1959; **9…♘b4** 10. ♘×d4 ♘×d3 11. c×d3⇄.

30 9. a3!? ♗d7! [9…0–0 10. h4 (10. ♘bd2 f5 11. ♕g3 a5 12. ♘b3 ♕b6 13. h4 a4 14. h5!?∞ Gershkovich–Petrosian, Tbilisi 1945) 10…♕c7 (10…♘×h4? 11. ♗×h7+ ♔×h7 12. ♘g5+ ♗×g5 13. ♗×g5 ♕c7 14. ♕×h4+ ♔g8 15. ♗f6+−) 11. ♗g5 (11. ♗×g6 f×g6 12. ♘bd2 ♖f5∓) 11…♗×g5 12. h×g5⇄] 10. b4 ♕c7 11. b5 h5 12. ♕g3 h4 13. ♕g4 ♘c×e5 14. ♘×e5 ♘×e5 15. ♕×g7 ♖h5!∓; **9. h4?!** ♗×h4∓.

31 9…♗d7 10. c×d4 ♘b4 11. ♖d1 h5 12. ♕h3 ♘×d3 13. ♖×d3 ♗a4 14. b3 ♗b5∓; **9…0–0** 10. c×d4 ♘b4 11. ♖d1 f5 12. ♕h5 ♕e8 13. ♘e1 ♗d7 14. ♘c3 ♕f7 15. ♗e2 ♖fc8⇄ Honfi–Uhlmann, Leipzig 1982.

32 11. ♗d2 (11. a3!?) 11…♘b4 12. ♗b1 ♖c8 13. a3 ♘c6 (13…♘a6 14. ♗d3 ♘c5 15. ♗c2⊼) 14. ♗d3 0–0∓ Sveshnikov–Komarov, Vrnjačka Banja 1999; 14…♘a5!?∓.

33 **4...c×d4** 5. ♕×d4!? (5. ♗d3 ♘e7!?
6. 0–0 ♘g6!? 7. ♗×g6 h×g6 8. ♕×d4 ♘c6
9. ♕f4= Short) 5...♘c6 6. ♕f4 ♕c7 7. ♘c3
a6 8. ♗d3 ♘ge7 9. 0–0 ♘g6 10. ♕g3 ♘g×e5
11. ♘×e5 ♘×e5 12. ♖e1 f6 13. ♘×d5 e×d5
14. f4∞ Velimirović – Kholmov, Yugoslavia –
USSR, Odessa 1975; **4...♕b6** 5. ♗d3 c×d4
6. 0–0 ♘d7 7. ♘bd2 ♘e7 8. ♘b3 ♘c6
9. ♖e1 g6 10. ♗f4 ♗g7 11. ♕d2 0–0 12. h4
♕c7?! Keres – Ståhlberg, 6th Olympiad, Warsaw 1935; 12...a5!?⇄.

34 5. d×c5 see 4. d×c5.

35

a) 6...f6!? 7. ♗b5 [7. ♕e2 (7...♕c7 8. ♗f4
g5 9. ♗g3 g4 10. ♘h4 f5 11. ♘d2?! (11. f3)
11...♗h6 12. ♘×f5?! (12. f4∞) 12...e×f5
13. e6 ♕g7!↑ Kogan – Glek, Copenhagen
1996) 7...f×e5 8. ♘×e5 ♘f6 9. ♗g5 (9. ♗f4
♗d6 10. ♘d2 0–0 11. ♖ae1 ⯑ ♕c7; 9. ♗b5
♕c7∓ 10. c3 d3!; 9. ♘d2 ♘×e5 10. ♕×e5
♗d6 11. ♕×d4 e5∓) 9...♗d6? Rauzer –
Grigoriev, Odessa 1929; 9...♘×e5! 10. ♕×e5
♗d6! 11. ♕×d4 0–0 12. ♘d2 ♕c7 13. ♕h4
h6∓] 7...♗d7 8. ♗×c6 b×c6 9. ♕×d4 f×e5
(9...♕b6!?) 10. ♕×e5 ♘f6 11. ♗f4 ♗c5⇄
Alekhine – Euwe, Nottingham 1936;

b) 6...f5 7. ♘bd2! (7. a3 a5 8. ♗b5 ♗d7
9. ♗×c6 b×c6 10. ♕×d4 c5 11. ♕f4 ♘h6
12. c4 d4∓ Crosa – Leitão, São Paulo 2002)
7...♘ge7 8. ♘b3 ♘g6 9. ♖e1 ♗e7 (9...♕b6
10. a4!? ♗b4 11. ♗d2 ♗×d2 12. ♕×d2±)

10. ♘b×d4 0–0 11. c4± (Keres) 11...♘×d4
12. ♘×d4 ♕b6 13. ♘f3±;
c) 6...♗c5 7. ♘bd2 (7. a3 ♘ge7 8. ♘bd2 ♘g6
9. ♘b3 ♗b6 10. ♖e1 ♗d7 11. g3 f6 12. ♗×g6+
h×g6 13. ♕d3 ♔f7 14. h4 ♕g8! 15. ♗d2
♕h7 16. ♗b4 g5!∓ Bondarevsky – Botvinnik,
Leningrad/Moscow 1941; 7. c3!?) 7...♘ge7
8. ♘b3 ♗b6 9. ♗f4 ♘g6 10. ♗g3 (10. ♗×g6
h×g6 11. ♖e1 ♗d7 12. ♗g3 ♖c8 13. ♖e2 ♘e7
14. ♘b×d4 ♘f5 15. ♘×f5 g×f5∓ Levenfish –
Botvinnik, Leningrad 1937) 10...f5 11. h4 0–0
12. h5 ♘h8∞;
d) 6...♗d7 7. ♖e1 h6 8. a3 ♗c5 (8...♘ge7)
9. ♘bd2 ♘ge7 10. b4! ♗b6 11. ♘b3
a6 12. ♗b2 0–0 13. ♕d2?! Hodgson –
Morozevich, Amsterdam 1996; 13. ♘b×d4
♘×d4 14. ♘×d4±.

36 **7. ♖e1** ♘g6 8. ♘bd2 [8. a3?! ♗d7
(8...♗e7 9. ♘bd2 0–0 10. ♘b3 f5⇄)
9. b4 ♕c7 10. ♕e2 ♗e7 11. b5 ♘a5
12. ♗g5? (12. ♘×d4∓ Short) 12...♘c4?!
Short – Bareev, Tilburg 1991; 12...♗×g5
13. ♘×g5 ♘c4 –+ Short] 8...♗e7 9. ♘b3 0–0
10. ♘b×d4 ♗d7⇄; **7. ♘bd2**.

37 **8...♕b6?!** 9. ♘bd2 ♕×b2 [9...♘b4!?
10. ♘b3 (10. ♗×g6 f×g6!? 11. ♘b3 ♗e7
12. ♘f×d4 0–0⇄ Gurevich) 10...♘×d3
11. ♕×d3 ♗d7 12. ♘f×d4 ♗e7 13. f4 0–0
14. ♔h1 ♔h8!? (14...f6 15. e×f6 ♗×f6
16. c3∞ Gurevich) 15. ♗e1 (15. f5? e×f5
16. ♘×f5 ♗b5∓) 15...a5⇄ Seul – Gurevich,
Bad Godesberg 1996; 15...♕a6!? 16. ♕×a6
b×a6⇄ Gurevich] 10. ♘b3 ⯑ [10. ♖b1 ♕×a2
(10...♕c3 11. h4!?↑) 11. ♘b3↑ Gurevich];
8...f5 9. e×f6 (9. h4?! h5∓) 9...g×f6 10. ♘×d4
♘×d4 11. ♗×g6+ h×g6 12. ♕×d4⇄.

38 9. ♖e1 ♕b6 10. ♘bd2 ♗d7 11. ♘b3
♖c8 12. a3 a6 13. h4 ♗d8 14. ♕d2 ⯑ Keres –
Hazenfuss, Kemeri 1937.

39 9...0–0 10. h4 [10. ♘b3 ♗d7 (10...f5
11. e×f6 g×f6 12. ♘f×d4 e5 13. ♘f5 e4
14. ♘×e7+ ♕×e7 15. ♗b5 f5 16. f4∞
Štoček – Matlak, Czech League 1999/2000)
11. ♘b×d4 ♘×d4 12. ♘×d4 ♕b6 13. ♗×g6
f×g6 14. ♕d2 g5!=] 10...f5∞.

40 10. h3 0–0 11. ♖e1 ♘h4 12. ♗xh4 ♗xh4 13. ♘b3 ♗d7 14. ♘xh4 ♕xh4 15. ♗b5= Hodgson–Ree, Wijk aan Zee 1986.

41 11. ♘h4 (11. ♖e1 e5 12. ♘h4 ♘xh4 13. ♕h5+ ♔d7 14. ♗xh4 ♔c7 15. ♗g3 ♗d6∓ Kivisto–Tukmakov, Moscow 1985) 11...♘ge5 (11...♘xh4! 12. ♕h5+ ♔d7 13. ♕xh4 e5 14. c4 dxc3 15. bxc3 ♔c7∓; 11...♔f7 12. ♕h5 f5∞; 11...f5 12. ♘xg6 hxg6 13. ♘f3 ♗f6 14. ♖e1 ⯍) 12. ♕h5+ ♔d7 13. ♗b5 ♕e8 14. ♕e2 a6 15. ♗xc6+ ♘xc6 16. c4 (16. c4 ⯍) 16...dxc3 17. bxc3 [17. ♘e4?! ♘d4 (17...cxb2 18. ♕xb2 ♕f7 19. ♘c3⇄) 18. ♕d3 cxb2 19. ♕xd4 bxa1♕ 20. ♖xa1 ♕f7∓] 17...♕f7 18. ♖ad1 ♖d8 (18...♔e8 19. c4⇄) 19. ♘c4 ♗c5 20. ♘e3 ♘e7 21. ♔h1 ♔e8⇄ Spraggett–Gurevich, Havana 1986.

42 4...♘e7 5. ♘f3 ♘ec6 (5...♘f5 6. h4 ♗e7 7. ♗d3 cxd4 8. cxd4 ♘c6 9. ♗xf5 exf5 10. ♗g5± Sveshnikov–Agrinsky, Moscow 1998)

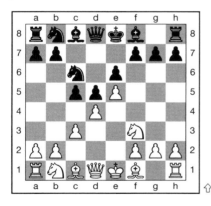

a) 6. h4 ♘d7 7. h5 f6!⇄ Sveshnikov–Kovačević, Belgrade 1988;

b) 6. ♗e3!? ♘d7 7. ♗d3 a5 8. ♘bd2 cxd4 9. cxd4 a4 10. a3 ♗e7 11. h4± Kupreichik–Kovačević, Ljubljana/Portorož 1989; 11. 0–0 f6 12. exf6 ♘xf6 13. ♘e5±;

c) 6. ♗g5 ♕d7?! (6...♕b6⇄) 7. dxc5 ♗xc5 8. ♗d3 Sveshnikov–Zeller, Böblingen 1991;

8. b4 ♗b6 9. b5±) 8...♕c7! 9. ♕e2 ♘d7 10. ♗f4 f6!⇄;

d) 6. ♗d3 b6 7. ♗g5 ♕d7 8. 0–0 ♗a6 9. dxc5 bxc5 10. ♗xa6 ♘xa6 11. c4± Sveshnikov–Lputian, Moscow 1989.

43 5. ♗d3 ♗d7 [5...cxd4 6. cxd4 ♘c6 (6...♗d7= Keres) 7. ♘f3 ♗d7 see 4...♘c6] 6. ♕e2!? (6. dxc5 ♗xc5 7. ♕e2) 6...cxd4 7. ♘f3 ♘c6 8. 0–0 ♘ge7!? 9. a3⯍ Garcia–Cardenas Serrano, Havana 1991.

44

6. a3 – See Table 2 on page 64 ff.

6. ♘a3!? cxd4 7. cxd4 ♗b4+ [7...♘c6 8. ♗e2 ♗b4+ 9. ♔f1!? ♗e7 10. h4 f6 11. ♖h3! ♘h6?! (⌂ 11...fxe5 12. dxe5 ♗c5 13. ♖g3 ♗xf2 14. ♖xg7 ♘ge7 15. ♗d3 ♗c5∞) 12. ♗xh6 gxh6 13. ♕d2↑ Kupreichik–Timoshchenko, Odessa 1968] 8. ♗d2 ♘c6 9. ♘c2 a5 10. ♗d3 ♗xd2+ 11. ♕xd2 ♘ge7⇄; 11...♘b4?! (Kupreichik–Zlotnik, Cheliabinsk 1975) 12. ♘xb4 ♕xb4 13. ♕xb4 axb4 14. ♔d2±;

6. ♘bd2

a) 6...a5?! 7. ♗d3 ♘c6 8. dxc5 ♗xc5 9. ♕e2! ♘ge7?! (9...a4 10. b4 axb3 11. ♘xb3 ♗e7 12. 0–0±) 10. ♘b3 a4 11. ♘xc5 ♕xc5 12. 0–0± Erenburg–Gunnarsson, Pardubice 2003;

b) 6...♘h6 7. ♘b3! ♗a4 8. ♗xh6 gxh6 9. dxc5 ♗xc5 10. ♕d2 ♗xb3 11. axb3 ♘c6 12. ♕c2 ♖c8 13. ♖a4± Dvoiris–Eingorn, Genf 2001;

c) 6...♗b5!?;

d) 6...c×d4 7. ♘×d4 (7. ♘b3) 7...♘c6
8. ♘2f3 ♘×d4 9. ♘×d4 ♗c5 10. ♕g4 ♘e7
11. ♗d3 ♗×d4 12. ♕×d4 ♕×d4 13. c×d4
♘f5 14. ♗e3 ♘×e3 15. f×e3 ♖c8 = Bareev –
Eingorn, Chalkidiki 2002;

6. ♕b3!? ♘c6 (6...c4?! 7. ♕c2±; 6...♕×b3
7. a×b3 ♘c6 8. d×c5!? ♗×c5 9. b4 ♗b6±;
6...c×d4 7. ♕×b6 a×b6 8. ♘×d4!±) 7. ♘a3
♘a5 8. ♕×b6 a×b6 9. ♘c2 ♘e7 10. ♗e2±
Aseev – Rustemov, St. Petersburg 1997;
10. ♗d3!?.

45 6...♘c6 See 4...♘c6; **6...c×d4** 7. c×d4
♗b5

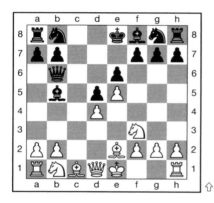

a) 8. 0–0 ♗×e2 9. ♕×e2 ♘c6 [9...♕a6
10. ♕d1 (10. ♕×a6 ♘×a6=) 10...♘c6 11. ♗e3
♘ge7 12. ♘c3 ♘f5 13. g4 ♘×e3 14. f×e3 ♗e7
15. ♘e2± Rozentalis – Schmidt, Zakopane
2000] 10. ♗e3 ♘ge7 11. ♘c3 ♘f5 12. ♖fc1
(12. g4 ♘×e3 13. f×e3 ♗e7=) 12...♗e7
13. ♘a4 ♕d8 14. a3 0–0 15. b4 ♕d7 16. ♘c5
♗×c5 17. ♖×c5 ♖fc8 = Hoffman – Psakhis,
Benasque 1994;

b) 8. ♕b3 ♗×e2 9. ♕×b6 a×b6 10. ♔×e2
♘e7 11. ♘c3 ♘ec6=;

c) 8. ♗×b5+ ♕×b5 9. ♘c3 ♗b4 10. ♗d2
♕a6 = Glek;

d) 8. ♘c3 ♗×e2 9. ♘×e2 ♘e7 (9...♗b4+!?
10. ♗d2 ♘e7=) 10. 0–0 ♘d7 11. ♘f4 h5
12. ♕d3 g6 13. ♗d2 ♘f5 14. ♖fc1± Naka-
mura – Paschall, Bermuda 2003.

46

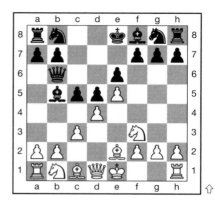

a) 7. 0–0 ♗×e2 8. ♕×e2 ♕a6!? 9. ♕d1
♘d7! (9...c4 10. ♖e1 ♘c6 11. ♘bd2 0–0–0
12. ♘f1± Hecht – Karpov, Moscow 1977)
10. ♗e3 (10. d×c5!? Kaidanov) 10...♘e7?
(10...♖c8!) 11. d×c5! ♘g6 12. b4± Sveshnikov – Zlotnik, Odessa 1975;

b) 7. d×c5!? ♗×c5 8. b4 [8. 0–0 ♗×e2
(8...a5?! 9. ♗×b5+ ♕×b5 10. ♘a3! ♗×a3?!
11. b×a3 ♘e7 12. a4 ♕c4 13. ♖b1 ± Gulko –
Vitolins, Tbilisi 1979) 9. ♕×e2 ♕a6 (9...a5!?
10. a4 ♘e7 11. ♘a3 0–0 12. ♘b5 ♘d7!
13. ♗d2 ♘c6= Lobzhanidze – Volkov, Bad
Wörishofen 1999) 10. ♕c2 ♘d7 11. a4
♖c8 12. ♘bd2 ♘e7⇄ Movsesian – Volkov,
ICC 2004] 8...♗×f2+ 9. ♔f1 ♗d7 10. ♕d2
[10. c4 ♘a6!? 11. c5 ♘×c5 12. b×c5 ♗×c5∞;
10...d×c4?! 11. ♘a3!± a6? 12. ♘×c4 ♕a7
13. ♘d6+ ♔f8 (13...♔e7 14. ♗g5+ f6
15. e×f6+ g×f6 16. ♘e4+–) 14. ♘c8!
1–0, Rogers – Sribar, Wijk aan Zee 1977]
10...♘h6! 11. ♗d3?? (11. c4⇄; 11. a4!?)
11...♘g4∓ Svidler – Shirov, León 2004;

c) 7. ♗e3!?N ♗×e2 8. ♕×e2 ♘c6 9. 0–0 a6
10. ♘bd2!? c×d4 (10...♕×b2 11. c4! c×d4
12. ♖ab1 ♕×a2 13. ♘×d4∞) 11. ♘×d4 ♘×d4
12. ♗×d4 ♗c5 13. ♕g4 g6 = Kupreichik –
Hába, Regensburg 2000.

47 7...d×c4!? 8. ♘c3 (8. a4 ♗c6
9. ♘a3⇄) 8...c×d4 9. ♘×d4 ♗a6!? (9...♗c6;
9...♗d7?!±) 10. ♗e3 (10. 0–0 ♘d7 11. ♕a4
♕b4 12. ♕×b4 ♗×b4 13. ♘cb5 ♗×b5

14. ♘xb5 ♔e7∞) 10...♛a5 (⌓ 10...♛xb2) 11. f4 ♘h6 12. ♛c2 (12. ♛d2 ♘d7 13. ♗f3 ⯑) 12...♗c5 13. 0-0 ⯑ Yagupov – Rustemov, Moscow 1994.

48 8...dxc4 9. d5 exd5 (9...♘e7 10. dxe6 ♛xe6! 11. ♘c3 ♘ec6! 12. 0-0 ♗e7 13. ♗g5! 0-0 14. ♗xe7 ♘xe7?! 15. ♘e4 ♘d7 16. ♘fg5 ♛c6 17. ♛c2! h6 18. ♖ad1 ♘d5 19. ♘c3 hxg5 20. ♖xd5±, Goloshchapov – Volkov, Abu Dhabi 2005) 10. ♛xd5 ♘e7 11. ♛e4 (11. ♛xc4 ♛b4+ 12. ♘bd2 ♛xc4 13. ♘xc4 ♘g6 14. h4 h5 15. ♗g5± Sax – Dreev, Tilburg 1992) 11...♛c6 (11...♘d7 12. 0-0 ♛c6 13. ♛xc4 ♘b6 14. ♛e2 ♘ed5 15. a4± Zaitsev – Doda, Riga 1968) 12. ♛xc4 ♛a6! (12...♘d7 13. 0-0 ♘b6 14. ♛e2 ♘ed5 15. a4± Salem – Volzhin, Abu Dhabi 2001) 13. ♛e4 (13. ♘a3± Zlotnik) 13...♘bc6 14. ♘bd2 0-0-0? Zaitsev – Krasnov, USSR 1968; 14...♘d4! 15. ♘xd4 cxd4 16. ♛xd4 ♘c6 ⯑.

49 10. 0-0 ♘c6 11. dxc5 ♗xc5 12. a3 ♛b5 13. ♘e4 (13. ♛e2 ♘ge7 14. ♘xc4 ♘f5 15. b4± Galdunts – Gavrilov, Naberezhnye Chelny 1988) 13...♘ge7 14. ♗e3 ♖d8 15. ♛e2 ♗xe3 16. ♘d6+ ♖xd6 17. exd6 ♗xf2+ 18. ♖xf2± Adams – Illescas Cordoba, Las Palmas 1994.

50 **10...♛a5** 11. 0-0 ♘c6 12. ♘xc4 ♛a6 13. ♘d6+!? ♗xd6 14. exd6 cxd4 15. d7+! ♔e7 16. ♘xd4 ♘f6 17. ♘f5+!→ Wolf – Gerbich, corr. 1988;

10...♛b5 11. 0-0 [11. ♛e2 cxd4 12. ♘xd4 ♛d5 13. ♘4f3! (13. ♘2f3 ♗c5 14. ♗e3 ♗xd4 15. ♗xd4 ♘c6 16. 0-0-0 ♘ge7∞ Ivell – Beliavsky, London 1985) 13...♘d7 14. ♘xc4 ♖c8 15. ♘e3 ♛e4 16. b4± Howell – Mestel, Swansea 1987] 11...♘e7 (11...♘c6) 12. ♘e4 ♘d5 13. dxc5 ♘d7 (13...♗xc5 14. ♛e2 ♘d7 15. b4 ♗e7 16. ♗g5 ⯑) 14. ♘d6+ ♗xd6 15. cxd6 0-0?! Illescas Cordoba – Beliavsky, Madrid 1995; 15...c3! ⇄.

Notes

Table 2

1. e4 e6 2. d4 d5 3. e5 c5 4. c3 ♛b6 5. ♘f3
♗d7 6. a3!?

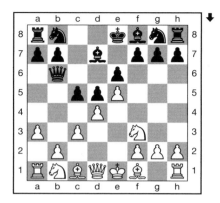

	6	7	8	9	10	11	12	13	
8	...	b3![51]	♗e3	♗d3	0-0[54]	♗xf5	♘bd2!?[56]	c4	
	a5	♘a6[52]	♖c8	♘e7[53]	♘f5[55]	exf5	♗e7	♗e6[57]	±
9	...	cxd4	♗xb5+	♘c3	♗d2!?[59]	b4!?[61]	♘e2[63]	0-0	
	cxd4	♗b5	♛xb5	♛a6[58]	♘d7[60]	♛d3[62]	♖c8	♘e7[64]	±
10	...	c4[65]	♘c3[67]	d5	d6[68]	♘xb5	♛c2	♘xe5	
	♗b5	dxc4!?[66]	♘c6	0-0-0!	f6	♛xb5	♘xe5	fxe5[69]	=
11	...	b4	♗xb5+[71]	cxd4[72]	♘c3	♘a4![75]	♗d2□	axb4[77]	
	...	cxd4[70]	♛xb5	♘d7[73]	♛c6[74]	a5!?[76]	axb4	♛a6[78]	∞

51 **7. ♝e2** a4 (7...♞e7 8. d×c5 ♛c7 9. b4 ♞bc6 10. ♝b2 ♞×e5 11. ♞bd2 ♞7g6 12. c4 d×c4 13. 0–0 ♝e7 14. ♞×e5 ♞×e5 15. f4 ♞g6 16. ♞×c4± Sveshnikov – Dambrauskas, Vilnius 1997) 8. 0–0 ♞c6 9. ♝d3 ♞a5 10. ♝c2 ♞c4 11. ♞g5!?∞ Sveshnikov – Volkov, Dubai 2002; (11. ♖a2);

7. ♝d3

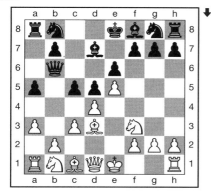

a) 7...♝b5 8. 0–0 ♝×d3 9. ♛×d3 ♞c6 10. d×c5 ♝×c5 11. c4 ♛a6 12. ♞bd2 ♞ge7 = Suetin – Lputian, Daugavpils 1978;

b) 7...c×d4!? 8. c×d4 ♞c6 9. 0–0 ♞×d4 10. ♞×d4 ♛×d4 11. ♞c3 (11. ♛e2 ⚌)

b1) 11...♞e7 12. ♞b5 ♛×e5 13. ♖e1 ♛b8 14. ♛f3 ♝×b5! 15. ♝×b5+ ♞c6 16. ♛×d5 ♛d6! 17. ♛c4 ⚌ I. Zaitsev – Lempert, Moscow 1994;

b2) 11...♖c8 12. ♛e2 ♞e7 13. ♔h1 ♛h4!? 14. f4 ♞f5 15. ♝×f5 e×f5 16. ♞×d5 ♝c5 17. ♝e3 0–0± Velimirović – Ivkov, Titograd 1965;

b3) 11...♞h6 12. ♞b5 ♛×e5 13. ♖e1 ♛b8 14. ♛f3 ♝d6 15. ♞×d6+ ♛×d6 16. ♝f4 ♛e7 17. ♛g3 f6 ⚌ I. Zaitsev – Geller, Moscow 1982;

b4) 11...♛b6 12. ♛g4 g6 (12...f5 13. e×f6?! ♞×f6 14. ♛g3 ♝e7! 15. ♛×g7 ♖g8 16. ♛h6 ♛d4 17. ♖d1 ♛g4 18. ♝f1 ♖g6 19. ♛f4 ♛h5 20. ♝e2 ♛h3 21. ♛f3 e5!∓ Steinberg – Shilov, Kharkov 1967; 13. ♛g3 ⚌) 13. ♝e3 ♝c5 14. ♞a4 ♝×a4 15. ♛×a4+ ♔f8

16. ♝×c5+ ♛×c5 17. ♖ac1 ♛b6 18. ♛d7 ⚌ Shirov – Anand, FIDE World Championship (1), New Delhi/Teheran 2000;

c) 7...a4 8. 0–0 ♝b5 9. c4 d×c4 10. ♝e2 c×d4 11. ♞×d4 ♞c6 12. ♞×b5 ♛×b5 13. ♞c3 ♛×e5 14. ♝×c4 ⚌ Sveshnikov – Minev, Moscow 1977.

d) 7...♞c6 8. ♝c2 ♞h6 9. 0–0 ♖c8 (9...c×d4 10. c×d4 ♞f5 11. ♝×f5 e×f5 12. ♞c3∞ Predojević) 10. d×c5 (10. h3!? c×d4 11. c×d4 ♞f5 12. ♝×f5 e×f5 13. ♞c3 ♝e6±) 10...♝×c5 11. b4?! a×b4 12. a×b4 ♝×f2+ 13. ♖×f2 ♞g4 14. ♞d4 (14. ♛e2 ♛×f2+ 15. ♛×f2 ♞×f2 16. ♔×f2 ♞×b4∓) 14...♞×f2 15. ♔×f2 ♞×e5 16. ♛h5=, Krapivin – Zakharevich, St. Petersburg 2005.

52 **7...♞e7** 8. d×c5 (8. ♝e2 c×d4 9. c×d4 ♝b5 10. ♝×b5+ ♛×b5 11. ♞c3 ♛a6 12. a4 ♞ec6 13. ♞b5 ♛b6= Zviagintsev – Volkov, St. Petersburg 1999) 8...♛×c5 9. c4 ♛c7 10. ♞c3 ♝c6 11. ♝b2 ♞d7 12. c×d5 ♞×d5 13. ♞b5 ♛b6 (Delchev – Volkov, Batumi 2002) 14. ♝d4!? (Psakhis) 14...♝c5 15. ♝×c5 ♛×c5 16. ♖c1±;

7...♞c6 8. ♝e3 ♞h6 9. ♝d3 ♞f5 10. ♝×f5 e×f5 11. 0–0 c×d4 12. c×d4 h6 13. ♞c3 ♝e6 14. ♞a4 ♛b5 15. ♞e1 ♝e7 16. ♞d3 ♖c8 17. ♞ac5 0–0 18. ♖c1 ♖fe8 19. ♖c3 ♞a7 20. a4 ♛b6 21. ♛h5± Vorobiov – Volkov, Moscow 2004.

53 **9...♞h6?!** 10. ♝×h6 g×h6 11. 0–0 ♝g7 12. ♖a2 c×d4 13. c×d4 ♝b5 14. ♖d2?! (14. ♝×b5+ ♛×b5 15. ♖c2 0–0 16. ♛c1± ♖c6 17. ♖×c6 b×c6 18. ♛e3 c5 19. ♖c1 ♖c8 20. ♞bd2±) 14...0–0 15. ♝×b5 ♛×b5= Sveshnikov – Volkov, Togliatti 2003;

9...c4!? 10. b×c4 ♛b2 11. ♞bd2 ♛×c3 12. ♛b1 d×c4 13. ♝e2 ♝×a3 14. 0–0 ♛b2 15. ♖a2 ♛×b1 16. ♖×b1 ⚌.

54 10. d×c5 ♞×c5 11. ♝c2 ♛a6∞ Svidler.

55 10...♝b5 11. c4±.

56 12. ♖e1 Svidler – Volkov, Russian Championship, Krasnoyarsk 2003.

57 14. c×d5 ♗×d5 15. ♘c4 ♕g6 16. ♖c1 0–0 17. d×c5 ♗×c4 18. ♖×c4 ♘×c5 19. b4 (19. ♗×c5 ♖×c5 20. ♕d7 ♖×c4 21. b×c4 ♗×a3 22. ♕×b7 ♗c5⇄) 19…a×b4 20. a×b4 ♖cd8 21. ♕b1 ♘e6 22. b5 ♖d5 23. ♖fc1 ♖fd8 24. ♕b3±.

58 **9…♕c4** 10. ♘e2 ♘c6 11. 0–0 ♘ge7 12. ♗d2 ♕a6 13. b4 ♕b6 14. ♕a4 a6 15. ♖fb1± Sveshnikov – Hulak, Brioni (Rapidplay) 1990;

9…♕d7 10. 0–0 ♘c6 11. b4 ♘ge7 12. ♕d3 ♘c8 13. ♗d2 a6 14. ♘a4!? ♘×e5 (14…b5 15. ♘c5 ♗×c5 16. d×c5 ♘8e7±) 15. ♘×e5 (15. d×e5 ♕×a4 16. ♗e3! ♘e7 17. ♘d4⩱) 15…♕×a4 16. f4?! Potkin – Asrian, Batumi 2002; 16. ♖ac1 ♗d6 17. ♕g3↑.

59 10. ♘e2 ♘e7 11. 0–0

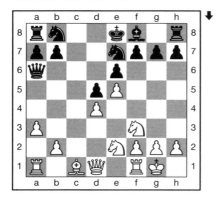

a) 11…♘g6 12. ♗e3 (12. ♘g3 ♗e7 13. ♘h5 0–0±) 12…♗e7 13. ♘e1 0–0 14. f4 f5 15. ♘d3 ♘d7 16. ♘c5 ♗×c5 17. d×c5 ♖fc8 18. b4± Markarov – Riazantsev, St. Petersburg 2000;

b) 11…♘f5!? 12. g4 ♘e7 13. ♘g3 ♘d7! 14. ♗e3 ♘c6 15. ♘e1! ♕b6 16. b4± Mukhametov – Fominikh, Prague 1994;

c) 11…♘d7 12. ♘f4 [12. ♘g3 ♘c6 13. ♘h5 (13. ♗e3±) 13…h6 14. ♗e3 0–0–0 15. b4 ♘b6 16. ♕b1 ♕b5 17. ♘f4± Sveshnikov – Repkova, Riga 1995] 12…♘c6 13. ♘g5 ♘d8 14. ♕g4!± (14. ♕h5 Sveshnikov – Danielian, Moscow (Rapidplay) 1996).

60 10…♘e7 11. b4 ♘f5 (11…♕d3 12. ♕a4+ ♘d7 13. ♘b5 0–0–0 14. ♖c1+ ♘c6 15. ♖×c6+ 1–0 Klünter – Hank, Cologne 1995) 12. g4 ♘e7 13. b5 ♕b6 14. ♕e2 ♘d7 15. ♘a4 ♕d8 16. 0–0 h5 17. h3± Korbut – Khasanova, Budva 2003.

61 **11. ♕b3** ♖c8 12. ♖c1 h6 13. ♖c2 ♘b6 14. ♘e2 ♖×c2 15. ♕×c2 ♕c4 16. ♗c3 ♘e7 17. 0–0 ♘c6 18. b3 ♕a6 19. ♖a1 ♗e7 20. ♘e1 0–0 21. ♕d3 ♕×d3 22. ♘×d3 ½–½ Oll – Rustemov, Vilnius 1997;

11. ♕e2!? ♕×e2+ 12. ♔×e2 0–0–0? (12…a6±) 13. ♖hc1+– ♔b8 14. ♘b5 ♘h6 15. ♗g5 1–0 Hengl – Luft, Schwarzach 2000.

62 11…♘e7?! 12. a4!± ♕b6 [12…♖c8?! 13. ♘b5! ♘c6 (13…♘f5 14. g4+–) 14. ♘d6+ ♗×d6 15. b5 ♕b6 16. b×c6 ♕×c6 17. e×d6 ♕×d6 18. ♕b3+– Fingerov – Vysochin, Ukrainian Championship, Sebastopol 2000] 13. a5 ♕d8 14. a6 b×a6 15. ♖×a6 ♘c8 16. ♘g5! ♗e7 17. ♖×e6! 0–0 18. ♕g4± Belov – Lisy, Vladimir 2002.

63 12. ♕e2 ♕×e2+ 13. ♔×e2 ♘b6 14. ♖hc1±.

64 14. ♘f4±.

65 7. ♗×b5+!? ♕×b5 8. a4 ♕b6 9. d×c5 ♗×c5 10. b4! ♗e7 (10…♗×f2+ 11. ♔e2 a5 12. ♖f1+–) 11. 0–0± Korchnoi.

66 7…♗×c4 8. ♗×c4 d×c4 9. ♘bd2! (9. d5 ♘e7 10. ♘c3 ♘×d5 11. ♘×d5 e×d5 12. ♕×d5 ♗e7 13. 0–0 ♘c6 14. e6 0–0 15. e×f7+ ♖×f7 16. ♗g5 ♕d8!=) 9…♕a6 (9…c3!? 10. b×c3 ♕a6 11. ♕e2±) 10. ♕e2 (10. ♕c2!?) 10…c×d4 (10…♘e7 11. ♘×c4 ♘d5 12. 0–0 ♘c6 13. d×c5 ♗×c5 14. b4 b5 Sveshnikov – Matveeva, Capelle la Grande 1995; 14…♗×b4⇄); 11. ♘×d4 (11. ♘×c4 ♘c6 12. 0–0? ♘a5∓) 11…♗c5 12. ♘4f3± Sveshnikov – Ehlvest, Leningrad 1984.

67 8. d5!?

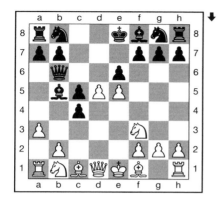

8...♘e7!?

a) 9. d6 ♘g6 10. ♘c3 ♘d7∓;

b) 9. a4 ♗a6 10. a5 ♕b4+ [10...♕d8 11. ♕a4+ ♕d7 12. dxe6 (12. d6 ♕xa4 13. ♖xa4 ♘ec6 14. ♘a3 ♗d7 15. ♗f4 ♘b4 16. ♘xc4∞) 12...fxe6 13. ♗xc4 ♕xa4 14. ♖xa4 ♘d5 15. ♘c3 ♗xc4 16. ♖xc4 ♘c6∞] 11. ♘fd2 ♘xd5 12. ♖a4 ♕b5 13. ♘a3 ♕d7 14. ♗xc4⩱;

c) 9. ♘c3 ♘xd5 (9...exd5 10. ♘xd5 ♕d8 11. ♘e3 ♕xd1+ 12. ♔xd1 ♗a4+ 13. ♔e1 b5 14. g3 ♘bc6 15. ♗g2 0-0-0∞) 10. ♘xd5 exd5 11. ♕xd5 ♗e7 12. ♗xc4 0-0 13. 0-0 ♘c6 14. b3 [14. ♕e4 ♖ad8 15. ♗e3 ♗xc4 16. ♕xc4 ♕xb2 17. ♗xc5 (17. ♖ab1 ♘xe5 18. ♘xe5 ♕xe5 19. ♖xb7) 17...♘xe5∓] 14...♖ad8 15. ♕e4± Sveshnikov – Lutsko, Minsk 1999;

8...exd5 9. ♕xd5 ♘e7 10. ♕e4 ♕c6 11. ♘c3 ♕xe4+ 12. ♘xe4∞.

68 10. ♕c2 exd5 11. ♕f5+ ♔b8 12. ♕xf7 ♘ge7∓.

69 14. ♗xc4 ♕c6□ 15. ♗xe6+ ♔b8 16. 0-0 (16. ♗xg8? ♕xg2∓) 16...♘f6! 17. ♗e3 (17. ♗g5 ♖xd6 18. ♗f5⩲) 17...♗xd6 18. b4= Sveshnikov – Vysochin, Yugoslavian League 1998; 18. ♖ac1↑.

70 7...cxb4 8. ♗xb5+ ♕xb5 9. axb4 ♘d7 10. ♖a5 ♕c4⇄.

71 8. ♕xd4 ♕a6 9. ♗xb5+ ♕xb5 10. a4 ♕d7⇄.

72 9. ♘xd4!? ♕d7 [9...♕c4 10. ♗e3 ♘c6 11. ♘d2 ♕xc3 (11...♕d3 12. ♕a4! ♖c8 13. ♘xc6 bxc6 14. ♕xa7±) 12. ♖c1 ♕xa3 13. ♘b5 ♕xb4 14. ♘c7+ ♔d7 15. ♘xa8∞] 10. 0-0 (10. ♘d2 ♕c7 11. ♘2f3 ♕xc3+ 12. ♗d2 ♕d3 13. ♕a4+ ♘d7 14. ♖c1 a6 15. ♖c3 ♕e4+ 16. ♗e3 ♕b1+ 17. ♗c1 ♕e4+ 18. ♗e3 ♕b1+=; 10. ♗f4!?) 10...♘e7 11. ♗f4!? ♘bc6 12. ♘f3 h6! 13. h4 (13. h3 g5 14. ♗g3 ♗g7∞) 13...g5!? 14. hxg5 ♘g6 15. ♗g3 hxg5 16. ♘xg5 (16. c4 g4 17. cxd5 ♕xd5∓; 16. b5 ♘ce7 17. ♘xg5 ♘f5⩰) 16...♘cxe5⇄ Kupreichik – Feigin, 2nd German League 1999/2000.

73 **9...a5!?** 10. ♘c3 (10. bxa5 ♘c6 11. ♘c3 ♕c4 12. ♘e2 ♖xa5⇄) 10...♕c6 (10...♕c4 11. ♗d2 axb4 12. axb4 ♖xa1 13. ♕xa1±) 11. ♗d2 axb4 12. axb4 ♖xa1 13. ♕xa1 ♕a6 14. ♕a4+!? (14. ♕b1 b5 15. 0-0 ♘e7 16. ♕d3 ♘ec6 17. ♘xb5 ♔d7 18. ♘g5± Shirov – Ljubojević, Monaco (blind) 2002) 14...♕xa4 15. ♘xa4 b5 16. ♘c3 ♗xb4 17. ♘xb5 ♗e7 (17...♗xd2+ 18. ♔xd2 ♗e7 19. ♖c1 ♘h6 20. ♘d6±) 18. ♔e2± Zviagintsev – Volkov, Samara 1998;

9...♘c6 10. ♗e3 a5 11. ♘c3 ♕c4 12. ♘a4!±.

74 10...♕c4 11. ♗b2 ♘e7 12. ♖c1 ♘c6 13. ♘e2 ♕b5 14. 0-0 a6 15. ♘e1!± Nisipeanu – Ionescu, Călimăneşti 1999.

75 **11. ♗d2** ♘b6 12. 0-0 ♘c4⇄;

11. ♗b2 ♘b6 12. ♘d2?! (12. 0-0 ♘e7 13. ♖c1 ♕d7∓) 12...♘e7 13. 0-0 ♘f5!? 14. ♖c1 ♕d7∓ Alekseev – Rustemov, Tomsk 2001.

76

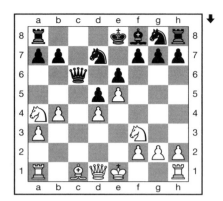

11...♘e7 12. ♗e3 ♘b6 13. ♘xb6 ♕xb6 14. 0–0 ♘f5 (14...♘c6 15. ♘e1 ♗e7 16. ♕g4 g6 17. ♘d3 0–0 18. ♘c5 ♕c7 19. ♖ac1

♖fc8 20. h4→ Grischuk – Gurevich, French League, Bordeaux 2003) 15. ♖c1 ♕d8 16. ♕a4+ ♕d7 17. ♕a5 ♗e7 18. ♖c7 b6 19. ♖xd7 bxa5 20. ♖b7 axb4 21. axb4 0–0 22. g4 ♘xe3= Carlsen – Rustemov, Moscow 2004;

11...♘b6 12. ♘xb6 axb6 13. 0–0 ♘e7 14. ♗b2 ♘c8 15. ♖c1 ♕d7 16. ♖c3 ♗e7 17. ♕c2 ♗d8 18. ♖c1 ± Torre – Bagamasbad, Greenhills 1997.

77 13. ♖c1 ? ♕a6! 14. ♕b3 b6−+.

78 14. b5 (14. ♗c3!?) 14...♕xb5 15. ♘c3 ♖xa1 16. ♘xb5 (16. ♕xa1!?) 16...♖xd1+ 17. ♔xd1 ∞ Sveshnikov – Grosar, Celje 2003.

Notes

Table 3

1. e4 e6 2. d4 d5 3. e5 c5 4. c3 ♘c6

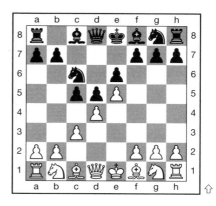

5	6	7	8	9	10	11	12	
12 ♗e3!? c×d4[79]	c×d4 ♘ge7[80]	♗d3[81] ♘f5[82]	♘f3![83] ♕b6[84]	♕d2 ♗d7	♘c3 ♘f×d4	♘×d4 ♘×d4	♗e2![85] ♗c5[86]	±
13 ♘f3 f6	♗b5[87] ♗d7	0-0 ♕b6[88]	♗×c6 b×c6	e×f6 ♘×f6	♘e5 ♗d6[89]	d×c5 ♗×c5[90]	♗g5 ♕d8?![91]	±
14 ... ♘ge7	♘a3![92] c×d4[93]	c×d4 ♘f5	♘c2 ♕b6[94]	♗d3[95] ♗b4+[96]	♔f1 ♗e7	h4[97] h5[98]	g3 a5[99]	±
15 ... ♘h6	♗d3?![100] c×d4[101]	c×d4[102] ♘f5	♗×f5 e×f5	♘c3[103] ♗e6[104]	♘e2[105] h6[106]	h4 ♕a5+[107]	♔f1[108] ♗e7[109]	⇄
16	d×c5! ♗×c5[110]	b4[111] ♗b6[112]	b5[113] ♘e7[114]	♗d3 ♘g6[115]	0-0 0-0	♗×h6 g×h6	a4[116] f6[117]	∞

79   **5...♗d7** 6. ♘f3 ♕b6 7. ♕d2

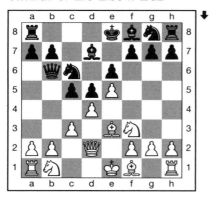

a) 7...f6 8. ♗d3 f×e5 9. d×e5?! (9. ♘×e5 ♘f6 10. 0–0 ♗d6 11. f4 0–0= Ulibin, Lysenko) 9...♘h6 10. 0–0 ♘f7 11. ♗f4 ♗e7 12. ♖e1 0–0–0∓ Westerinen – Ulibin, Benidorm 1993;

b) 7...c×d4 8. c×d4 ♖c8 9. ♘c3 ♘a5!? 10. ♗d3 ♗b4⇄ Kupreichik – Kaminski, Bad Endbach 1995;

c) 7...♘h6 8. d×c5 ♗×c5 9. ♗×h6 g×h6 10. ♗d3 ♕c7 11. ♕e2 f6 12. e×f6 ♕f4 13. ♘bd2 0–0 14. 0–0–0⇄ Kupreichik – Kruppa, St. Petersburg 1996;

5...♕b6 6. ♕d2 ♗d7 [6...♘h6 7. ♗d3 (7. ♘f3 c×d4 8. c×d4 ♗d7 9. ♘c3 ♖c8 (9...♘f5⇄) 10. ♗d3 ♘g4 11. 0–0± Kupre-ichik – Nikolenko, Berlin 1994) 7...♘g4 8. ♘f3 (8. d×c5!?) 8...♗d7!? (8...♘×e3 9. f×e3 ♗e7 10. 0–0 0–0 11. ♔h1 g6!? 12. ♘a3!?∞ Kupreichik – Vasiljević, Yugoslavian League, Cetinje 1993) 9. 0–0 ♘×e3 10. f×e3 ♗e7 11. ♔h1 0–0 12. e4 d×e4 (12...c×d4 13. e×d5 e×d5 14. c×d4 ♗e6 15. ♘c3∞) 13. ♗×e4 ♖ad8 14. d×c5!± Kupreichik – Libeau, Germany 1993] 7. f4 ♖c8 8. ♘f3 c×d4 9. c×d4 ♗b4 10. ♘c3 ♘ge7=.

80   6...♕b6 7. ♕d2!? ♘ge7 (7...♘h6!? 8. ♗×h6 g×h6 9. ♘f3 ♗g7 10. ♘c3 0–0⇄) 8. ♘c3 (8. ♗d3 ♘f5 9. ♘c3 ♗b4 10. ♘ge2 ♗d7 11. 0–0 ♘ce7 12. a3 ♗×c3 13. b×c3! 0–0

14. ♖ab1 ♕c7 15. ♗g5± Kupreichik – Faragó, Passau 1993) 8...♘f5 9. ♘f3 ♗d7 10. ♗d3! (10. ♗e2 ♘a5 11. 0–0 ♗b4 12. ♖ac1 ♖c8 13. ♗d3 ♘c4 14. ♕e2 ♕a5⇄ Ács – Párkányi, Budapest 1994) 10...♘f×d4 11. ♘×d4 ♘×d4 12. ♗e2 ♗c5 13. b4 ♘c2+ 14. ♕×c2 ♗×e3 15. f×e3 ♕×e3 16. ♕d3 ♕×e5 17. 0–0±.

81   7. ♘c3 ♘g6 8. ♘f3 ♗e7 9. ♗d3 ♗d7 10. 0–0 0–0 11. ♖c1 ♗e8 12. ♘e2 f6 13. e×f6 ♗×f6± Pegoraro – Salami, Bratto 1996.

82   7...♕b6 8. ♕d2 ♘b4 9. ♗e2 ♘f5 10. ♘c3 ♘×d4? 11. ♗d1! ♘bc6 12. ♘ge2 ♗c5 13. ♘a4+– Kupreichik – Charochkin, Schwäbisch Gmünd 2002.

83   8. ♗×f5 e×f5 9. ♘c3 ♗e6 10. ♘ge2±;

8. ♘e2?! ♗e7? [8...♘×e3! 9. f×e3 ♕g5 10. ♘f4 (10. 0–0 ♕×e3+ 11. ♔h1 ♗d7 12. ♖f3 ♕g5 13. ♘bc3 f5! 14. ♘b5 ♖c8∓ Rodríguez – Gleizerov, Málaga 2000) 10...♘×d4! 11. e×d4 ♕×f4 12. ♗b5+ ♗d7 13. ♗×d7+ ♔×d7 14. ♕a4+ ♔d8∓] 9. 0–0 0–0 10. ♘bc3 ♘×e3 11. f×e3 ♗d7 12. ♘f4 f5 13. g4 g6 14. g×f5 g×f5 15. ♔h1 ♔h8 16. ♖g1± Kupreichik – Jorgensen, Copenhagen 1993.

84   **8...♗d7** 9. ♘c3 ♕b6 10. 0–0 ♘×e3 11. f×e3 ♗e7 12. a3 0–0 13. ♖c1 f5 14. e×f6 ♖×f6 15. ♘a4± Pavasović – Bukal, Nova Gorica 1999;

8...♘×e3 9. f×e3 ♗e7 (9...g6 10. ♘c3 ♗g7 11. h4 ♕e7 12. ♕e2 ♗d7 13. 0–0–0!? f6 14. e×f6 ♗×f6 15. ♔b1 0–0–0 16. g4± Kupre-ichik – Kacheishvili, Schwäbisch Gmünd 2001) 10. 0–0 0–0 11. ♘c3 ♗d7 12. ♖c1 f5 13. e×f6 ♗×f6⇄ Jerić – Gleizerov, Ljubljana 2000.

85   12. 0–0? ♗c5∓ Vazelaki – Stamiris, Athens 1999.

86   13. b4 ♘c2+ 14. ♕×c2 ♗×e3 15. f×e3 ♕×e3 16. ♕d3 ♕×e5 17. 0–0±.

87

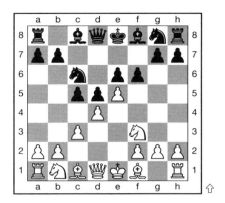

6. ♗d3

a) 6...f×e5 7. d×e5 g6 8. h4! ♗g7 9. h5±
Paulsen – Schwarz, Vienna 1882;

b) 6...♗d7 7. ♕c2 f5 8. g4 g6 9. g×f5 g×f5
10. d×c5 ♗×c5 11. ♕e2 ♕c7 12. ♘bd2 ♘ge7
13. ♘b3 ♗b6 14. ♘bd4= Muffang – Alekhine,
Paris 1923;

c) 6...♕c7 7. 0–0!? (7. ♗f4 f5 8. 0–0±
Paulsen – Blackburne, Nuremberg 1883;
8. d×c5!? ♗×c5 9. b4 ♗f8 10. 0–0±) 7...f×e5
8. d×e5 c4 (8...♘×e5 9. ♘×e5 ♕×e5 10. ♖e1
♕d6 11. ♕h5+ ⯑) 9. ♗c2 ♗c5 10. b3 c×b3
11. a×b3 ♘×e5 12. ♘×e5 ♕×e5 13. ♖a4!?
♘f6 14. ♖h4 ⯑ Dvoiris – Bertholee, Dieren
2002.

88 7...♘×e5 8. ♘×e5 ♗×b5 9. ♕h5+ g6
(9...♔e7 10. ♕f7+ ♔d6 11. ♕×b7 ♕e7
12. ♘f7+ +−) 10. ♘×g6 h×g6 11. ♕×h8
♗×f1 12. ♕×g8 ♗d3 13. ♕×e6+ ♕e7
14. ♕×e7+ ♗×e7 15. d×c5 ♗×c5 16. ♗e3
♗×e3 17. f×e3±.

89 10...c×d4 11. c×d4 c5 12. ♘×d7 ♘×d7
13. ♖e1 ♗e7 14. ♕h5+ g6 15. ♕h3±.

90 11...♕×c5±.

91 12...♕×b2!? 13. ♘d2 ♕×c3 14. ♘×d7
♘×d7 (14...♔×d7 15. ♖c1±) 15. ♕g4 ⯑

12...♕d8?! 13. ♗×f6 ♕×f6 14. ♕h5+ g6
15. ♕e2 ♖d8 16. ♘d2± Nimzowitsch –
Levenfish, Carlsbad 1911.

92 **6. a3** ♘f5 (6...c4!?) 7. b4 c×d4 8. c×d4
♕b6 see 5...♕b6 6. a3;

6. ♗e2 ♘f5 (6...♗d7 see 5...♗d7) 7. g4!?
♘h4 8. ♘×h4 ♕×h4 9. ♗e3 ♗d7 10. 0–0
♕d8!? 11. ♘d2 ♕b6 12. ♖b1 c×d4 13. c×d4
a5 14. ♔h1 a4 ⇄ Sax – Glek, German League
1993/94;

6. ♗e3 ♘f5 7. ♗d3 ♘×e3 8. f×e3 ♗e7 9. 0–0
0–0 10. ♘bd2 ♗d7 11. a3 c4 12. ♗c2 b5
13. ♕e1 a5 14. ♕g3 b4∓ Kosić – Abramović,
Yugoslav Championship, Tivat 1994;

6. ♗d3 c×d4 7. c×d4 ♘f5 see 5...♘h6 6.
♗d3.

93 6...♘f5 7. ♘c2 ♗d7? (7...c×d4) 8. ♗d3
c4 (8...c×d4 9. ♗×f5 e×f5 10. ♘c×d4 ♗e6
11. h4 h6 12. ♖h3!? Sveshnikov – Dvoiris,
Cheliabinsk 1990; 12. ♗e3 ♗e7 13. ♕d2±)
9. ♗×f5 e×f5 10. ♘e3 ♗e6 11. g3 ♗e7 12. h4±
Kupreichik – Furman, 37th USSR Championship, Moscow 1969.

94

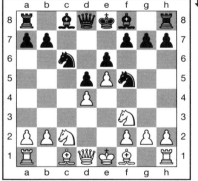

8...♘b4

a) 9. ♗d2 ♘×c2+ 10. ♕×c2 ♕b6 11. ♗c3
♗e7 12. ♗d3 ♗d7 13. g4 ♘h4 14. ♘×h4
♗×h4 15. 0–0–0 h5?! (15...♗b5!? 16. f4
♗e7 ⇄) 16. ♖hg1 ♗g5+ 17. ♔b1 h4 18. ♖df1±
Sveshnikov – Nikolenko, Moscow (Rapidplay) 1989;

b) 9. ♘×b4 ♗×b4+ 10. ♗d2 ♗×d2+ (10...♕a5
11. ♗d3 ♗×d2+ 12. ♕×d2 ♕×d2+ 13. ♔×d2±
Karpachev – Lukov, Hyères 2001) 11. ♕×d2
♕b6 12. ♗d3 ♗d7 13. ♗×f5 e×f5 14. 0–0±
Psakhis – Chernin, 52nd USSR Championship, Riga 1985;

c) 9. ♗e2 ♘xc2+ 10. ♕xc2 ♕a5+ 11. ♗d2 ♗b4 12. a3 ♗xd2+ 13. ♕xd2 ♕xd2+ 14. ♔xd2 ♗d7 15. b4 0–0 16. b5 f6 17. ♖hc1± Grischuk–Pert, French League 2003;

8...♗d7 9. ♗d3 (9. ♗e2 ♘b4 10. ♘xb4 ♗xb4+ 11. ♗d2 ♕a5 12. ♗xb4 ♕xb4+ 13. ♕d2 ♕xd2+ 14. ♔xd2 ♘e7 15. ♖hc1 f6± Sieiro González–Gurevich, Havana 1986) 9...♘b4 10. ♗xf5 (10. ♘xb4 ♗xb4+ 11. ♗d2 ♗xd2+ 12. ♕xd2 ♕b6 13. ♗xf5 exf5 14. 0–0 0–0 15. ♖fc1 ♖fc8± Romero Holmes–Bukal, Rom 1986) 10...exf5 11. 0–0 ♖c8? 12. ♘xb4 ♗xb4 13. ♕b3+– Sveshnikov–Suleimanov, Moscow (Rapidplay) 1990;

8...♗e7 9. ♗d3 ♘b4 (9...0–0? 10. g4! ♘h4 11. ♘xh4 ♗xh4 12. g5 ♗xg5 13. ♕h5 h6 14. ♖g1 ♗xc1 15. ♖xc1→ Sveshnikov–Faragó, Hastings 1984/85) 10. ♘xb4 ♗xb4+ 11. ♔f1 ♗d7 12. a3 ♗e7 13. g4 ♘h4 14. ♘xh4 ♗xh4 15. g5 ♗xg5 16. ♕g4 ♗xc1 17. ♕xg7 ♖f8 18. ♖xc1 ♕b6⇄ Sveshnikov–Tunik, Podolsk 1992.

95 9. ♗e2 ♗d7 see 5...♗d7 6. ♗e2.

96 9...♗d7!? 10. 0–0 a5! 11. ♗xf5 exf5 12. ♗e3 ♘d8 13. ♖b1 h6 14. h4 ♗e7 15. h5 ♘e6 16. g3 g5⇄ Jonkman–Gurevich, Vlissingen 1997.

97 11. g3 ♗d7 12. ♔g2 ♖c8 13. ♗xf5?! exf5= Short–Vaganian, Candidates Tournament, Montpellier 1985.

98 11...♗d7 12. g4 ♘h6 13. ♖g1 ♘g8 14. ♖b1 a5 15. ♕e2 ♘b4 16. ♘xb4 axb4 17. a3± Rohde–Spraggett, New York 1986.

99 13. ♔g2 ♗d7 14. ♗xf5 exf5 15. ♗g5 ♗xg5 16. ♘xg5 f4 17. ♕f3!± Malaniuk–Lputian, 53rd USSR Championship, Kiev 1986

100 6. ♗e2 ♘f5 see 5...♘ge7;

6. a3 ♘f5 7. b4 cxd4 8. cxd4 ♕b6 siehe 5...♕b6 (8...♗e7 9. ♗b2 0–0 10. ♗d3 a6 11. 0–0 f6 12. ♗xf5 exf5 13. ♘c3 f4 14. ♖e1± Grischuk–Najer, St. Petersburg 1999);

6. ♗xh6 gxh6 7. dxc5 see 6. dxc5;

6. ♘a3 ♘f5 (6...cxd4 7. cxd4 ♗xa3 8. bxa3 ♘f5 9. ♗d3 ♕a5+ 10. ♗d2 ♕xa3 11. ♕b1 a6 12. 0–0 h6 13. ♖c1 ∞ I. Zaitsev–Mesropov, Moscow 1996) 7. ♘c2 ♗d7 8. ♗e2 cxd4 9. cxd4 ♗e7 10. 0–0 ♖c8 11. ♔h1 h5 12. a3 ♘a5⇄ Jonkman–Sadvakasov, Philadelphia 2003.

101 6...♕b6 7. dxc5 ♗xc5 8. 0–0 ♘g4 9. ♕e2 f6 10. exf6 gxf6± 11. h3 ♘ge5 12. ♘xe5 ♘xe5 13. b4 ♗d6 14. ♗h6 ♕c7 15. ♗b5+ ♗d7 16. ♘a3⇄.

102 7. ♗xh6!? gxh6 8. cxd4 ♗d7 (8...♗g7 9. ♘c3 0–0 10. 0–0 f6 11. ♖e1 fxe5 12. dxe5±) 9. ♘c3 ♕b6 10. ♗b5 ♖g8 11. 0–0 ♘xe5?! (11...♖c8 12. ♖c1±; 11...a6!? 12. ♗xc6 ♗xc6±) 12. ♘xe5 ♗xb5 13. ♕h5 ♖g7 (13...0–0–0 14. ♘xb5 ♕xb5 15. ♕xf7+–) 14. ♖fe1↑ Grischuk–Bareev, 17th EU Cup, Pánormos 2001.

103 9. 0–0!? ♗e7 10. ♘c3 g5 11. ♘e1 f4 12. h4 h6 13. ♕h5 ♘xd4 14. hxg5 ♗xg5 15. ♕d1 ♘c6 16. ♕xd5±.

104 9...♗b4 10. ♗d2 ♗xc3 11. ♗xc3 ♗e6 12. ♕d2 a5 13. a4 h6 14. h4 0–0 15. 0–0± Sveshnikov–Chernin, Sochi 1986;

9...h6 10. ♕b3 ♗b4 11. ♗d2 0–0 12. 0–0 ♗e6 13. ♘e2 a5 14. ♗xb4 axb4 15. ♘f4 ♕b6 16. ♖fd1 ♖a5⇄ Sveshnikov–Lputian, Djermuk 1987.

105

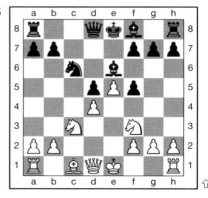

10. 0–0 ♗e7 (10...h6 11. ♘e1 ♗e7 12. f4 g5 13. ♘c2 ♕b6 14. ♕d3 0–0–0 15. ♗d2

♔b8 16. ♘a4 ♕c7 17. b4± I. Zaitsev – Volke, Podolsk 1991) 11. ♘e1 (11. ♕b3 ♖b8 12. ♘e2 g5 13. ♗d2 f4∓ Kholmov – Vasyukov, Beltsy 1979; 11. ♘e2 g5 12. ♕b3 ♖b8 13. ♗d2 f4! 14. ♖ac1 ♕d7 15. ♔h1 ♗f5 16. ♘e1 0–0 17. ♘d3 f6!⇄ Zhuravliov – Sveshnikov, Moscow 1975) 11...♖c8 12. ♘c2 0–0 13. ♕d3 ♕d7 14. f4 a6 15. ♗d2 f6 16. e×f6 ♗×f6 = I. Zaitsev – Moskalenko, Moscow 1992;

10. h4 h6 (10...♗b4 11. ♗d2 ♗×c3 12. b×c3 h6 13. ♘g1 0–0 14. ♘e2 f6 15. ♘f4 ♗f7 16. e×f6± Vasyukov – Popović, Palma de Mallorca 1989) 11. ♔f1!? (11. ♗f4 ♕b6 12. ♕e2 a6 13. ♖d1 0–0–0!? 14. ♔f1 ♗e7 = Edelman – Glek, Philadelphia 1990; 11. ♘e2 ♗e7) 11...♕d7 12. ♗d2 ♗e7 13. ♘e2 0–0–0 14. ♔g1 ♔b8 15. ♘f4± Christiansen – Andersson, FIDE World Championship (1), Groningen 1997.

106   10...♕b6 11. ♘f4 h6 12. h4 g6 13. ♔f1 (13. 0–0 ♗e7 14. g3 a5 15. ♔g2 a4 16. ♖b1±) 13...♗e7 14. g3 0–0–0 15. ♔g2± Sax – Gurevich, German League 1992/93.

107

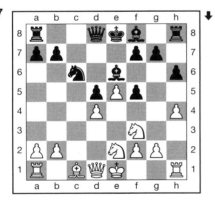

11...g6 12. ♗d2 ♕b6 13. ♖b1 a5 14. ♔f1 ♗e7 15. ♔g1 ♔d7 16. a3 ♕a6 17. ♗e3 a4 18. ♘f4 g5 19. h×g5 h×g5 20. ♖×h8 ♖×h8 21. ♘×e6 f×e6 22. ♗×g5 ♗×g5 23. ♘×g5 ♖h4 24. ♘f3 ♖g4 ⇆ Adams – Vaganian, Lucerne 1997;

11...♗e7 12. h5! (12. ♔f1 ♕b6! 13. h5 0–0–0 14. g3 ♔b8 15. ♔g2 ♖c8 16. ♘f4 ♘b4 17. ♘e1 ♖c4 = Schlosser – Glek, Odessa

1989; 12. ♘f4 ♕b6 13. ♖h3 g6 14. ♔f1 0–0–0 15. ♔g1 ♖dg8 16. ♖b1 g5 ⇄ Sveshnikov – Temirbaev, Kuibyshev 1986) 12...♕b6 (12...♕a5+ 13. ♔f1 ♖c8 14. ♔g1 ♘d7 15. ♘f4 ♖c7 16. ♖h3 ♖hc8 ⇄ Khalifman – Akopian, Dortmund 2000) 13. ♘f4 ♕a6 (13...♖c8 14. a3 ♘a5 15. b4 ♘c4 16. ♖h3 a5 ⇄ Kharlov – Kuporosov, Helsinki 1992; 13...0–0 14. 0–0 ♖fc8 15. ♖e1 ♖c7 16. ♖e2 ♖ac8 17. ♗e3 ♘b4 ⇄ Tiviakov – Arizmendi Martínez, Istanbul 2003) 14. ♗d2 ♖c8 15. ♖h3 0–0 16. ♖g3± Sveshnikov – Naumkin, Moscow 1987.

108   12. ♗d2 ♕a6.

109   13. ♔g1 ♖c8 14. ♘f4 ♕b6 [14...g6 15. a3?! (15. ♖h3±) 15...♕b6 16. b4 a5 17. ♖b1 a×b4 18. a×b4 ♘a7 = Adams – Lputian, Pula 1997] 15. h5 0–0⇄; 15...♘b4?! 16. ♗d2 ♘c2? (△ 16...♖c6⇄) 17. ♘×e6 f×e6 18. ♖c1 ♕×b2 19. ♘e1!± Sveshnikov – Psakhis, Sochi 1997.

110   **6...♘g4?** 7. ♕a4! h5 8. h3 ♘h6 9. ♗e3 ♘f5 10. ♗d4± Sveshnikov – Bareev, European Club Cup, Moscow 1991;

6...♕c7?! 7. b4! ♘g4 (7...♘×e5!? Lempert) 8. ♗f4 f6 (Mukhametov – Lempert, Moscow 1992) 9. ♗b5!±.

111   7. ♗×h6 g×h6 8. b4 [8. ♗d3 f6 9. e×f6 (9. b4 ♗f8 10. b5 ♘×e5 11. ♘×e5 f×e5 12. ♕h5+ ♔d7 13. ♕×e5 ♖g8 14. g3 ♗d6∓ Khalifman – Kaidanov, Moscow 1987) 9...♕×f6 10. 0–0 0–0 11. ♗c2 ♖f7 12. ♘bd2 ♗d7 13. ♘b3 ♗b6 14. ♕e2 e5⇄ Short – Glek, Cap d'Agde (Rapidplay) 1996] 8...♗f8 9. b5 ♘e7! 10. ♗d3 ♗g7 11. 0–0 ♘g6⇄ Sveshnikov – Glek, Moscow 1991.

112   **7...♗f8** 8. b5 ♘a5 (8...♘e7 9. ♗d3 ♘ef5 10. 0–0±) 9. ♗d3 f6 10. ♗×h6 g×h6 11. ♘d4 ♕c7 12. e×f6 ♕e5+ 13. ♗e2 ♗d6 14. f7+!± (Sveshnikov – Jolles, Torcy 1991) 14...♔×f7 15. g3 ♔g7 16. 0–0;

7...♗×f2+?! 8. ♔×f2 ♘g4+ 9. ♔g3 ♘c×e5 10. ♗b5+ ♗d7 11. ♕e2±.

113 8. ♗xh6 gxh6 9. b5 ♘e7 10. ♗d3
(10. ♕d2 ♘g6 11. ♕xh6 ♕c7 12. ♕g5 ♗d7 ⩱)
10... ♘g6 11. 0–0 ♕c7! (11...f6 12. ♗xg6+
hxg6 13. ♕d3 ♔f7 14. exf6 ♕xf6 15. ♘bd2
♖d8?! 16. ♖ae1 a6 17. ♘e5+ ± Sveshnikov –
Dukhov, Moscow 1992) 12. ♖e1 0–0 13. a4
♗d7 14. ♖a2 (14. ♕d2!? ±) 14...f6 15. ♗xg6
(15. exf6 ♖xf6 16. c4 ⇄) 15...hxg6 16. ♕d3
f5 17. ♘bd2 ♖fc8 18. ♖c2 a6 ∞ Sveshnikov –
Nikolaev, Moscow 1992.

114 8...♘a5 9. ♗xh6 gxh6 10. ♕d2 ♗d7
11. ♕xh6 ♕e7!? [11...♕c7 12. ♕f6 ♖f8
13. ♗e2!? (13. ♗d3 ♘c4 14. 0–0 ♗xb5
15. ♘bd2 ±) 13...♘c4 14. a4 ♕c5 (14...♗c5
15. ♗xc4 ♗e7 16. ♕f4 ♕xc4 17. ♕xc4
dxc4 18. ♘bd2 a6 19. 0–0±; 14...a6
15. bxa6 ♖xa6 16. 0–0 ♖xa4 17. ♖xa4
♗xa4 18. ♗d3 ∞ Sveshnikov – Moskalenko,
PCA 1994) 15. ♘g5 ♗d8 16. ♕g7 ♗xg5
17. ♕xg5 ♕c7 ⇄] 12. ♗d3 0–0–0 13. 0–0
♖df8 14. ♘bd2 ♔b8 15. a4 f6 16. c4 ♗c8 ∞
Sveshnikov – Cherniaev, Moscow 1996.

115 9...♘g4 10. 0–0 ♘g6 11. ♗xg6 fxg6
(11...hxg6 12. ♕a4 ±) 12. ♕a4 (12. h3 ♘h6
13. ♗xh6 gxh6 14. ♘bd2 0–0 15. c4 a6 ⇄
Grischuk – Bareev, Cannes (Rapidplay) 2001)
12...♘h6 13. ♘bd2 (13. ♗a3 ±) 13...0–0
14. ♗a3 ♖f7 15. c4 ±;

9...♘hf5 10. g4 ♘h6 11. ♗xh6 gxh6
12. ♕d2 ±.

116 **12. ♕a4?!** ♗d7 13. h4 f5 14. h5
♘h8 15. ♘bd2 ♘f7 16. c4 ♘g5 17. cxd5
exd5 18. ♖ae1 Gallagher – Glek, Dubai 1993
18...♘e6!? ∓;

12. ♕c2!? ±.

117 12...f6 13. ♗xg6 hxg6 14. ♕d3 ♔g7
15. ♘bd2 ♗d7 16. c4 ± fxe5 17. cxd5
[17. ♘xe5! ♗e8 18. ♘df3 ♖c8 (18...a6 19. a5
♗c5 20. cxd5 ♕xd5 21. ♕c2 ±) 19. ♖ad1
dxc4 20. ♕e4 ♕c7 21. ♘d4↑] 17...exd5
18. ♕xd5 ♗f5 19. ♕xe5+ ♕f6 ⩱ Sveshnikov –
Moskalenko, Rostov on Don 1993.

Notes

Table 4

1. e4 e6 2. d4 d5 3. e5 c5 4. c3 ♘c6 5. ♘f3 ♗d7

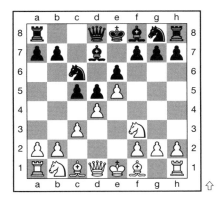

	6	7	8	9	10	11	12	13	
17	a3	♗d3[119]	0-0[121]	♖e1[123]	dxe5[124]	♗c2	♘bd2[125]	b4	
	f6[118]	♕c7[120]	0-0-0[122]	fxe5	c4!?	♗c5	♘h6	♗b6[126]	⇄
18	dxc5!	b4[128]	b5	♗d3	a4	♕e2	bxa6	0-0	
	♗xc5[127]	♗b6	♘a5[129]	♘c4[130]	♕c7	a6	♖xa6	♘e7[131]	=
19	♗e2	0-0	♘xe5[134]	dxe5	c4[137]	♗g5[138]	♗g4[140]	♘c3	
	f6[132]	fxe5[133]	♘xe5[135]	♗c6[136]	♘e7	♕d7[139]	♘g6[141]	dxc4[142]	±
20	...	0-0[143]	cxd4	♘c3	♗e3!?[146]	♗d3	fxe3	e4!	
	♘ge7	cxd4[144]	♘f5	a6[145]	♗e7	♘xe3	0-0	♘b4[147]	⇄
21	...	...	♘a3[148]	cxd4	bxa3	♗e3	fxe3	♖b1!?[152]	
	...	♘f5	cxd4	♗xa3[149]	♕b6!?[150]	♘xe3[151]	♕d8	b6[153]	=
22	...	...	♗e3[154]	dxc5!?[156]	♘a3	♘xe5	♘b5[158]	♗xb5+	
	...	♘g6!?	♗e7[155]	♕c7[157]	♘cxe5	♘xe5	♗xb5	♘c6[159]	⇄

118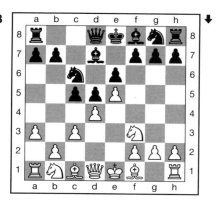

6...c4!? 7. g3 (7. ♗f4 ♛b6 8. ♕c2 f6 9. ♘bd2 g5 10. ♗g3 g4 11. ♘h4 fxe5 12. dxe5 ♘h6 13. ♗e2 ♗g7∓ Sveshnikov – Gulko, Volgodonsk 1981) 7...♛b6 8. ♘bd2 ♘a5 9. ♗h3 0–0–0 10. 0–0 ♗e7 11. ♘e1 h5 12. f4 g6 13. ♘df3± Sveshnikov – Kalinin, Kharkov 1978;

6...a5 7. ♗d3 ♘ge7 8. h4 ♛b6 9. ♗c2 ♘f5 10. 0–0 ♘h6 11. h5± Sveshnikov – Gulko, Cheliabinsk 1981;

6...♘ge7 7. ♗d3 ♘g6 8. h4 cxd4 9. cxd4 ♛b6 10. ♗c2 ♖c8 11. ♘c3 ♘ge7 12. ♖b1 ♘a5 13. 0–0 ♘c4 14. ♕e2 ♘c6 15. ♖d1± Sveshnikov – Torre, Wijk aan Zee 1981;

6...♖c8 7. ♗d3 cxd4 8. cxd4 ♛b6 9. ♗c2 g5!? (9...♘xd4?! 10. ♘xd4 ♗c5 11. ♘f3 ♗xf2+ 12. ♔e2±) 10. h3 ♘xd4 11. ♘xd4 ♗c5 12. ♘e2 ♗xf2+ 13. ♔f1 f6 (Sveshnikov – Chernin, 52nd USSR Championship, Riga 1985) 14. ♘bc3!±.

119 7. b4 c4! (7...fxe5 8. b5!? ♘a5 9. ♘xe5 ♘f6 10. ♗g5!? ♗e7 11. ♗d3 0–0 12. ♘d2±) 8. ♗f4 ♘h6 9. exf6 gxf6 10. g3 ♘f7 11. ♗g2 ♗g7 12. ♗e3 ♘e7 13. ♘h4 ♘g6 14. ♕h5 ♘xh4 15. ♕xh4 0–0⇄ Sveshnikov – Razuvaev, Sochi 1986.

120 **7...fxe5!?** 8. ♘xe5 ♘xe5 9. dxe5 ♘e7 (9...♛h4!?⇄) 10. 0–0 ♕c7∞;

7...cxd4 8. cxd4 ♘h6 9. 0–0 ♘f7 10. ♖e1 ♗e7 11. ♘c3 0–0 12. ♕c2 f5 13. ♘xd5!? exd5 14. e6±.

121 8. ♗f4!? 0–0–0 9. b4 [9. 0–0 c4 10. ♗c2 ♛b6 11. b3 cxb3 12. ♗xb3 g5 13. ♗e3 g4 14. ♘e1 f5 15. ♘d3 ♘a5 16. ♗c2 ♔b8 17. a4 (17. ♘d2 ♖c8 18. ♖b1 ♕c7 19. ♘b3 ♘xb3 20. ♖xb3 ♗a4 21. ♖b2 ♗xc2 22. ♕xc2 ♗xa3 23. ♖b3 ♗f8 24. ♖fb1 b6 25. ♘c5↑) 17...♖c8 18. ♕e2 ♛a6±, van Wely – Topalov, Dortmund 2005] 9...c4 10. ♗c2 fxe5 11. ♗xe5! ♘xe5 12. ♘xe5 ♘h6 13. ♘d2±, Karmov – Kalinichenko, corr. 1993/94.

122 **8...fxe5** 9. ♘xe5 ♘xe5 10. ♗f4! ♛b6 11. ♗xe5 ♛xb2 12. ♕h5+ ♔e7 13. ♕g5+ ♘f6 14. ♘d2→;

8...c4 9. ♗c2 0–0–0 10. ♖e1 fxe5 11. ♘xe5 ♘xe5 12. dxe5 ♗c5 13. ♗e3 ♗xe3 14. ♖xe3 ♘e7= Hába – Potkin, Pardubice 2002.

123 **9. ♗f4** c4 10. ♗c2 h6! 11. h4 ♗e8 12. b3 cxb3 13. ♗xb3 ♗h5 14. ♘bd2 fxe5 15. dxe5 ♗c5∓ Adams – Epishin, Ter Apel 1992;

9. ♕e2 h6 10. b4 c4 11. ♗c2 f5 12. ♘h4 ♗e8 13. f4 ♗e7∞ Grischuk – Short, Reykjavík 2000.

124 **10. ♘xe5** ♘xe5 11. dxe5 (11. ♗f4?! c4 12. ♗c2 ♛b6 13. ♗xe5 ♛xb2 14. ♘d2 ♛xc3∓).

125 **12. ♗e3** ♗xe3 13. ♖xe3 ♘h6 14. h3 ♘f7 15. ♕e2 g5 16. ♘bd2 ♖dg8 17. b3 h5⇄.

126 **14. h3** ♘f7 15. ♕e2⇄ Alekseev – S. Ivanov, St. Petersburg, 1999.

127 **6...♛c7?!** 7. ♗f4 (7. ♘a3!? ♘xe5 8. ♘b5 ♘xf3+ 9. ♕xf3 ♕e5+ 10. ♔d1 ♖c8 11. ♗f4 ♛f6 12. ♕g3 ♛g6 13. ♘xa7± Nikolenko – Shur, Asov 1991) 7... ♘ge7 8. ♗d3 ♘g6 9. ♗xg6 fxg6 10. b4 a5 11. ♛d2 axb4 12. cxb4 b6 13. b5 ♘a5 14. c6 ♗xc6 15. bxc6 ♘b3 16. axb3 ♖xa1 17. 0–0± Sveshnikov – Katishonok, Riga (Rapidplay) 1990.

128 7. ♗d3 ♘ge7 (7...a5!?; 7...f6 8. b4 ♗e7 9. b5 ♘xe5 10. ♘xe5 fxe5 11. ♕h5+ ♔f8 12. ♕xe5 ♗f6 13. ♕d6+ ♘e7 14. 0–0 e5∞ Sveshnikov–Savon, Zonal Tournament, Lvov 1978) 8. b4 (8. 0–0 ♘g6 9. ♖e1 ♕c7 10. ♗xg6 fxg6!? 11. ♗f4 0–0 12. ♗g3 ♘e7∓ Sveshnikov–Balashov, 44th USSR Championship, Moscow 1976) 8...♗b6 9. b5 ♘a5 10. 0–0 ♖c8! 11. a4 ♘g6 12. ♖e1 (12. ♗a3 ♗c5 13. ♗xc5 ♖xc5 14. g3 ♕c7 15. ♖e1 ♘c4= Sveshnikov–Balashov, Zonal Tournament, Lvov 1978) 12...f6 13. ♖a2 0–0 14. ♗xg6 hxg6 15. ♕d3 ♔f7 16. ♗e3 ♖h8 17. ♖ae2 ♘c4 18. ♗d4± Sveshnikov–Naumkin, Moscow 1989.

129 8...♘ce7 9. ♗d3 ♕c7 10. 0–0 ♘g6 11. ♖e1 ♘8e7 12. a4 f6 13. ♗xg6+ ♘xg6 (13...hxg6 14. ♗a3∞) 14. exf6 gxf6 15. ♕xd5∞ Kharlov–Dolmatov, Moscow 1991.

130 9...♕c7

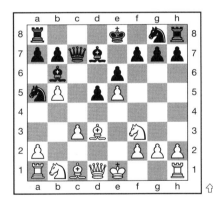

a) 10. ♕e2 ♘c4 (10...♘e7 11. 0–0 ♘g6 12. ♖e1 0–0–0 13. ♘a3 ♔b8 14. ♗d2 f6 15. ♗xg6 hxg6 16. ♗f4 ♗c5 17. ♘c2 ♘c4 18. a4 ♖hf8 19. ♗g3 f5 20. ♗f4 ♕a5 21. ♖ec1± Sveshnikov–Shabalov, Riga (Rapidplay) 1990) 11. ♗xc4!? dxc4 12. ♘bd2 ♗xb5 13. ♘e4 ♗c5! 14. a4 ♗c6! 15. ♘xc5 ♗xf3 16. ♕xf3 ♕xc5 17. 0–0 ♕d5⇄ Kharlov–Zakharevich, Russian Championship, Elista 1996;

b) 10. 0–0 ♘e7 11. a4 ♘g6 12. ♖e1 ♗c5 13. ♖a2 0–0–0 14. ♗e3± Sveshnikov–Popović, Palma de Mallorca 1989.

131 13...♖xa4 14. ♖xa4 ♗xa4 15. ♘a3⧴;

13...♘e7 14. ♘a3 ♖xa4 15. ♘xc4 dxc4 (15...♖xa1? 16. ♘d6+ ♔f8 17. ♘g5+−) 16. ♖xa4 ♗xa4 17. ♗xc4 0–0 18. ♗d3! ♘g6! 19. h4 ♗c6 20. h5 ♗xf3 21. gxf3 ♕xe5! 22. hxg6 ♕g3+ 23. ♔h1 ♕h3+= Sveshnikov–Kharlov, Böblingen 1992

132 6...♖c8 7. 0–0 a6

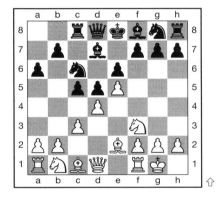

a) 8. dxc5!? ♗xc5 9. ♗f4 ♘ge7 10. ♗d3 f5 11. exf6 gxf6 12. ♘h4 0–0 13. ♕g4+ ♔h8 14. ♕h5 f5 15. b4 ♗b6 16. ♘d2 ♗c7∞ Oll–Ivanchuk, Polanica Zdrój 1998;

b) 8. a3 cxd4 9. cxd4 ♘ge7 10. ♘c3 ♘f5 11. g4 [11. ♗e3 ♗e7 12. ♗d3 ♘xe3 13. fxe3 0–0 14. ♖f2 f6 15. ♕c2 f5= Ivanović–Bareev, Moscow (Blitz) 1993] 11...♘h4 12. ♘xh4 ♕xh4 13. ♗e3 g5 14. ♘a4 h5⇄ Xie Jun–Karpov, Guanzhou (Rapidplay) 2000;

c) 8. b3 ♘ge7 9. ♗b2 ♘f5 10. ♗d3 cxd4 11. ♗xf5 exf5 12. ♘xd4 ♗e7 13. ♖e1 0–0 14. ♕d3 ♘xd4 15. cxd4 ♕a5 16. ♘c3 ♖c6 17. a3 ♗e6 18. b4 ♕c7 19. f4± Sveshnikov–Epishin, Moscow 1992;

d) 8. ♔h1 cxd4! (8...♘ge7 9. dxc5! ♘g6 10. ♗e3 ♘cxe5 11. ♘xe5 ♘xe5 12. b4 ♗e7 13. ♘d2 ♘c6 14. f4± Grischuk–Radjabov, Dubai 2002) 9. cxd4 ♘ge7 10. ♘c3 ♘g6 11. ♗d3 ♗e7 12. ♗e3 0–0 13. ♖e1 ♘a5

14. ♖c1 ♘c4 15. ♖c2 ♘xe3 16. fxe3 b5⇄ Grischuk – Radjabov, Dubai 2002;

e) 8. g3 h6 9. h4 ♕c7 10. h5 ♘ge7 11. ♖e1 cxd4 12. cxd4 ♕b6 13. g4 g6 14. hxg6 ♘xg6 15. ♘c3 ♖g8∞ Grischuk – Bareev, Chalkidiki 2002;

f) 8. ♘a3!? ♘ge7 9. ♘c2 ♘g6 10. ♗d3 ♗e7 11. g3 c4 12. ♗e2 f6 13. exf6 ♗xf6 14. h4 h6 15. h5 ♘ge7 16. ♗f4± Sveshnikov – Razuvaev, Moscow (Rapidplay) 1992.

133

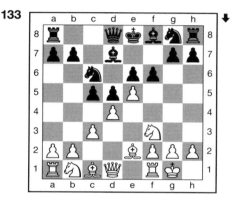

7...♕c7 8. ♗f4 0-0-0 (8...♘ge7 9. ♗g3 ♘f5 10. exf6 ♘xg3 11. f7+ ♔xf7 12. fxg3 ♔g8 13. dxc5 ♗xc5+ 14. ♔h1 ♖f8 15. c4 d4 16. a3± Prié – Dimitrov, Sofia 1990) 9. ♗g3 ♕b6 10. ♕c1 fxe5 11. ♘xe5 ♘xe5 12. ♗xe5 ♘f6 13. b4 c4 14. a4 ♗d6 15. a5 ♕c7 16. ♕e3 ♔b8 17. ♘d2 ♗c8 18. ♖ae1± Sveshnikov – Atanasov, Berlin 1989;

7...♕b6 8. dxc5 (8. a3 fxe5 9. dxe5 c4 10. ♘bd2 ♘a5 11. ♘d4 ♗c5 12. ♘2f3 ♘e7∓ Jonkman – Stellwagen, Wijk aan Zee 2003) 8...♗xc5 9. b4 ♗e7 10. ♗f4 (10. c4 dxc4 11. ♘a3 ♘xe5 12. ♘xe5 fxe5 13. ♘xc4 ♕xb4 14. a4⯑ Degraeve – Bricard, French Championship, Val d'Isère 2002) 10...fxe5 11. ♘xe5 ♘xe5 12. ♗xe5 ♘f6 13. a4 a5 14. bxa5 ♖xa5 15. ♘d2 0-0 16. ♖b1 ♕a7 17. ♗b5± Polgár – Topalov, Dos Hermanas 1994.

134   8. dxe5 ♕c7 9. c4!? (9. ♘a3 a6 10. ♗f4 ♘h6 11. ♘c2 ♘f7 12. c4 d4 13. ♗d3

♗e7 14. ♕e2 g5 15. ♗g3 0-0-0∓ Kupreichik – Gulko, 44th USSR Championship, Moscow 1976; 9. ♖e1 0-0-0 10. ♗d3 ♘h6 11. ♘a3 a6 12. ♗g5 ♖e8 13. ♗f4 ♗e7 14. ♕d2 ♖ef8 15. ♘c2 c4 16. ♗f1 ♖hg8∓ Movsesian – Shirov, German League 1999/2000) 9...d4 10. ♗f4 ♘h6 11. ♘bd2 ♘f7 12. ♘e4 ♗e7 13. ♗d3 0-0-0 14. ♖e1 ♖df8 15. ♗g3 g5 16. ♘f6 h5 17. h3∞ Motylev – J. Ivanov, St. Petersburg 1997.

135   8...♗d6 9. ♘xc6 ♗xc6 10. ♗h5+ g6 11. ♗g4±.

136   **9...♕c7** 10. c4

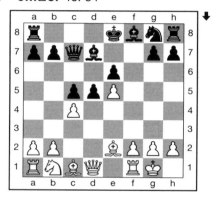

a) 10...♕xe5 11. ♗h5+! g6 12. ♗f3 0-0-0 13. ♖e1 ♕d6 14. ♘c3± Romanishin – Ivanchuk, Irkutsk 1986;

b) 10...d4 11. ♗f4 ♘e7 (11...0-0-0 12. ♘d2 ♗c6 13. ♗d3 g5!?↑ Jonkman – Smeets, Groningen 2002) 12. ♘d2 ♘f5 13. ♗d3 ♗e7 14. ♘e4 0-0 15. ♕g4 ♔h8 16. ♕h3 ♕d8 17. ♗d2 ♗e8 18. g4 ♘h4 19. f4± I. Zaitsev – Tarjan, Quito 1977;

c) 10...♘e7 11. ♘c3 d4 12. ♘e4 ♕xe5 13. ♖e1 0-0-0 14. ♗f3 ♖e8 15. b4 cxb4 16. a3⯑ Milos – Rodríguez, Santos 2003;

d) 10...0-0-0 11. cxd5 ♕xe5 12. ♗f3 exd5 [12...♗d6 13. g3 exd5 14. ♗f4 ♕f6 15. ♘c3 ♗c6 16. ♘xd5 ♕d4 (Sveshnikov – Psakhis, Sochi 1984) 17. ♕c2!±] 13. ♖e1 ♕d6! 14. g3!? ♘f6 15. ♗f4 ♕a6! 16. ♘c3 d4 17. ♘e4 ♘xe4 18. ♖xe4⯑ Sveshnikov – Vaisser, Sochi 1984;

9...♘e7 10. ♗g5 (10. c4!?) 10...♕c7 11. ♗h5+ g6 12. ♗f6 ♖g8 13. ♗g4 ♗g7 14. ♖e1 ♔f7?! (14...♘c6!? 15. ♕e2 ♗×f6 16. e×f6 0–0–0! 17. ♗×e6 ♗×e6 18. ♕×e6+ ♕d7∞ Glek) 15. c4!± Glek – Yurtaev, Tashkent 1987.

137 10. ♗d3 ♕d7 11. ♗g5 ♘h6 12. ♘d2 ♘f7 13. ♗h4 ♗e7 14. ♗×e7 ♕×e7 15. f4 0–0–0 16. ♕e2 ♔b8 17. ♖ae1 g6 18. a3 c4!∞ Ivanchuk – Short, 34ᵗʰ Olympiad, Novi Sad 1990.

138 11. ♗g4 ♕d7 12. ♘c3 d×c4 13. ♕e2 ♘f5 14. ♕×c4 ♘d4 15. a4 h5 16. ♗h3 ♕f7∞ Sax – Speelman, Hastings 1990/91.

139 11...d×c4 12. ♘d2! (12. ♗×c4 ♕×d1 13. ♖×d1 ♘d5 14. ♘c3 h6 15. ♗h4 g5 16. ♗g3±) 12...♕d5 13. ♗h5+ ♘g6 14. ♕g4 ♗e7□ 15. ♗×g6+ h×g6 16. ♗×e7 ♔×e7 17. ♘×c4 ♕e4 18. ♕g5+± Benjamin – Gulko, Groningen 1993.

140 12. ♗h5+! g6 (12...♘g6 13. ♕c2 ♕f7 14. c×d5±) 13. ♗f6 ♖g8 14. ♗f3±.

141 12...d×c4 13. ♕×d7+! ♗×d7 14. ♘d2±.

142 **13...d4** 14. ♘d5;

13...d×c4 14. ♕e2 ♗e7 (14...♕d3 15. ♕e1! h6 16. ♖d1 h×g5 17. ♖×d3 c×d3 18. g3!±) 15. ♖ad1± ♕c7 16. ♗×e7 (16. ♗c1?! Sveshnikov – Panbukchian, Anapa 1991) 16...♕×e7 17. f4!±.

143

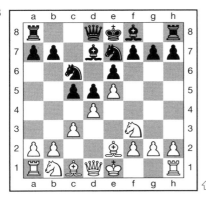

7. d×c5!? ♘g6 8. ♗e3 ♘g×e5 9. ♘×e5 ♘×e5 10. f4 ♘c6 11. ♘d2 b6 12. ♘b3 b×c5 13. ♘×c5 ♕b6 14. ♘×e6!? (14. ♘×d7 ♕×e3 15. ♘×f8 ♔×f8 16. ♕d2 ♕×d2+ 17. ♔×d2 ♔e7 18. b4⇄ Velimirović – Züger, Lucerne 1989) 14...♕×e3 15. ♘c7+ ♔d8 16. ♘×d5 ⯑ (16. ♘×d5 ♕e6 17. ♕d2⯑; 16. ♘×a8 ♗c5 17. ♕×d5 ♕f2+ 18. ♔d1 ♖e8∞);

7. h4!?

a) 7...h5 8. ♘a3 c×d4 9. c×d4 ♘f5 10. ♘c2 ♕b6 11. 0–0 ♘b4 12. ♘e3 ♘×e3 13. f×e3 ♗e7 14. a3 ♘c6 15. b4± Sveshnikov – Kholopov, Cheliabinsk (Rapidplay) 1997;

b) 7...♕c7 8. ♘a3 a6 9. ♘c2 c×d4 10. c×d4 ♘a5 11. b3 ♖c8 12. ♘e3 ♘ec6 13. 0–0 ♗e7 14. ♗d2 0–0 15. ♗d3 f5 16. e×f6 ♗×f6 17. ♖c1± Sveshnikov – Sæther, Gausdal 1992;

c) 7...♕b6 8. d×c5! ♕×c5 9. h5 ♕b6 10. ♘a3 ♘f5 11. ♕b3 ♗c5 12. ♕×b6 ♗×b6 13. g4 ♘h6 14. ♖g1 ♗c7 15. ♘b5 ♗b8 16. ♗f4± Sveshnikov – Bashkov, Satka (Rapidplay) 2003;

d) 7...c×d4!? 8. c×d4 ♕b6 9. ♘a3 ♘f5 10. ♘c2 ♘b4 (10...♗b4+ 11. ♔f1 h5 12. a3 ♗e7 13. b4 ♖c8 14. g3 f6 15. ♗d3 f×e5 16. ♗×f5 e×f5 17. d×e5± Topalov – Nikolić, Monte Carlo (blind) 1997) 11. ♘×b4 (11. ♔f1 h5 12. g3 ♗b5 13. ♗×b5+ ♕×b5+ 14. ♔g2∓ Movsesian – Nikolić, German League 2002/03) 11...♗×b4+ 12. ♔f1 ♖c8 13. g4 ♘h6 14. ♗×h6 g×h6 15. ♖c1 ♖×c1 16. ♕×c1⇄.

144 7...♖c8 8. ♘a3 (8. ♖e1 c×d4 9. c×d4 ♘f5 10. ♘c3 ♗e7 11. a3 0–0= Menvielle Lacourrelle – Larsen, Las Palmas 1976; 8. d×c5 ♘g6 9. b4 ♗e7 10. ♗e3 ♘c×e5 11. ♘×e5 ♘×e5 12. ♘d2⇄ Peng Xiaomin – Yusupov, 33ʳᵈ Olympiad, Elista 1998) 8...c×d4 9. c×d4! ♘f5 10. ♘c2

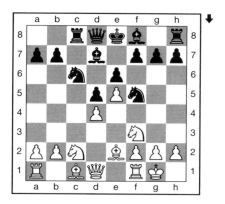

10...♛b6

a) 11. ♗d3!? a5 (11...♞f×d4? 12. ♞f×d4 ♞×d4 13. ♗e3 ♗c5 14. b4+−; 11...♞b4 12. ♞×b4 ♗×b4 13. a3 ♗e7 14. ♗×f5 e×f5 15. ♗g5 ♗×g5 16. ♞×g5 0–0 17. ♛d2 ♖c4= Benjamin – Gulko, US Championship, Key West 1994) 12. a3 a4 13. ♗×f5 e×f5 14. ♞e3 ♛b5 15. b3! a×b3 16. ♖b1↑ Guido – Foisor, Montecatini Terme 1994; 16. a4? b2!−+;

b) 11. ♛d3?! a6 12. a4 (12. g4 ♞fe7 13. a4?! ♞a5 14. b4 ♞c4 15. ♛b3 ♞c6∓ Yanovsky – Kindermann, Biel 1991) 12...♞b4 13. ♞×b4 ♗×b4 14. h4 h6 15. h5 ♞e7 16. ♗f4 ♞c6 17. ♖fc1 ♗a5⇄ Sveshnikov – Dizdar, Slovenian League, Celje 2003;

c) 11. ♔h1!? ♞a5 [11...♞b4 12. ♞×b4 ♛×b4 13. a4!? a5 (⌓ 13...♛a5) 14. ♗d2 ♛b6 15. g4 ♞e7 16. b4 a×b4 17. a5 ♛c7 18. ♗×b4 ♞g6 19. ♗d2!± Dvoiris – Gleizerov, Hoogeveen 2000] 12. g4 ♞e7 13. ♞fe1 ♗b5 14. ♞d3! h5!? 15. g×h5 ♞f5 16. ♗e3± Grischuk – Gulko, Esbjerg 2000;

d) 11. g4! ♞fe7 12. ♞fe1 [12. ♞h4!? ♞b4 (12...♞g6 13. ♞g2 f6 14. e×f6 g×f6⇄ Sveshnikov – Atalik, Slovenian League, Bled 1999) 13. ♞×b4 ♛×b4 14. f4 ♞c6 (14...♗b5 15. ♛d2 ♛a4 16. b3 ♛a6 17. ♗×b5+ ♛×b5 18. f5 ♞c6 19. ♗b2= Sveshnikov – Gleizerov, Russian League, Podolsk 1992) 15. ♗e3 ♗e7 16. ♞g2± Sveshnikov – Ulibin, Russian League, Podolsk 1992] 12...h5?! (12...g6;

12...♞d8) 13. g×h5 ♞f5 14. ♗e3!± Sveshnikov – Skalkotas, Athens 1983;

10...♗e7 11. g4 ♞h4 12. ♞×h4 ♗×h4 13. f4∞.

145

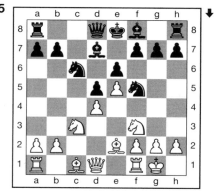

9...♗e7 10. g4 ♞h4 (10...♞h6 11. h3 0–0 12. ♗e3 f6 13. e×f6 ♖×f6 14. ♞e5 ♖f8 15. f4 ♗b4 16. ♗f3 ♗×c3 17. b×c3± Sveshnikov – Lalić, Sochi 1987) 11. ♞×h4 ♗×h4 12. ♗e3 0–0 13. f4 f6 14. e×f6 ♗×f6 15. ♖c1 g6 16. ♛d2= Nunn – Anand, Munich 1991;

9...♖c8 10. ♔h1!? (10. ♗e3) 10...a6 11. g4 ♞fe7 12. ♗d3 ♞a5 13. ♖g1 ♞ec6 14. ♖g3 ♛b6⇄ Vatter – Kindermann, Baden-Baden 1993;

9...h5?! 10. ♗g5 ♗e7 11. ♗×e7 ♛×e7 12. ♛d2± Romero Holmes – Korchnoi, Wijk aan Zee 1992.

146   10. g4 ♞h4 11. ♞×h4 ♛×h4 12. ♗e3 ♗e7 13. f4 f6⇄;

10. ♗f4!? ♛b6 11. ♞a4 ♛a7 12. ♗e3 b5 13. ♞c3 b4 (13...f6 14. ♗d3±) 14. ♞a4±;

10. ♔h1 ♖c8 11. ♗e3 ♗e7 12. ♗d3 ♞×e3 13. f×e3 0–0 14. ♖c1 f6 15. e×f6 ♗×f6⇄ Palleja – Dizdar, Montpellier 1997.

147   14. e×d5 ♞×d3 (14...e×d5 15. ♗b1 ♗e6 16. ♞e2± Kharlov – Dokhoian, 58th USSR Championship, Moscow 1991) 15. d×e6! ♞×e5! 16. ♞×e5 ♗×e6 17. d5 ♛b6+! (17...♗f6 18. ♛d4 ♗×e5 19. ♛×e5 ♗d7± Kharlov) 18. ♔h1 ♖ad8 19. ♛f3 ♗c8⇄.

148   8. ♗d3!?

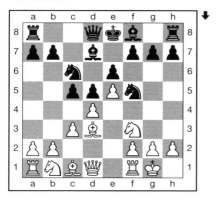

8...♘h4 9. ♘×h4 [9. ♘g5!? c×d4 10. c×d4 (10. f4!?) 10...♘×d4 11. ♕h5 ♘g6 12. ♘c3 ⯗ Kupreichik–Levitt, Badenweiler 1990] 9...♕×h4 10. ♗e3 ♕d8!? [10...c×d4 11. c×d4 ♗b4 (11...♕d8!?) 12. a3 ♗a5 13. g3 ♕e7 14. ♘c3 f5 15. b4± Kupreichik–Levitt, Copenhagen 1988] 11. ♘d2 ♕b6 12. b3 (12. ♕b1 c×d4 13. c×d4 ♘b4 14. ♗e2 ♗b5 15. ♗×b5+ ♕×b5 16. ♖c1 ♗e7 17. ♖c3 ♘c6 18. ♖b3 ♕a6 19. ♕d1 0–0=; 12. ♘f3 c4 13. ♗c2 ♕×b2 14. ♕d2 ♕b6 15. ♘g5 ⯗ Vasyukov–Levitt, Græsted 1990) 12...c×d4 13. c×d4 ♘b4 14. ♗e2 ♗b5 15. ♗×b5+ ♕×b5 16. a3 ♘c6 17. ♕g4±;

8...c×d4 9. ♗×f5 e×f5 10. ♘×d4 ♗e7 11. ♕b3 (11. ♘f3 ♗e6 12. ♗e3 g5! 13. ♘a3! f4 14. ♗d4 ♖g8 15. ♘e1 ∞ Romanishin–Hort, Biel 1987) 11...♘×d4 (11...♗c8 12. f4 0–0 13. ♗e3 f6 14. e×f6 ♗×f6 15. ♘d2± Kupreichik–Kosten, Val Maubuée 1989) 12. c×d4 ♕b6 (12...♗c6 13. ♕g3±) 13. ♕×b6 (13. ♘c3 ♗e6 14. ♕a4+ ♗d7 15. ♕b3= Stević–Dizdar, Croatian League, Medulin 2002) 13...a×b6 14. ♘c3 ♗e6 15. a3 (15. f4!? ♔d7 ⇄) 15...♔d7 16. f4 ♖hc8= Reefat–Barsov, Dhaka 2001.

149   9...♗e7 10. ♘c2 0–0 11. g4 ♘h4 12. ♘×h4 ♗×h4 13. f4 f6 (13...f5 14. ♗d3±) 14. ♗e3 ♖c8 15. ♗d3 g6 16. ♕d2± Sveshnikov–Leito, (Rapidplay) 2000.

150   10...0–0 11. ♖b1 ♕c7 12. ♗d3 ♖fc8 ∞ Sax–Dreev, Tilburg (Rapidplay) 1992.

151   11...0–0 12. ♗d3 ♖ac8 13. g4 ♘×e3 14. f×e3 ♕d8 15. ♕e1 f5 16. g×f5 e×f5 17. ♖b1 b6 18. ♕g3± Rozentalis–Züger, Chiasso 1991.

152

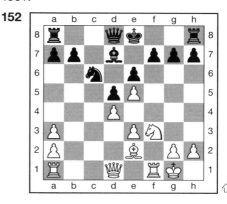

13. ♗d3 ♖c8 14. ♖c1 ♕e7 15. ♖c5 0–0! 16. ♕b1 b6 17. ♖c2 (17. ♖c3? ♘×d4!! 18. ♗×h7+ ♔h8 19. ♖×c8 ♘×f3+ 20. ♖×f3 ♖×c8 21. ♖h3 ♕×a3–+; 17. ♗×h7+? ♔h8 18. ♖cc1 g6 19. ♗×g6 f×g6 20. ♕×g6 ♕h7!∓) 17...h6 18. ♗a6 ♖cd8= Shirov–Topalov, Dos Hermanas 1997;

13. ♕b1!? b6 14. e4 0–0 15. ♗d3 h6 16. e×d5 e×d5 17. h3± Sveshnikov–Iskusnykh, St. Petersburg 1997.

153   **13...♘a5!** 14. ♕e1 0–0 15. ♗d3 ♖c8 16. e4 ♗c6=.

13...b6 14. ♗b5 ♖c8 15. ♕a4 0–0 16. ♗×c6 ♖×c6 17. ♕×a7 ♗e8 18. ♖fc1 ♖×c1+ 19. ♖×c1 f6 20. ♕c7± Sveshnikov–Luther, Nova Gorica 2000.

154

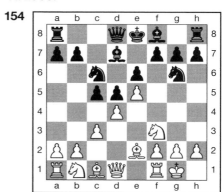

8. g3!?

a) 8...f6!? 9. ♗d3 (9. e×f6 g×f6 10. h4 ♖g8 11. h5 ♘h8 12. ♔g2 c×d4 13. c×d4 ♗d6 14. ♗e3 ♕c7 15. ♖g1 0-0-0⇄ Gurevich) 9...c×d4!? 10. c×d4 ♘b4 11. ♗e2 f×e5 12. ♘×e5 ♘×e5 13. d×e5 ♗c5⇄ Meessen-Gurevich, Belgian Championship, Charleroi 2001;

b) 8...♕b6 9. a3 c4 10. h4 h6 11. ♘bd2 ♘a5 12. ♖e1 0-0-0 13. ♖b1± Adams-Vaganian, Oviedo (Fischer Blitz) 1992;

c) 8...♗e7 9. h4 0-0 (9...c×d4 10. c×d4 0-0 11. h5!? ♘h8 12. h6 g6 13. ♘bd2 f6 14. e×f6 ♗×f6 15. ♘b3 ♘f7 16. ♘h2! ♘d6 17. ♗g4⇄ Hjartarson-Korchnoi, Amsterdam 1991) 10. h5 ♘h8 11. h6 g6 12. d×c5 [12...♗×c5!? 13. c4 f6! (13...d×c4 14. ♘c3 ♗e7 15. ♘e4 g5 16. ♗×g5 ♗×g5 17. ♘f×g5 ♘×e5 18. f4± Gdański-Przewoźnik, 49th Polish Championship, Częstochowa 1992) 14. c×d5 ♘×e5 15. ♕b3 ♘×f3+ 16. ♗×f3 e5 17. ♘c3 ♘f7 18. d6 ♔h8 19. ♕×b7 ♖b8 (19...♖c8!) 20. ♕c7 ♗×d6 21. ♕×a7↑ Timman-Ljubojević, Amsterdam 1999] 12...f6 13. e×f6 ♗×c5 14. ♗g5!? ♘f7 15. ♗h4 ♕c7 16. ♕d2 ♘ce5∞ Timman-Nikolić, Amsterdam 1999;

8. a3 ♗e7 9. b4 c×d4 10. c×d4 ♖c8 11. ♗e3 0-0 12. ♕d2 f6 13. e×f6 ♗×f6 14. ♘c3 ♘ce7 15. ♗d3 ♗e8 16. ♗g5 h6 17. ♗×f6 ♖×f6

18. ♘e5 ♘×e5 19. d×e5 ♖f8 20. ♘e2 ♗g6= Romero Holmes-Nikolić, Wijk aan Zee 1992.

155   8...c×d4 9. c×d4 ♗e7 10. ♘c3 0-0 11. ♗d3 ♗e8 12. ♖c1 f6 13. e×f6 ♗×f6 14. ♕d2 ♔h8 15. ♗b1 ♖c8 16. ♖fe1± Sax-Korchnoi, Candidates Tournament (m/10), Wijk aan Zee 1991.

156   9. ♘e1?! 0-0 10. f4 ♕b6 11. ♕d2 c×d4 12. c×d4 f6= Kupreichik-Nikolić, Ljubljana/Portorož 1989; 12...♘h4!?∓;

9. g3 c×d4 10. c×d4 f6 11. e×f6 ♗×f6 12. ♘c3 0-0 13. ♕d2 ♘ge7 14. ♗d3 h6!?⇄ Romanishin-Nikolić, Leningrad 1987.

157   9...♘g×e5 10. ♘×e5 ♘×e5 11. f4 ♘c6 (11...♘g6 12. b4 0-0 13. ♘d2 b6 14. ♘b3 ♕c7 15. ♕d2 ♗a4 16. f5 ♘e5 17. c×b6 a×b6 18. ♘d4± Cherniaev-Fernández Hernández, Spain 1997) 12. ♘d2 0-0 13. ♗d3± Kharlov-Sakaev, São Paulo 1991.

158   12. b4 0-0 13. f4 ♘g6 14. ♕d2 b6 15. c×b6 a×b6 16. ♘b5 ♗×b5 17. ♗×b5 ♗f6 18. ♗d4 ♗×d4+ 19. c×d4 ♖a3⇄ Mukhametov-Stojanović, Bela Crkva 1996.

159   14. ♖e1!? 0-0 15. ♗d3 f5 (15...b6 16. c×b6 a×b6 17. ♕h5↑) 16. b4⇄;

14. c4 ♖d8 15. c×d5 (Kharlov-Sakaev, Russian League, Podolsk 1992) 15...♖×d5= Sakaev.

Notes

Table 5

**1. e4 e6 2. d4 d5 3. e5 c5 4. c3 ♘c6 5. ♘f3
♗d7 6. ♗e2 ♘ge7 7. ♘a3 c×d4[160] 8. c×d4
♘f5[161] 9. ♘c2[162]**

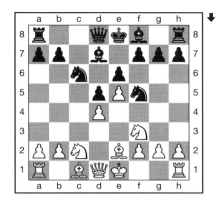

	9	10	11	12	13	14	15	16	
23	...	0–0[164]	g4![166]	♘fe1	g×h5	♘d3	♗e3[169]	b4[171]	
	♛b6[163]	♘a5[165]	♘e7[167]	h5[168]	♗b5	♘f5	♖c8[170]	♘c6[172]	⇄
24	...	...	g4[173]	♘fe1[174]	g×h5	♗e3	♗d3	♗×f5	
	...	a5	♘fe7	h5!?[175]	♘f5	f6	0–0–0[176]	e×f5[177]	∞
25	...	...	♔h1!?	♘e3	♘×f5	♗d2	a3	♗c3[181]	
	...	...	♘b4[178]	♖c8[179]	e×f5	♗e7	♘c6[180]		±
26	...	0–0[182]	g4!?[184]	b4	♖b1[187]	e×f6	a4		
	♗e7	g5!?[183]	♘g7[185]	a6[186]	f5!?[188]	♗×f6	h6[189]		±
27	...	0–0[190]	♕×c2	♕d3	♗d2[194]	♖fc1	♗×d3	♗×f5	
	♘b4	♘×c2[191]	♕b6[192]	a6[193]	♕b5[195]	♕×d3	♗e7	e×f5[196]	±
28	...	...	...	...	g4!?[197]	♗d2[198]	h3	a4[199]	
	...	...	...	♖c8	♘e7	h5	a6	h×g4[200]	±

160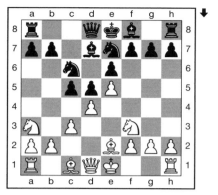

7...♘f5 8. ♘c2 ♗e7 9. 0–0 see 7...c×d4 8. c×d4 ♘f5 9. ♘c2 ♗e7; 9. ♗d3!?± c×d4 10. ♗×f5 e×f5 11. ♘c×d4±;

7...♘g6 8. h4!? c×d4 9. c×d4

a) 9...♗b4+ 10. ♔f1 h6 (10...♘ge7 11. ♘c2 ♗a5 12. g3 f6 13. ♔g2 0–0 14. e×f6 g×f6 15. ♘e3 ♔h8 16. b3 ♗c7 17. ♗b2 ♗e8 18. ♗d3± Sveshnikov – Graf, Kiev (Rapidplay) 1989; 10...♗e7!? Movsesian – Kindermann, German League 2005/06) 11. ♘c2 ♗e7 12. ♗d3! (12. h5 ♘f8 13. b4 ♘h7 14. ♗d2 0–0 15. ♗d3 ♖c8 16. ♕e1 a6 17. a4 f5⇄ Sveshnikov – Gulko, Tashkent 1984) 12...♘f8 13. ♖h3 ♕b6 14. ♖g3 g6 15. ♔g1± Ehlvest – Minasian, Ohrid 2001;

b) 9...♗×a3 10. b×a3 h6 11. h5 ♘ge7 12. 0–0 ♘a5 13. ♖b1 ♗c6 14. ♗d3 ♘c4 15. ♘h4!↑ Grischuk – Graf, 35th Olympiad, Bled 2002.

161 8...♘g6 9. h4 ♗b4+ [9...h6 10. h5 ♗×a3 11. b×a3 ♘ge7 12. ♖b1 (12. 0–0 Grischuk – Graf, 35th Olympiad, Bled 2002) 12...♘a5 13. ♗d2 ♗c6 14. ♗b4 ♘c4 15. ♘d2 ♘f5 16. 0–0 ♘×d4 17. ♗×c4 d×c4 18. ♘×c4 ♘f3+ 19. g×f3 ♕g5+ 20. ♔h2 ♕h4+ 21. ♔g1 ♕×c4∓ Stević – Nikolić, Slovenian League, Celje 2003] 10. ♔f1 0–0 11. h5 ♘h8 12. ♗d3 h6 13. ♕c2 f5 14. ♕e2 ♗e7 15. ♘c2± Sandipan – Hertneck, German League 2002/03.

162 9. 0–0 ♗×a3 – see 7. 0–0.

163 9...♕a5+ 10. ♗d2 ♕b6 11. ♗c3 ♗e7 (11...a5 12. g4 ♘fe7 13. h4 h5 14. g×h5

♘f5 15. ♘e3 ♘×e3 16. f×e3± Sveshnikov – Furlan, Slovenia (Rapidplay) 1997) 12. 0–0 [12. ♕d2 a5 13. 0–0 0–0 14. ♔h1 ♔h8!? (14...♗b4=) 15. g4 ♘h6 16. ♖g1 ♘g8⇄ Cifuentes Parada – Sokolov, Dutch Championship, Amsterdam 1994] 12...a5!? 13. a3 (13. g4 ♘h6 14. ♘fe1 f6 15. ♘d3 ♘f7 16. ♗f3 f×e5 17. d×e5 0–0∓ Marković – Sokolov, Yugoslavia 1987) 13...0–0 14. ♗d3 ♔h8 15. ♖e1 ♘a7 16. a4 ♘c6⇄ Timman – Sokolov, Dutch Championship (m/3), Amsterdam 1996;

164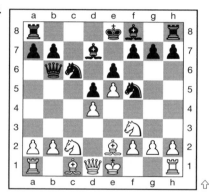

10. g4 ♘fe7 11. 0–0 (11. ♘h4 ♘b4 12. ♘a3 ♘ec6 13. ♗e3 ♗e7 14. ♘g2 f6 15. ♘b5 f×e5 16. 0–0 0–0 17. d×e5 ♗c5∓ Wemmers – Gurevich, Belgian League 2003/04) 11...h5 12. h3!? h×g4 13. h×g4 f6 (13...♘g6!? van Wely) 14. ♗d3! 0–0–0 15. b4± Shirov – van Wely, Wijk aan Zee 2001;

10. h4

a) 10...♗b4+ 11. ♔f1 h5 12. a3 ♗e7 13. b4 ♖c8 14. g3 f6 15. ♗d3 f×e5 16. ♗×f5 e×f5 17. d×e5 d4± Topalov – Nikolić, Monte Carlo (blind) 1997;

b) 10...f6 11. g4 ♘f×d4! (11...♘fe7 12. e×f6 g×f6 13. g5 ♗g7∞) 12. ♘c×d4 ♘×e5 13. g5 ♗c5 14. 0–0 ♘×f3+ 15. ♘×f3 ♕b4 16. ♘e1 ♕×h4 17. ♘g2 ♕b4⇄ Movsesian – Gurevich, Sarajevo 2000;

c) 10...♘b4 11. ♘×b4 ♗×b4+ (11...♕×b4+ 12. ♔f1 ♗b5 13. g4 ♗×e2+ 14. ♔×e2 ♕c4+

15. ♕d3 ♘e7 16. h5± Movsesian – Ulibin, Pula 1999) 12. ♔f1 h5 (12…♗b5!? 13. g4 ♘h6 14. ♗×h6 g×h6 15. ♕b3 ♖g8 16. a3 ♗×e2+ 17. ♔×e2 ♕a6+ 18. ♕d3 ♗e7 = Pilaj – Moor, Leipzig 2002) 13. a4! ♖c8 14. g3 ♗e7 15. ♔g2 ♖c7 16. a5 ♕b4 17. b3± Shirov – Gurevich, Prague (Rapidplay) 2002.

165   10…♖c8!?

a) 11. ♗d3 a5 12. a3 a4 13. ♗×f5 e×f5 14. ♘e3 ♕b5∓;

b) 11. g4!? ♘fe7 12. ♘h4 (12. ♘fe1 h5 13. g×h5∞ Sveshnikov – Skalkotas, Athens 1983) 12…♘g6 [12…♘b4 13. ♘×b4 ♕×b4 14. f4 ♗b5 (14…♘c6 15. ♗e3 ♗e7 16. ♘g2 f6± Sveshnikov – Ulibin, Russian League, Podolsk 1992) 15. ♕d2 ♕a4 16. b3 ♕a6 17. ♗×b5+ ♕×b5 18. f5 ♘c6 19. ♗b2 = Sveshnikov – Gleizerov, Russian League, Podolsk 1992] 13. ♘g2 (13. ♘×g6 h×g6 =) 13…♗e7 ⇄;

c) 11. ♔h1 ♘a5 12. g4 ♘e7 13. ♘fe1 h5 14. g×h5 ♘f5 15. ♗g4 ♘h6 16. ♗h3 ♘c6 17. b3 ⇄ Charbonneau – Barsov, Montréal 2003.

166   11. ♘e3 ♘×e3 12. f×e3 ♗e7 ⇄.

167   11…♘h6 12. h3±.

168   12…♗b5 13. ♘d3 h5 14. b4 ♘ac6 15. a4 ♗c4 16. a5 ♕c7∓ Stević – Dizdar, Croatian League, Poreč 1998.

169   15. b4 ♘c6 16. a4 ♗c4 17. a5 ♕d8 18. ♗e3 ♕h4 (Grosar – Dizdar, Nova Gorica 1997) 19. ♘f4 ♗×e2 20. ♕×e2 g5∓.

170

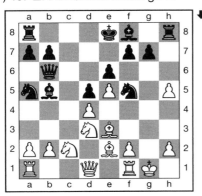

15…♗e7 16. a4 ♗×d3 17. ♗×d3 g6 18. h×g6 f×g6 19. b4 ♘c4 20. ♗×c4 d×c4 21. d5 ♘×e3 22. f×e3 Sveshnikov – Dolmatov, Moscow (Rapidplay) 1991; 22. ♘×e3±;

15…♘c4 16. a4 ♘c×e3 17. f×e3 ♗c4 18. ♘f4! ♗b3 19. ♗b5+ ♔d8 20. ♕e2 ♗×c2 21. a5! ♕c7 22. ♖fc1 ♖c8 23. a6! b6 24. ♗a4 ♕c4! 25. ♖×c2 ♕×e2 26. ♖×c8+? = Sveshnikov – Dolmatov, Russian League, Naberezhnye Chelny 1988; 26. ♖×e2 ♗e7 27. ♖g2! ♖c4 28. ♔f2 ♖b4 (28…♗h4+?! 29. ♔e2 ♖b4? 30. b3±) 29. ♖a2±;

15…♘c6! (Shirov; △♕d8–h4→) 16. a4 ♗c4 17. b4 ♕d8! (17…♗b3 18. a5 ♕d8 19. ♘de1 ♖c8 20. ♖b1 ♗c4 21. ♘g2 ♗×e2 22. ♕×e2 ♘h4 23. ♘ge1 ♘f5 24. ♘g2 ♘h4 25. ♘ge1 ½–½ Grosar – Dizdar, Ljubljana 1997) 18. ♗g4!? (18. ♕d2 a5!⇄; 18. a5!? transposes to Grosar – Dizdar, Nova Gorica 1997, see Note 169) 18…♘×e3!? (18…♕h4 19. h3 ♘×e3 20. f×e3 ♕g3+ 21. ♔h1 ♖×h5! 22. ♗×h5 ♕×h3+ 23. ♔g1 ♕g3+=) 19. f×e3 ♕g5 20. h3 ♖×h5 21. ♕f3 0–0–0!?⇄ Shabalov – Shirov, Edmonton 2005.

171   16. b3 ♘c6 17. ♖c1 a5 18. ♕d2 ♗e7 19. ♗g4 ♕a6⇄ Bergstrom – Kiriakov, Port Erin 2000.

172   17. a4 ♗c4 18. ♖b1 ♕d8 19. ♘f4 ♗×e2 20. ♕×e2 ♕h4 21. h3⇄ Sveshnikov – Kiriakov, Russian Championship, Elista 1994.

173   11. b3 ♖c8 (11…♘b4 12. ♘e3 ♗e7 13. ♘×f5 e×f5 14. a3 ♘c6 15. ♗b2 0–0 16. ♘e1 ♖fc8 17. f4∞ Delchev – Gurevich, Batumi 2002) 12. ♗b2 (12. ♗e3 ♘b4 13. ♘ce1 ♗b5 14. ♖c1 ♖×c1 15. ♗×b5+ ♕×b5 16. ♕×c1 ♘c6 = Greenfeld – Sher, Swiss Championship 1995) 12…♘b4 13. ♘×b4 a×b4 14. ♖e1 [14. ♕d3± ♗e7 15. g4! (15. a4 b×a3 16. ♗×a3 ♗×a3 17. ♖×a3 0–0=) 15…♘h4 (15…♘h6 16. h3 0–0 17. ♖fc1±) 16. ♘×h4 ♗×h4 17. a4 0–0 18. ♖ac1±] 14…♗b5 15. ♖c1 ♖×c1 (15…♖c6) 16. ♕×c1 ♗e7 17. g4 ♘h6 18. ♕c8+ ♗d8 19. h3± Timman – Jóhannesson, Reykjavík 2004.

174   12. ♘h4 ♘g6 (12…f6 13. ♗e3 f×e5 14. d×e5 ♕c7 15. f4 g5 16. f×g5 ♕×e5 17. ♘f3 ♕b8 18. ♘fd4 ♗g7 ∞ Kupreichik – Pilaj, Graz 2002) 13. ♘g2 ♗e7 14. f4 0–0 15. ♗e3 f5 16. e×f6 ♖×f6 17. h4 (17. ♗d3 ♗d6 18. h4 ♖af8 19. g5 ♖6f7 20. ♗×g6 h×g6 21. h5 g×h5 22. ♕×h5 g6! ⯑ Benjamin – Gulko, US Championship, Durango 1992) 17…♗d6 18. h5 ♘ge7 19. ♗d3 ♖f7!? (19…♖c8 20. ♕e2 ♖ff8 21. ♘h4 h6 22. g5 h×g5 23. f×g5 ♘f5 24. h6! → Sveshnikov – Gulko, 52nd USSR Championship, Riga 1985) 20. ♕e2 a4 (20…♖af8 21. ♖ad1 g6 22. h6 ♘b4 23. ♘×b4 a×b4 ⇄ Sveshnikov – Mencinger, Finkenstein 1994) 21. ♖ab1 ♖af8 ∞ Yagupov – Piskov, Rostov on Don 1993.

175   12…♘g6 13. f4 h5 14. g×h5?! ♘h4 15. ♗e3 ♘f5 16. ♗f2 ♕×b2 ⯑ Orak – Dizdar, Pula 1999.

176   15…♘×e3!? ⯑.

177   **17. ♘d3** ♗e8 18. ♕f3 ♖×h5 19. e×f6 g×f6 20. ♗f4 ♗d6 ⇄ Ermenkov – Spassov, Albena 1985.

17. e×f6 ♗e8 18. h6 g×f6 19. ♕d2 ♖d7 ∞ Sveshnikov – Razuvaev, Moscow 1985.

178

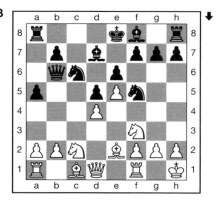

11…♖c8 12. b3 (12. g4 ♘fe7 13. ♘h4 ♘b4 ⇄ Ni Hua – Kristjánsson, Goa 2002) 12…♘b4 13. ♘e3 ♘×e3 14. ♗×e3 ♗e7 15. ♘e1 ♗b5 16. f4 ± Hadzimanolis – Barsov, Ikaros 2001;

11…h5!?

a) 12. ♗g5 ♗e7 13. ♗×e7 ♘c×e7 14. ♕d3 ♖c8 15. ♖ab1 0–0 16. ♘e3 g6 17. h3 ± Dvoiris – Willemze, Dieren 2002;

b) 12. ♗d3 ♗e7 13. ♗×f5 e×f5 14. ♗g5 ♕×b2 15. ♖b1 ♕×a2 16. ♖×b7 ♘d8 17. e6 f×e6 18. ♖×d7 ♗×g5 19. ♖×g7 ♗f6 20. ♖c7 ⯑ Gwaze – Summerscale, Edinburgh 2003;

c) 12. b3 ♗e7 (12…h4 13. h3 ♗e7 14. ♗d3 ♕d8 15. ♖b1 ♘b4 16. ♘×b4 a×b4 17. ♖b2 g6 18. ♗f4 ± Cherniaev – Pert, Hastings 2002/03) 13. ♗d3 ♘h4 14. ♘g5 a4 15. ♖b1 a×b3 16. ♖×b3 ♕d8 17. ♘h3 ♖×a2 18. ♖×b7 ♘a5 19. ♖b2 ♖×b2 20. ♗×b2 ± Ehlvest – Barsov, Dhaka 2001.

179   12…♗e7 13. ♘×f5 e×f5 14. ♗d2 0–0 15. a3 (15. ♗c3 ♗b5 16. a3 ♗×e2 17. ♕×e2 ♘c6 18. e6 ♗f6 19. e×f7+ ♔×f7 20. ♕d3 ½–½ Predojević – Galyas, Budapest 2002) 15…♘c6 16. ♗c3 ♖fb8 17. ♕d2 ♕d8 18. b3 ± Cherniaev – Dzhakaev, Istanbul 2003.

180   15…♘a6 16. b4 a×b4 17. a×b4 ♘c7 18. b5 ± Vescovi – Vučković, Bermuda 2002.

181   Grischuk – Gurevich, Esbjerg 2000.

182   10. g4!? ♘h4 11. ♘×h4 ♗×h4 12. 0–0 f5 13. f4 (13. g×f5!? ±) 13…f×g4 14. ♗×g4 0–0 15. b3 ♖c8 16. ♘e3 ♕b6 17. ♗b2 ♘e7 18. ♗h3 ♖f7 19. ♕h5 ♘g6 20. f5↑ Sveshnikov – Karer, Nova Gorica 1999.

183

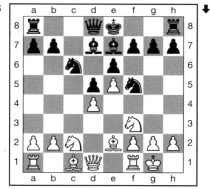

10…h5?!

a) 11. ♖b1 ♕b6 (11…g5 12. b4 g4 13. ♘fe1 ♕b6 14. ♗e3 ±) 12. b4! a5 13. a3 a×b4

14. a×b4± Grischuk – Kaidanov, New York 2000;

b) 11. ♘e3!? g5 12. ♘×f5 e×f5 13. h4 g4 14. ♘g5 ♕b6 15. ♗e3 f4! 16. ♗×f4 ♕×d4∓ Dolmatov – Hertneck, Tilburg (Rapidplay) 1992;

c) 11. ♔h1 g5 12. ♘fe1 g4 13. ♗e3 ♕b6 14. ♘d3 a5 15. a4 ♖c8 16. ♕d2 ♕b3 17. ♖fc1 ♘×e3 18. f×e3 ♘d8 19. ♗d1 ♕b6 20. b4↑ Movsesian – Schlindwein, German League 2000/01;

d) 11. b4!? ♖c8 (11...♘×b4 12. ♘×b4 ♗×b4 13. ♖b1 ♗a5! 14. ♖×b7 ♗b6 15. ♗g5 ♕c8 16. ♗a6 ♕c6 17. ♕d3±) 12. ♖b1 a6 13. a4! ♕b6 14. b5 a×b5 15. ♗×b5 ♕c7 16. ♘e3 ♘×e3 17. ♗×e3 ♘a5 18. ♗g5!± Sveshnikov – Fominikh, Russian Championship, Elista 1996;

10...♖c8 11. ♗d3! ♕b6 12. ♔h1! ♘b4 [12...0–0 13. g4 ♘h6 (13...♘h4 14. ♘×h4 ♗×h4 15. g5 ♘e7 16. a4!? ♘g6 17. ♕g4 ♖c4 18. ♗×c4 d×c4 19. a5 ♗c6+ 20. ♔g1 ♕b5 21. ♘e3±) 14. ♖g1↑ Párkányi – Bagoly, Miskolc 1998] 13. ♘×b4 ♕×b4 14. ♗d2 ♕b6 15. a4 a5 16. ♗c3± Voronovsky – Lukonin, Sosnowi Bor 2002.

184 11. b4 g4 (11...a6 12. a4 f6∞ 13. b5 a×b5 14. a×b5 ♘a5 15. e×f6 ♗×f6 16. ♗a3±) 12. ♘fe1 h5 13. b5 ♘a5 14. ♗a3 ♗×a3 15. ♘×a3 ♖c8 16. ♘ec2±.

185 11...♘h6!? 12. h3 f6 13. e×f6 ♗×f6 14. b4 ♘f7 15. b5 ♘e7 16. ♗d3 ♕c7 17. a4 ♘g6 18. ♗×g6 h×g6 19. ♔g2 0–0–0 20. ♘b4± Goloshchapov – Zakharevich, St. Petersburg 2002.

186 12...h5!?⇄.

187 13. a4!?.

188 13...b5!?⇄.

189 Dvoiris – Zakharevich, Russian Championship, Elista 2001.

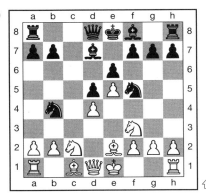

190

10. ♘e3 ♘×e3 11. f×e3 ♗e7 12. a3 [12. 0–0 0–0 13. ♗d2 ♕b6 (13...a5 14. a3 ♘c6 15. ♗d3 ♕b6 16. ♗c3 f5 17. e×f6 ♗×f6 18. ♕c2 h6 19. ♖f2 ♘e7 20. g4± Peng Xi-aomin – Kacheishvili, 34th Olympiad, Istanbul 2000) 14. a3 ♘c6 15. b4 f5 16. e×f6 ♗×f6 17. ♗d3 ♘e7 18. ♕b1 h6 19. a4 ♘f5 20. b5 a5 21. ♗c1 ♖fc8 22. ♖a2 ♕d8 23. ♖af2± Sax – Brenninkmeijer, Wijk aan Zee 1992] 12...♘c6 13. b4⇄ Spassky – Korchnoi, Candidates match, Belgrade 1977; 13. 0–0 0–0 14. ♗d2 f6 15. e×f6 ♗×f6 16. ♗c3 ♖c8 17. ♗d3±);

10. ♘×b4 ♗×b4+ 11. ♗d2 ♕a5 12. a3! [12. ♗×b4 ♕×b4+ 13. ♕d2 ♕×d2+ (13...a5 14. a3 ♕×d2+ 15. ♔×d2 a4 16. h4 ♘e7 17. h5 h6 18. ♔e3 ♘c6 19. g4 ♘a5⇄ Wempe – Glek, Hoogeveen 2003) 14. ♔×d2 ♘e7 15. ♖hc1 (15. ♖ac1 ♘c6 16. ♔e3 f6 17. ♗b5 ♘b4 18. a3 ♗×b5 19. a×b4 ♔d7 20. ♖c3 ♖hc8 21. ♖hc1 ♖×c3+ 22. ♖×c3 ♖f8= Popchev – Morozevich, Krasnodar 1997) 15...f6 16. ♖c5 ♔d8 17. ♗d3 ♖c8 18. ♖ac1 ♖×c5 19. ♖×c5 ♗e8= Sieiro González – Gurevich, Havana 1986] 12...♗×d2+ 13. ♕×d2 ♕×d2+ 14. ♔×d2 f6 15. ♖ac1 ♘e7 16. b4± Anand – Gurevich, Interzonal, Manila 1990.

191 10...♖c8 11. ♘×b4 (11. ♘e3 ♘×e3 12. ♗×e3 ♘c2 13. ♖c1 ♘×e3 14. f×e3 ♖×c1 15. ♕×c1 ♗e7⇄) 11...♗×b4 12. a3 ♗e7 13. g4 ♘h4 14. ♘×h4 ♗×h4 15. ♗e3 0–0 16. ♕b3 ♕b6?! (16...♗c6 17. f4 f6 18. ♗d3±) 17. ♕×b6 a×b6 18. ♗d3± Sveshnikov – Bashkov, Cheliabinsk 2003;

10...♗a4?! 11. b3 ♗d7 12. ♘e3 a5 13. a3 ♘c6 14. ♗b2 ♗e7 15. ♗d3 g6? (15...♘xe3 16. fxe3±) 16. ♕d2 ♕b6 17. ♗c2 h5 18. ♗c3 ♔f8 19. ♗xf5! gxf5 20. g3± Sveshnikov – Gurevich, Ekaterinburg 2002.

192

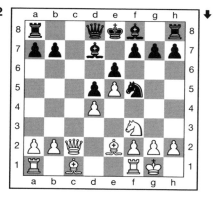

11...♖c8 12. ♕d3 (12. ♕b3 ♕b6 13. ♕xb6 axb6 14. ♗d2 ♘e7 15. ♖fc1 ♘c6 16. ♖c3= Grosar – Dizdar, Slovenian League, Bled 1996) 12...a6 13. a4 (13. ♕b3±) 13...♗b4 14. ♗g5 ♕b6 15. h4 h6 16. ♗d2!? ♕a5 17. ♗f4! ♖g8!? 18. g3 ♔d8!∞ Movsesian – Morozevich, Sarajevo 2000;

11...h5 12. ♗d2 ♗e7 13. ♗d3 ♕b6 14. ♗xf5 ♖c8! (14...exf5 15. ♗g5 ♗xg5 16. ♘xg5 ♕xd4 17. ♖fd1 ♕h4 18. ♕d2 ♕c4 19. ♖ac1± Sveshnikov – Dreev, St. Petersburg 1993) 15. ♕b3 exf5 16. ♕xd5 ♗e6 17. ♕a5 ♕xa5 18. ♗xa5 b6 19. ♗d2 ♗d5∓ Yagupov – Dreev, Rostov on Don 1993.

193 **12...♗e7** 13. a4 (13. g4 ♘h4 14. ♘xh4 ♗xh4 15. f4 h6 16. ♗e3± Sveshnikov – Foisor, Oviedo (Rapidplay) 1993) 13...0–0 14. a5 ♕c7 15. ♗d2 a6 16. ♖fc1 ♗c6 17. ♕b3± Sveshnikov – Nikolaev, Šibenik 1990;

12...h6 13. b3 a6 14. a4 ♗b4 15. ♗b2 g5?! (15...0–0 16. ♗d1! ♖fc8 17. ♗c2 g6 18. ♖fc1±; 15...♖c8 16. ♗d1!? 0–0 17. ♗c2 ♖c6 18. g4!±) 16. ♖ac1 ♖c8 17. ♖xc8+ ♗xc8 18. ♘e1! ♗d7 19. ♘c2 ♗e7 20. ♘e3 ♕b4 21. ♗d1! ♘xe3 22. ♗c3! ♕b6 23. fxe3± Sveshnikov – Brumen, Bled 2000.

194 13. a4 ♗b4 14. g4 (14. b3!? ♖c8 15. ♗b2 0–0 16. g4 ♘e7 17. ♘g5 ♘g6 18. f4 f6 19. exf6 ♖xf6 20. ♖f2± Sveshnikov – Ulibin, Moscow (Rapidplay) 1990) 14...♘e7 15. ♘g5 h6 16. ♘h3 ♖c8 17. ♗e3 a5 18. ♘f4 g6 19. h4± Sveshnikov – Shulman, Riga (Rapidplay) 1987.

195 **13...h5?!** 14. a4 a5 15. ♖fd1 ♗e7 16. h3 ♖c8 17. ♗c3! h4 18. ♕d2± Sveshnikov – Zlotnik, Moscow 1991;

13...♗e7 14. a4 0–0 15. g4 ♘h6 16. h3 ♔h8 17. ♘h2± Sveshnikov – Bashkov, Herfurd (Rapidplay) 1992.

196 17. ♗g5 ♗f8 18. ♖c7 h6 19. ♗d2 ♗c6 20. e6 fxe6 21. ♖e1 ♗d7 22. ♘e5± Sveshnikov – Totsky, Cheliabinsk (Rapidplay) 1990.

197

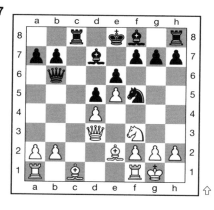

13. a4!? ♗b4 14. h4 h6 (14...h5 15. ♗g5⇄) 15. h5 ♘e7 16. ♘d2 0–0 17. ♘b3 f5 18. a5 ♕d8 19. ♗d2± Sveshnikov – Rublevsky, Russian Championship, Elista 1994;

13. ♗d2!? ♗b4! (Filipenko; 13...♗e7?! 14. g4!±) 14. ♖fc1 (14. ♗xb4 ♕xb4 15. a3 ♕b6; 14. ♗f4?! a6! 15. a4 ♘e7!? 16. h4 ♗a5 17. ♖fc1 ♖xc1+ 18. ♗xc1 h6 ½–½ Sveshnikov – Dreev, Rostov on Don 1993) 14...0–0 15. ♗xb4 ♕xb4 16. a3 ♕b6 17. b4 ♖c4 18. ♕d2 ♖xc1+ 19. ♖xc1 ♗b5 20. ♗xb5 ♕xb5 21. ♖c5±.

13. ♖d1 h6 14. h4 a6 15. a4 ♗b4 16. h5 ♘e7
17. ♕e3 ♘c6 18. ♗d3 ♘a5 19. ♗b1 ♗e7 ∞
Campora – Dreev, Biel 1995.
198   14. ♗e3 h5 15. h3 h×g4 16. h×g4 a6
17. ♖fc1 ♖×c1+ 18. ♖×c1 ♗b5 19. ♕d2 ♗×e2
20. ♕×e2 ♘c6 ⇄ Grosar – Dražić, Bratto
1997.

199   16. ♖fc1 ? h×g4 17. h×g4 ♖×c1+
18. ♗×c1 ♗b5 19. ♕c2 ♗×e2 20. ♕×e2 ♘c6
21. ♗e3 ♗e7 ∓ Sveshnikov – Dizdar, Slovenian League, Bled 2002.

200   16...h×g4 17. h×g4 ♘c6 (17...♘g6
18. b4 ⇄) 18. a5 ♕c7 19. ♖fc1 ±.

Notes

Table 6

1. e4 e6 2. d4 d5 3. e5 c5 4. c3 ♘c6 5. ♘f3 ♛b6

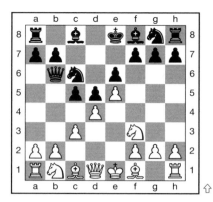

	6	7	8	9	10	11	12	13	
29	♗d3?!	c×d4	♘c3[202]	♘×d4	0–0[203]	♖e1	♘b5[206]	♗e3	
	c×d4![201]	♗d7	♘×d4	♛×d4	♛×e5?![204]	♛d6[205]	♛b6[207]	♛a5[208]	=
30	...	...	...	...	...	♛e2	♔h1![210]	f4	
	...	...	...	...	a6!	♘e7[209]	♘c6	♘b4[211]	∓
31	♗e2?!	♗×h6!?[213]	♛d2	0–0	♘a3!	c×d4	♘c2	e×f6[218]	
	♘h6[212]	g×h6[214]	♗g7[215]	0–0	c×d4[216]	♗d7[217]	f6	♖×f6[219]	±
32	...	c×d4	♘c3!?[221]	♘a4[222]	♗d2[224]	♗c3	a3	♘×c3	
	c×d4!?	♘h6!?[220]	♘f5	♛a5+[223]	♗b4	b5![225]	♗×c3+	b4[226]	⇄
33	a3!?	b4[228]	c×d4	♗b2[230]	♘bd2	♘×c4[232]	♖c1	♘d2![234]	
	♗d7[227]	c×d4	♖c8[229]	♘a5[231]	♘c4	d×c4	a5[233]	a×b4[235]	±
34	...	...	...	♗e3	♗d3	0–0	f×e3	♘bd2[240]	
	...	...	...	♘h6[236]	♘g4[237]	♘×e3[238]	g6[239]	♗h6[241]	±

201 6...♗d7?! 7. d×c5! ♗×c5

a) 8. 0–0 a5 (8...♘ge7?? 9. b4+–; 8...f6? 9. b4! ♗e7 10. ♗f4 f×e5 11. ♘×e5 ♘×e5 12. ♗×e5 ♘f6 13. ♘d2 0–0 14. ♘f3 ♗d6 15. ♛e2± Nimzowitsch–Salwe, Carlsbad 1911; 8...a6 9. b4 ♗e7 10. ♖e1 d4? 11. a3!+– Euwe–Graves, Amsterdam 1923) 9. ♛e2 ♘ge7 (9...f6!?⇄) 10. ♗f4 ♘g6 11. ♗g3 0–0 12. h4 f6! 13. ♗×g6 (13. e×f6 ♖×f6∓) 13...h×g6 14. e×f6 ♖×f6∞ Nun–Kupreichik, Germany 1991/92; 14...g×f6!?∓;

b) 8. ♛e2!? a5 9. ♘bd2 a4 10. b4 a×b3 11. ♘×b3 ♗a3 12. 0–0 ♘ge7 (12... ♗×c1 13. ♖f×c1 ♘ge7 14. ♘bd4±) 13. ♗d2 ♘g6 14. ♘bd4± Hort–Andersson, Reykjavík 1972.

202 **8. ♗c2** ♘b4 9. 0–0 ♘×c2 10. ♛×c2 ♘e7 11. ♘c3 ♖c8 12. ♗e3 ♘c6?! Steinitz–Burn, Vienna 1898; 12...♘f5∓;

8. 0–0 ♘×d4 9. ♘c3 See 8. ♘c3; 9. ♘bd2 ♘c6 10. ♘b3 ♘ge7 11. ♗e3 ♛c7 12. ♖c1 ♘g6 13. ♘c5 ♗×c5 (13...♗e7 14. b4=) 14. ♗×c5 ♘g×e5 15. ♘×e5=, Pap–Kosić, Bosnjaci 2005; (15. ♖e1 ♖c8 16. ♗a3 ♘×d3 17. ♛×d3 ♘e5–+).

203 10. ♛e2 a6 11. 0–0 See 10. 0–0 a6 11. ♛e2.

204 **10...♛b6** 11. ♛e2 (11. ♛g4 ⯑) 11...a6 12. ♔h1 ♘e7 13. f4 g6 14. ♗e3 ♛c7 15. ♖ac1 ♛d8 16. f5 e×f5 17. ♗g5 ⯑ Penalver–Chaumont, Aix-les-Bains 2003;

10...♘e7 11. ♘b5 ♛×e5 12. f4! ♛b8 13. f5 a6 (13...e5 14. f6 ⯑) (14. ♛f3!± Glek 14...a×b5

15. f6 (15. f×e6 ♗×e6–+) 15...♘f5! 16. ♗×f5 e×f5 17. ♖e1+ ♗e6 18. ♛×f5 ♛d6–+; 14. f×e6! f×e6 (14...♗×b5 15. e×f7+±) 15. ♗f4 e5 16. ♛h5+ g6 17. ♛×e5+–;

10...a6.

205

11...♛c7 12. ♘×d5 ♛a5

a) 13. ♖e5!? ♛d8 14. ♗g5 ♘e7 (14...♗e7 15. ♘×e7 ♘×e7 16. ♛h5→) 15. ♛h5 (15. ♛e2 h6 16. ♗×e7 ♗×e7 17. ♘×e7 ♛×e7=) 15...e×d5 16. ♖ae1 ♖c8 17. ♗×e7 ♗×e7 18. ♖×e7+ ♛×e7 19. ♖×e7+ ♔×e7 20. ♛g5+ ♔d6 21. ♛f4+=;

b) 13. ♖×e6+!⯑ (Glek) 13...f×e6 14. ♛h5+ ♔d8 15. ♗g5+ ♘f6 16. ♘×f6 ♗e7 17. ♘e4 ♛d5 18. ♗×e7+ ♔×e7 19. ♛h4+ g5 20. ♛h6 ♛e5∞;

11...♛b8 12. ♘×d5 ♗d6

a) 13. ♛g4 ♔f8 14. ♗d2 (14. ♘f4 ♘f6 15. ♛h4 h6 16. ♘e2 ♘d5∓ Glek–Zlotnik, Moscow 1980) 14...h5!? 15. ♛h3 ♗c6! (15...e×d5?! 16. ♛×d7 ♗×h2+ 17. ♔h1 ♘f6 18. ♛f5 ♗d6 19. ♖ac1!± Borg–Nikolić, Kavála 1985; 15...♘h6 16. ♘e3 ♔g8 17. ♗c3 ♘g4 18. ♘×g4 h×g4 19. ♛×g4 ♗×h2+ 20. ♔f1 ♛f8∞) 16. ♘e3 ♘f6 17. ♘c4 ♗c7 18. ♗c3 ♘d5 19. ♘e5!?∞ Salnikov–Prudnikova, USSR 1991;

b) 13. ♛h5!? ♔f8 14. ♘c3 ♘f6 15. ♛h4 ♗c6 16. ♗g5 ♗e5 17. ♖ad1 ⯑; 17. f4?! ♗d4+∓ Bisguier–Westerinen, Netanya 1971.

206 12. ♛f3 ♘f6 13. ♘b5 ♛b6 14. ♗e3 ♛a5 15. ♘d4 ♗b4∓ Dolmadian–Inkiov, Sofia 1978.

207   12...♗×b5? 13. ♗×b5+ ♔d8 14. ♗d2 (14. ♕f3 ♘f6 15. ♗f4 ♕b6 16. a4 a6 17. ♗d3 ♗d6 18. a5 ♕b4 19. ♗g5 ♔d7 ∓ Gossell – Shulman, Stillwater 2002) 14...♕b6 15. ♕a4 a5□ 16. ♖ac1 ♗c5 17. ♖×c5 ♕×c5 18. ♖c1 +– ♕b6 19. ♗e3 ♕d6 20. ♗c5 ♕b8 21. ♕a3! b6 22. ♗×b6+ 1-0 Sveshnikov – Genov, Bulgaria 1988;

12...♕b8?! 13. ♕f3 ♗d6 14. ♘×d6+! (14. ♕×d5) 14...♕×d6 15. ♗f4 [15...♕e7 16. ♕g3 f6 (16...♕f8 17. ♖ac1 ±) 17. ♖ac1! ± (Glek; 17. ♗×h7± ♖×h7 18. ♕g6+ ♕f7 19. ♕×h7 g5 20. ♕×f7+ ♔×f7 21. ♗d2±)] 15...♕b6 16. ♕g3 g6 17. ♗e5 f6 18. ♗×g6+!→ Strauts – Kantoris, USSR 1985.

208   13...♕d8?! 14. ♗f4 ♖c8 15. ♘×a7 ± ;

13...♕a5

a) 14. ♕b3 a6 15. ♗d2 ♕d8 16. ♘d4 ♘f6 17. ♕×b7 ♗c5 (17...♕b8 18. ♕×b8+ ♖×b8 ∓) 18. ♗e3 ♕c8?! (18...♕b8!? 19. ♕×b8+ ♖×b8 20. ♘×e6 ♗×e3 21. ♘d4 0-0 22. ♖×e3 ♖×b2 ∓) 19. ♕×c8+ ♖×c8 20. ♗×a6 ♖a8 21. ♗d3 ♗b4 22. ♖ec1 ♘g4 ⇄ Krasnov – Glek, Moscow 1989;

b) 14. ♗d2 ♕b6 15. ♗e3 (15. a4?! a6 16. a5 ♕d8 17. ♘d4 ♘f6 ∓) 15...♕a5 16. ♗d2 = Adorján – Faragó, Hastings 1976/77.

209

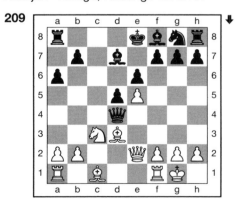

11...♖c8!? 12. ♔h1 [12...♗c5 13. ♗g5 (13. f4 ♘h6 14. h3 0-0 15. ♗d2 f6 16. ♖f3 f×e5 17. ♗e3 ♕b4 18. a3 ♕b6 19. ♗×c5 ♖×c5 20. ♕×e5 ♘f5 ∓ Möhring – Thormann,

GDR 1977) 13...h6 14. ♗d2 ♘e7 15. ♖ac1 ♕h4 16. f4 ♘f5 17. ♗×f5 e×f5 18. b4 ♗a7 19. ♘×d5 0-0 = Padevsky – Darga, 19th Olympiad, Siegen 1970] 12...♕h4!? 13. f4 ♘h6! ∓ 14. f5?! ♘×f5 15. ♗×f5 e×f5 16. ♖f4 ♕d8 (16...♕e7!?) 17. ♘×d5 ♗e6 ∓ Schuh – Namyslo, Germany 1992;

11...♕h4!? 12. f4 ♘h6 13. ♗e3 ♖c8 (13...♗c6 14. f5 ♕g4 ∞ Maciejewski – Glek, Prague 1985) 14. ♖f3 ♗c5 15. ♗×c5 ♖×c5 16. ♖af1 ♕e7 17. ♖h3 ∞ Rozentalis – Epishin, 57th USSR Championship, Leningrad 1990.

210   12. ♖d1 ♘c6 13. ♗×a6 ♕×e5 14. ♕×e5 ♘×e5 15. ♗×b7 ♖a7 16. ♗×d5 e×d5 17. ♖e1 f6 18. f4 ♗c5+ 19. ♔h1 d4 ∓ Mnatsakanian – Monin, USSR 1979.

211   14. ♖d1!

14...♗c5!? (Piskov) 15. ♗×a6 (15. ♗×h7 ♕f2 16. ♕×f2 ♗×f2 17. ♗b1 ♔e7 ∓ Blasek – Kishnev, Gelsenkirchen 1991) 15...♕f2 16. ♕×f2 ♗×f2 △ 17. ♗b5 (17. ♗×b7 ♖a7 18. a3 ♘c2 19. ♖a2 ♘e3 20. ♗×e3 ♗×e3 21. ♗×d5 e×d5 22. ♘×d5 ♗e6 ∓) 17...♔e7 18. ♗×d7 ♔×d7 19. a3 ♘c6 ∓;

14...♘×d3 15. ♖×d3 ♕c4?! (15...♕b6 16. ♗e3 ♗c5! 17. ♗×c5 ♕×c5 18. f5!? ⚌ ♗c6! 19. ♖ad1 0-0-0 20. f×e6 f×e6 21. ♕g4 d4 22. ♕×e6+ ♔b8 23. ♕g4 ♕×e5 24. ♖×d4 ♖×d4 25. ♕×d4 ♕×d4 26. ♖×d4 ♖e8 27. ♔g1 = Öchslein – Tischer, German League 1980/81) 16. b3! ♕c7 17. ♗b2

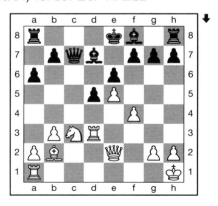

a) 17...♖c8 18. f5 ♛a5 19. ♖ad1 ♗a3 20. ♗×a3 ♛×a3 21. f6→ Möhring – Casper, GDR Championship, Frankfurt/Oder 1977;

b) 17...♗c6 18. ♖c1 ♖d8 19. ♛f2! ♗e7 20. ♘e2 0–0 21. ♘d4∞ Sveshnikov – Razuvaev, Belgrade 1988;

c) 17...♗c5 18. ♖c1 ♗c6 19. ♘×d5 ♗×d5 20. ♗a3 b6 21. b4 0–0 22. b×c5 b×c5 23. f5?! (△ 23. ♖×c5 ♛b7 24. ♖c×d5 e×d5 25. ♗×f8 ♖×f8 26. ♖d1±) 23...c4 24. ♖h3? (24. ♖g3! e×f5 25. ♛d2∞) 24...e×f5 25. ♗×f8 ♖×f8∓ Sveshnikov – S. Ivanov, Kiev 1988;

d) 17...b5 18. ♖c1 ♛b7

d1) 19. f5 ♖c8!

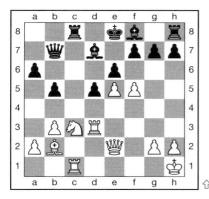

d11) 20. f×e6 f×e6! [20...♗×e6 21. ♛f3 ♗e7 (21...♖d8 22. ♖cd1±) 22. ♘×d5 ♖×c1+ 23. ♗×c1 ♗×d5 24. ♖×d5 0–0=] 21. ♖f1 b4 22. ♛h5+ ♔d8 (22...g6 23. ♛f3 ♗e7 24. ♘×d5 e×d5 25. ♛f7+ ♔d8 26. e6 ♖f8 27. ♗f6 ♖×f7 28. e×f7 ♔c7 29. ♗×e7 ♗b5 30. f8♛ ♖×f8 31. ♗×f8 ♛c6 32. ♖f7+ ♔b6 33. ♖d1 ♛c2 34. ♖f6+∓) 23. ♘e2 ♖c2 24. ♗c1 ♗b5 25. ♖d2 ♖c6∓;

d12) 20. ♖f1 b4 21. f×e6□ (21. ♘×d5? e×d5 22. e6 ♗b5!∓ Smirnov – Beliakov, Alushta 1994) 21...f×e6 22. ♛h5+ g6!? 23. ♛f3 ♗e7 24. ♛f7+ ♔d8 25. ♛g7!? ♖e8 26. ♘×d5 e×d5 27. ♖fd1 ♗e6 28. ♛×h7 g5∓;

d2) 19. ♛d2 ♖c8! 20. ♖d1 ♗e7 21. f5!? b4 22. ♘×d5 e×d5 23. f6 ♗e6! 24. f×e7 ♛×e7 25. ♖g3 g6∓ Wallyn – Mednis, Cannes 1992.

212

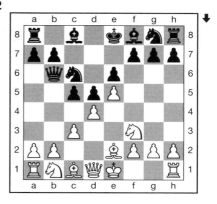

6...♘ge7 7. d×c5!?

a) 7...♛c7 8. ♘d4 ♛×e5 (8...♘×e5? 9. ♘b5! ♛×c5 10. ♛d4+– Euwe – Kramer, Zaanstreek 1946) 9. 0–0±;

b) 7...♛×c5

b1) 8. ♗d3 ♘g6 9. ♛e2 d4!? (9...f6?! 10. e×f6 g×f6 11. 0–0 ♗g7±) 10. ♗×g6 (10. 0–0 ♘g×e5 11. ♘×d4 ♘×d3 12. ♛×d3 ♘×d4 13. c×d4 ♛c7 14. ♗e3 ♗d7 15. ♘c3 ♗d6⇄) 10...h×g6 11. 0–0 d3 12. ♛e4 ♛d5=;

b2) 8. ♗f4 ♘g6 9. ♗g3 ♛b6! 10. b4 ♗d7 11. ♗d3 a5 12. b5 ♘ce7 13. ♘bd2 ♘f5 14. ♛e2 (Benjamin – Korchnoi, Horgen 1994) 14...h5∓;

b3) 8. b4 ♛b6 9. b5!? (Glek) 9...♘a5 10. 0–0 ♗d7 11. ♗e3 (11. ♘d4?! ♘g6 12. f4 ♗c5 13. ♗e3 0–0 14. a4 f6 15. e×f6 ♖×f6 16. g3 e5∓ Vysochin – Wojtaszek, Polanica Zdrój 2001) 11...♛c7 12. ♘bd2 ♘f5 13. ♗d4±;

6...f6 7. 0–0 f×e5 8. ♘×e5 ♘×e5 9. d×e5 ♗d7 10. c4±;

6...♗d7 7. 0–0 ♖c8 8. d×c5! ♗×c5 9. b4 ♗f8 10. ♗d3 ♘ge7 11. ♗f4 ♘g6 12. ♗g3 ♗e7 13. h4± Castro Rojas – Korchnoi, Linares 1979.

213

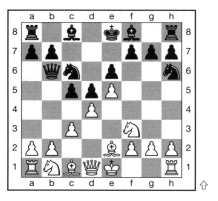

7. ⌗f1?! ♗d7 8. ♘a3 c×d4 9. c×d4 ♘f5
10. ♘c2 h5 11. ♗d3 ♖c8 12. g3 ♘b4
13. ♘×b4 ♗×b4 14. ⌗g2∞ Kupreichik–
Bagirov, USSR 1973;

7. b3!? c×d4 8. c×d4 ♘f5 9. ♗b2 ♗b4+
(9...♗d7 10. g4 ♘fe7 11. ♘c3 h5 12. ♘a4
♕d8 13. g5 ♘g6 14. ♕d2 ♖c8⇄ Kupreichik–Korchnoi, Münster 1996) 10. ⌗f1 ♗e7
11. h4!? (11. ♘c3 ♕d8 12. g3 f6 13. ⌗g2 f×e5
14. d×e5 0–0 15. ♖c1 ♗d7 16. ♗d3 ♕e8⇄
Sveshnikov–Portisch, Interzonal Biel 1993)
11...♕d8 12. h5 f6 13. a3 f×e5 14. d×e5 0–0
15. ♗d3± Movsesian–Priehoda, Kaskády
2002;

7. ♗d3 c×d4 8. c×d4 ♗d7 9. ♗c2 ♘f5
10. ♗×f5 e×f5 11. ♘c3 ♗b4 12. ⌗f1 0–0
13. ⌗g1 ♗×c3 14. b×c3 ♖fc8 15. h4 ♘d8
16. ♗d2 ♖c4 17. h5 ♗a4 18. ♕c1 ♘e6⇄ Benjamin–Grétarsson, Bermuda 1999.

214   7...♕×b2?

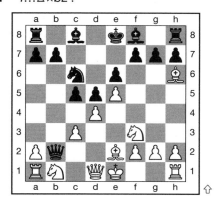

8. ♗c1?! ♕×a1 9. ♕c2 c×d4 10. 0–0
(10. ♘fd2 ♘×e5 11. 0–0 d3∓) 10...♗d7!
(10...d×c3? 11. ♘×c3± d4 12. ♘b5 ♘b4
13. ♘c7+ ⌗d8 14. ♗g5+ f6 15. e×f6 ♘×c2
16. f×g7+ ⌗×c7 17. g×h8♕ 1–0 Karpachev–
Siedentopf, Leutersdorf 2002) 11. ♗d2 ♖c8
12. ♘a3 ♕×f1+ 13. ♗×f1 ♗×a3 14. ♕b3 d×c3
15. ♗×c3 ♗c5 16. ♕×b7 ♖b8 17. ♕c7 ♖b1
18. ♗d2 h6∓;

8. ♗e3! ♕×a1 9. ♕c2 c×d4 10. ♘×d4
a) 10...♘×d4? 11. ♗×d4 ♗a3 12. ♗b5+ ⌗d8
13. 0–0 ♕b2 14. ♕a4 ♗e7 15. ♕a5++−
Survila–Skoblikov, Podolsk 1978;
b) 10...♘b4? 11. ♗b5+ ♗d7 12. ♗×d7+
⌗×d7 13. c×b4+− ♗×b4+ 14. ⌗e2 a5
15. ♖c1 ♖hc8 16. ♘c3!+− Drvota–Schmidt,
Děčín 1979;
c) 10...♗a3□ 11. ♘b5!± (11. 0–0 ♕b2
12. ♘×a3 ♕×a3 13. ♘b5 ♕a5 14. ♘d6+
⌗f8∞) 11...♗b2 (11...0–0 12. ♘5×a3 b6
13. 0–0 d4 14. ♗f4+−) 12. ♘c7+ ⌗d7
13. ♘×a8 ♗×c3+ 14. ♕×c3 ♕×b1+ 15. ♗d1
b6 (15...♕e4 16. 0–0 d4 17. ♕d2+−)
16. 0–0 ♕×a2 17. ♗×b6! (17. ♘×b6+
a×b6 18. ♗×b6 ♕c4±) 17...♗b7 (17...a×b6
18. ♗a4!) 18. ♕f3! (18. ♕c5 ♗×a8 19. ♕d6+
⌗e8 20. ♗e3∞; 18. ♗b3 ♕e2!∞)
c1) 18...f5 19. e×f6 ♖×a8 20. ♕g3 a×b6
21. ♕×g7+ ⌗d6 22. f7±;
c2) 18...♖e8 19. ♕×f7+ ♖e7 20. ♕f8 a×b6±
(20...♕c4 21. ♗h5 g6 22. ♗×a7 ♗×a8
23. ♕×a8 g×h5 24. ♖b1 ♘d8 25. ♗b6+−);
c3) 18...♘×e5 19. ♕c3 ♘c6 (19...♖×a8
20. ♕c7+ ⌗e8 21. ♗c5 ♘d7 22. ♕×b7 ♖b8
23. ♕c6+−) 20. ♕×g7 ♖e8 21. ♗c5 ♘d8
22. ♗h5 ♗×a8 23. ♗×f7 ♘×f7 24. ♕×f7+ ⌗d8
25. ♗d6 ♕c2 26. ♗f4 h6 27. ♖c1+−.

215   8...♗d7 9. 0–0 0–0–0!? 10. d×c5
(10. b4!? c×b4 11. ♖c1 ⌗b8 12. c×b4 ♗×b4
13. ♘c3⯗) 10...♕c7 (10...♗×c5 11. b4 ♗e7
12. b5 ♘a5 13. ♕f4↑) 11. ♕f4±.

216   10...f6 11. e×f6 ♖×f6 12. d×c5 ♕×c5
13. b4 ♕f8 14. ♘c2 ♗d7 15. b5 ♘e7 16. ♘e5
♖d8 17. ♘d4 ♘g6 18. ♘×d7 ♖×d7 19. ♗g4±
Kupreichik–Huzman, Sverdlovsk 1987.

217 11...f6!? 12. e×f6 ♖×f6 13. ♘c2 a5!? ⇄ Jonkman–Uhlmann, Chemnitz 1998.

218 13. ♗d3 f×e5 14. ♘×e5 ♘×e5 15. d×e5 ♗×e5! (15...♛×b2?! Sveshnikov–Filipenko, Cheliabinsk 1975) 16. ♛×h6 ♖f7 17. ♖ae1 ♛×b2 18. ♛g5+ ♗g7 19. ♛h5 ♗f6∓ (19...h6∓).

219 14. b4

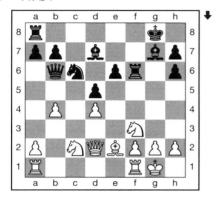

14...♖×f3!? 15. ♗×f3 ♘×d4 16. ♘×d4 ♛×d4 17. ♛×d4 ♗×d4 18. ♖ac1 ♗b6⯑ Hort–Spassky, Moscow 1999;

14...a6 15. a4 ♖ff8 16. ♖a3 ♗e8 17. ♖e3 (17. ♖e1!? ♘e7 18. a5 ♛d6 19. ♘e5 ♘g6 20. ♖g3± McShane–Gdański, Istanbul 2003) 17... ♘e7 18. a5 ♛d6 19. ♗d3 ♘f5!? (19...♘c6 20. ♖fe1± Savić–Antić, Yugoslav Championship, Banja Koviljača 2002) 20. ♗×f5 ♖×f5 21. ♖fe1 ♖f6 22. ♘e5 ♗a4 23. ♖g3 ♖af8 24. ♘e3! (24. ♘d3 ♔h8 25. ♘e3 h5⇄ Antonio–Lputian, Shenzhen 1992) 24...♖f4 [24...♖×f2 25. ♘3g4! ♖×d2 (25...♛×e5 26. ♘×f2±) 26. ♘×h6+ ♔h8 27. ♘ef7+ ♖×f7 28. ♘×f7+ ♔g8 29. ♘×d6 ♔h8 30. ♘f7+ ♔g8 31. ♘d8 ♔h8 32. ♘×e6 ♗×d4+ 33. ♘×d4 ♖×d4 34. ♖e5±] 25. ♘3g4 ♔h8 26. ♘f3 (26. ♖h3 ♗e8±) 26...h5 27. ♘ge5 h4 28. ♖h3±;

14...♖af8 15. b5 ♘e7 16. ♘e5 (16. a4±) 16...♗e8 17. g3 (17. a4 ♘f5 18. a5± Kislov–Vysochin, Voronezh 2001) 17...h5 (17...♘g6 18. ♘g4 ♖6f7⇄; 17...♔h8 18. a4 h5 19. f4 ♘f5 20. a5 ♛d8 21. ♘e3 ♘d6 22. ♛b4±

Karpachev–Bauer, Montpellier 2003) 18. a4 ♘f5 (18...h4 19. ♗d3 h×g3 20. h×g3 h5 21. ♘e3 ♗h6 22. a5 ♛d8 23. f4 ♔h8 24. ♛h2± Topalov–Bareev, Novgorod 1997) 19. a5 ♛c7 20. ♖ac1± Kupreichik–Lautier, Belgrade 1988.

220

7...♘ge7 8. ♘a3 (8. b3 ♘f5 9. ♗b2 ♗b4+ 10. ♔f1 ♗e7 11. h4 ♗d7 12. ♘c3 ♘c×d4 13. ♘×d5 e×d5 14. ♘×d4 ♘×d4 15. ♗×d4 ♗c5 16. ♗×c5 ♛×c5 17. ♖c1 ♛a5= Kosten–Lputian, Altensteig 1989) 8...♘f5 9. ♘c2 ♗b4+ (9...♘b4 10. 0–0 ♘×c2 11. ♛×c2 ♗d7 12. ♛d3 ♖c8 13. a3± Sveshnikov–Lputian, Training match, Sochi 1993; 13. a4!?±) 10. ♔f1 ♗e7 11. h4 h5 12. b4⇄ Benjamin–Bareev, Munich 1994;

7...♗b4+ 8. ♘c3 ♘ge7 9. 0–0 ♘f5 10. ♘a4 ♛d8 11. a3 ♗e7 12. b4 a6 13. ♗b2 ♗d7 14. ♖c1 b5 15. ♘c5 h5 16. ♗d3 ♗×c5 17. ♖×c5± Paulsen–Stern, Frankfurt (M.) 1878.

221

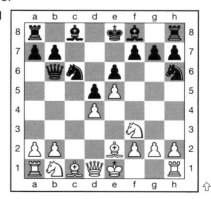

8. ♗×h6 ♕×b2! (8…g×h6 9. ♕d2±) 9. ♘bd2 g×h6 10. 0–0∞;

8. b3 ♘f5 9. ♗b2 ♗b4+ (9…♗e7 10. 0–0 ♗d7 11. g4 ♘h4 12. ♘×h4 ♗×h4 13. ♘a3 0–0 14. f4 f6 15. ♔g2 f×e5 16. d×e5 ♖f7∞ Kupreichik–Hertneck, Debrecen 1992) 10. ♔f1 ♗e7 11. ♘c3 ♕d8 12. g3 f6 13. ♔g2 f×e5 14. d×e5 0–0 15. ♖c1 ♗d7 16. ♗d3 ♕e8 17. ♘e2 ♕f7 18. ♖f1 ⇄ Sveshnikov–Portisch, Interzonal, Biel 1993;

8. ♗d3?! ♗d7 9. ♘c3 ♘×d4 10. 0–0 ♗c5 11. a4 ♕b3 12. ♕d2 ♘×f3+ 13. g×f3 ♖c8 14. ♕e2 ♘f5 15. ♗c2 ♕c4 16. ♗d3 ♕b3 17. ♗c2 ♕c4 18. ♗d3 ♕h4 19. ♗×f5 e×f5 20. ♘×d5 ♗c6∓ Movsesian–S. Ivanov, 18th EU Cup, Chalkidiki 2002;

222   9. ♔f1? ♘f×d4! 10. ♗e3 (10. ♘a4 ♕b4 11. ♗d2 ♕e7 12. ♗g5 f6∓) 10…♕×b2 11. ♘×d5 ♕×e2+! 12. ♕×e2 ♘×e2 13. ♘c7+ ♔d7 14. ♘×a8 ♘c3∓ Schürmans–Claesen, Belgian Championship 1987.

223   9…♗b4+!? 10. ♔f1 (10. ♗d2 ♕a5 siehe 9…♕a5+ 10. ♗d2) 10…♕d8 11. g4 (11. ♗g5 ♗e7 12. ♗×e7 ♕×e7 13. ♕d2 0–0 14. g3 ♗d7 15. ♘c3 f6 16. g4 ♘f×d4!∓ Camilleri–Uhlmann, Zonal Tournament, Raach 1969) 11…♘h4 12. ♘×h4 ♕×h4 13. ♗f4 f6 14. ♔g2 f×e5 15. d×e5 0–0 16. ♗g3∞ Kupreichik–Lputian, Blagoveshchensk 1988.

224   10. ♔f1 ♗d7 (10…b5 11. ♘c3 b4 12. ♘b5 ♗a6 13. ♘c7+ ♕×c7 14. ♗×a6 ♕a5 15. ♗e2 ♗e7∓) 11. ♗d2 ♕d8 12. ♗e1 ♖c8 13. ♖c1 ♘h4 14. ♘c3 ♘×f3 15. ♗×f3 ♕b6 16. ♘a4 ♕d8∓ Steinitz–Maróczy, Vienna 1898.

225   11…♗d7?! 12. a3 ♗×c3+ 13. ♘×c3± h5 14. 0–0 ♖c8 15. ♕d2 ♕d8 16. h3 ♘a5 17. ♖ad1 ♕b6 18. ♖fe1± Nimzowitsch–Spielmann, Stockholm 1920.

226   **14. a×b4** ♕×b4 15. ♕a4 (15. 0–0 ♘f×d4 16. ♘×d4 ♘×d4 17. ♗d3 ♗d7 18. ♕g4 g6 19. ♕g5⯑ Kuzmin–Lempert, St. Petersburg 1993) 15…♗d7 16. ♕×b4!? (16. ♗b5

♕×a4 17. ♖×a4 0–0 18. ♔d2 ♖fb8 19. ♗×c6 ½–½ Kupreichik–Libeau, Münster 1991) 16…♘×b4 17. ♔d2 ♘c6 18. ♘b5±;

14. ♗b5 ♗d7 15. a×b4 ♕×b4

a) 16. 0–0 ♘×e5 17. d×e5 ♗×b5 18. ♘×b5 ♕×b5 19. g4 ♘e7 20. ♘d4 ♕b4∓;

b) 16. ♕a4 ♕×b2 17. ♘×d5 e×d5 18. 0–0 ♘f×d4 19. ♖fb1 ♘×f3+ 20. g×f3 ♕c3 21. ♖c1 ♕b4 22. ♗×c6 ♕×a4 23. ♖×a4 ♗×c6 24. ♖×c6 ♔e7∓ Kupreichik–Ulibin, Moscow 1989;

c) 16. ♗×c6 ♗×c6 17. 0–0 (17. ♕d2 0–0 18. 0–0 ♖fb8= Epstein–Saunina, Tbilisi 1976) 17…0–0–0⇄; 17…♕×b2 [18. ♕d3 ♕b7 19. g4 ♘e7 (19…♘h6 20. h3 0–0 21. ♘g5 g6 22. ♖a5⯑) 20. ♖fb1 ♕d7 21. ♖b3 (21. ♘b5 0–0 22. ♘d6 f5∓) 21…0–0∓] 18. ♘a4 ♕b4 19. ♕c2 ♕c4 20. ♖fc1 ♕×c2 21. ♖×c2 ♘e7 22. ♘c5 0–0 23. ♖ca2 ♖fb8∓ Sankovich–Bareev, Naberezhnye Chelny 1988.

227   6…♘ge7 7. d×c5 (7. b4 c×d4 8. c×d4 ♘f5 see 6…♘h6) 7…♕×c5 [7…♕c7 8. ♗b5 (8. ♗e3 ♘g6 9. ♘bd2 ♘g×e5 10. ♘×e5 ♘×e5 11. b4±) 8…♗d7 9. ♗f4 ♘g6 10. ♗g3 ♗×c5 11. ♕e2 h5 12. h4 0–0–0 13. ♗d3 ♖h6 14. b4 ♗b6 15. a4± Nikitin–Ragozin, Leningrad 1957] 8. ♗d3 ♘g6 9. ♕e2 ♕b6 10. 0–0 ♗e7 11. c4 d×c4 12. ♗×c4 0–0± Timman–Korchnoi, Reykjavík 2000.

228   7. ♗e2 ♘h6 8. b4 c×d4 9. ♗×h6 d3!? (9…g×h6 10. c×d4±) 10. ♗×d3 g×h6 11. 0–0 ♗g7 12. ♖e1 0–0 13. ♘bd2 f6 14. e×f6 ♗×f6 15. ♖a2 ♔h8 16. c4↑ Sveshnikov–Razuvaev, Palma de Mallorca 1989; 16. ♘b3 ♗×c3 17. ♘c5 ♕c7 18. ♘×e6 ♗×e6 19. ♖×e6±.

229   **8…f6** 9. ♗d3 (9. ♘c3±) 9…f×e5 10. d×e5 ♘h6 11. 0–0 ♘f7 12. ♗b2 g6 13. ♕e2 ♗g7 14. ♘bd2± Smeets–Stellwagen, Wijk aan Zee 2002;

8…♘ge7 9. ♘c3 ♘f5 10. ♘a4±.

230 9. ♗e2? a5! (9...♘ge7 10. 0–0 ♘f5 11. ♗b2 ♗e7 12. ♛d2 0–0 13. ♖d1 f6 14. ♘c3± Sveshnikov–Lputian, Russian League, Podolsk 1990) 10. b5 ♘xd4! 11. ♘xd4 ♖xc1 12. ♛xc1 ♛xd4= (Sveshnikov) 13. ♛c3 (13. ♛c7!=; 13. ♘d2 ♛xe5 14. ♘f3 ♛f6 15. 0–0 ♗d6⇄) 13...♗c5∓ Sveshnikov–Hoàng, Cheliabinsk 1989.

231

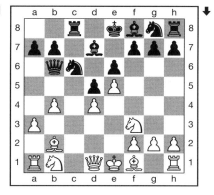

9...♘h6!?

a) 10. ♗d3 ♘a5 11. 0–0 ♘c4 12. ♗xc4 ♖xc4 13. ♘c3 ♛a6 14. ♖c1 ♗e7 15. ♘d2!? ♖c8 (15...♖xd4!? 16. ♘e2 ♖h4 17. g3 ♗a4!? 18. ♛e1 ♗b5 19. ♖c8+ ♗d8 20. gxh4 ♗xe2 21. ♛c1 0–0⇄) 16. ♘b3± Korchnoi–Kotsur, 34th Olympiad, Istanbul 2000;

b) 10. ♘c3

b1) 10...♘f5 11. ♘a4 ♛d8 12. h4 (12. ♗d3 b6 13. 0–0 ♗e7 14. ♘c3 g6 15. ♗a6 ♖b8 16. ♖c1 Portisch–Milić, Olympiad, Moscow 1956; 16. ♛d3±) 12...♗e7 13. ♗d3 f6 14. ♗xf5 exf5 15. ♘c3 fxe5 16. dxe5 d4 17. ♘e2 ♗e6 18. ♘exd4 ♘xd4 19. ♘xd4± Sveshnikov–Poljakov, Latvian Championship 1992;

b2) 10...♘a5 11. ♘a4 ♛c6 [12. ♘c5 ♘c4 13. ♗xc4?! (13. ♗c1⇄) 13...dxc4 14. 0–0 ♛d5 15. ♛e2 (15. ♘xd7 ♛xd7∓) 15...♗c6! 16. ♖fe1 ♗e7 17. ♖ac1 0–0 18. ♘e4 ♘f5∓ Korchnoi–Iruzubieta Villaluenga, Oviedo (Rapidplay) 1992] 12. ♖c1 ♘c4 13. ♗xc4 dxc4 14. ♘c3 ♗e7 15. 0–0 0–0 16. d5 exd5 17. ♘d4 ♛g6 18. ♘xd5 ♗g5 19. f4± Dür–Damjanović, Graz 1979;

9...♘xb4?! 10. axb4 ♛xb4+ 11. ♛d2 ♖c2 12. ♗c3 (12. ♗a3 ♛a4±) 12...♛b3 13. ♛e3 ♘h6 14. ♗d3 ♖xc3 15. ♘xc3 ♛xc3+ 16. ♔e2 ♛b2+ 17. ♛d2 ♛xd2+ 18. ♘xd2 a6±.

232 11. ♗xc4!? dxc4 12. ♖c1 c3 (12...♛a6 13. 0–0 ♘e7 14. ♘g5 h6 15. ♛h5 g6 16. ♛h3 ♘d5 17. ♘ge4± Rodriguez Boado–Masip Rodriguez, Mondariz 2000) 13. ♗xc3 ♘e7 14. 0–0 ♘d5 15. ♘e4 ♗e7 16. ♗d2 0–0 17. ♘c5 ♗c6∞ Sax–Nogueiras, Lucerne 1989.

233 12...♛a6 13. d5 (13. ♘d2 b5 14. ♘e4 ♗c6⇄; 13. ♘g5!?±) 13...exd5 14. ♛xd5±.

234 13. ♗xc4!? ♗b4+ (13...axb4 14. ♛b3∞) 14. axb4 ♛xb4+ 15. ♘d2 (15. ♛d2 ♖xc4 16. ♖xc4 ♛xc4 17. ♛xa5 ♘e7 18. ♘d2 ♛c2 19. ♗a3 ♘c6= Yagupov–Rychagov, Russia 1993) 15...♛xb2 16. ♘e4 ♛b4+ 17. ♔e2 ♖c6!⇄; 17...♔e7? 18. ♘d6 ♖xc4 19. ♖xc4 ♗b5 20. ♛d3 ♗xc4 21. ♘xc4 b5 22. ♘d6 ♛b2+ 23. ♔f3± Hába–Stojanov, Datteln 2002.

235 14. ♘xc4 ♛d8! [14...♖xc4?! 15. ♗xc4 bxa3 16. ♗c3 ♛c6 17. ♗e2 ♛xg2 (17...♘e7 18. 0–0±) 18. ♗f3 ♛h3 19. ♗xb7 ♘h6 20. ♛f3± Grosar–Weinzettl, Austrian League 2003/04; 14...♛a7?! 15. axb4 ♗xb4+ 16. ♗c3 ♗xc3+ 17. ♖xc3± Sveshnikov–Nevednichy, Bled 1991] 15. axb4 [15. a4!? ♗c6 16. a5! ♗e7 (16...♖c7? 17. ♘d6+! ♗xd6 18. exd6 ♛xd6 19. d5+−) 17. ♘b6 ♖c7 18. d5!?↑ Fressinet–Soćko, German League 2002/03] 15...♗xb4+ [15...b5?! 16. ♘d6+! ♗xd6 17. exd6 ♘f6□ 18. ♗d3! (18. ♖c5? Sveshnikov–Lputian, Moscow 1991) 18...0–0 19. 0–0 ♗c6 20. d5↑ ♘xd5 (20...exd5 21. ♗f5 ♛xd6 22. ♗xc8±) 21. ♛g4!; 15...♗c6!? 16. b5!? ♗d5 17. ♗e2 ♗xg2 18. ♖g1 ♗d5 19. ♘e3⇄] 16. ♗c3 ♗xc3+ 17. ♖xc3 ♔f8 18. ♖a3 ♗c6 19. ♘d6± Peng Xiaomin–Soćko, 34th Olympiad, Istanbul 2000.

236   9...♘ge7 10. ♗d3 a6 11. ♕d2 ♘a7 12. ♘c3 ♕c7 13. ♖c1 ♘b5 14. ♘a2 ♕d8 15. ♕b2 ♖×c1+ 16. ♗×c1 ♘c8 17. 0–0 ♗e7 18. a4 ♘ba7 19. b5± Grosar – Raičević, Yugoslav Championship, Kladovo 1991.

237   10...♘f5 11. 0–0 ♗e7 12. ♘bd2 0–0 13. ♗×f5 e×f5 14. ♘b3 ♗e6 15. ♕d2 ♖c7 16. h4 ♖fc8 17. h5 h6 18. ♘c5± Najer – Soćko, ACP Blitz 2004.

238   11...♗e7 12. ♘bd2!? (12. ♕d2 f5 13. e×f6 ♗×f6 14. ♘c3 ♘×e3 15. f×e3 0–0 16. ♖f2 ♕c7 17. ♖c1 ♘e7 18. ♕c2 h6 19. ♕b3 ♔h8 20. ♘e2 ♕d6 21. ♖cf1 ⇄ Movsesian – Heberla, Czech League 2003/04) 12...♘×e3 13. f×e3 ♘b8 14. ♕b1 ♗a4 15. e4 ♘c6 16. ♕b2 a5 17. e×d5 e×d5 18. b5 ♘d8 19. ♖ac1 ♖×c1 20. ♖×c1 0–0 21. ♘b1 ♘e6 22. ♔h1 ♘g5 23. ♘c3 ♘×f3 24. ♘×d5 ♕d8 25. ♘×e7+ ♕×e7 26. g×f3± Balashov – Belozerov, Elista 2001.

239

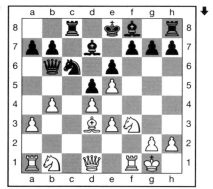

12...♗e7

a) 13. ♘bd2 ♘d8 (13...♘b8 14. ♕e2 ♗a4 15. e4 ♘c6 16. ♕e3 0–0 17. ♖ab1 a5 18. b×a5 ♕a7 19. e×d5 e×d5 20. ♖b6!? ♘×a5 21. ♖h6 ♗c2 22. ♖h3 ⇄ Motylev – Rychagov, Kolontayevo 1997; 13...0–0 14. ♘b3 ♘b8 15. ♕e2 ♖c7 16. h4± Torre – Chernin, New Delhi 1990) 14. ♕e2 ♖c3 15. ♖fe1 0–0 16. g4 a6 17. ♘b1 ♖c8 18. ♕d2 ♕c7 19. ♖a2 ♗a4 20. ♕g2 f6 ⇄ Baklan – Moskalenko, Zonal Tournament, Donetsk 1998;

b) 13. ♕e2 0–0 14. ♘bd2 f6 15. b5 ♘d8 16. e×f6 ♗×f6 17. ♘e5 ♗e8 18. ♕g4 ♖c3 ⇄ Smirnov – Belozerov, Novosibirsk 1999;

12...f6   13. ♘bd2 f×e5 14. ♘×e5 ♘×e5 15. ♕h5+ ♔d8 16. ♕×e5±.

240

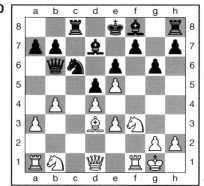

13. ♕e1 ♗g7 14. ♘c3 ♘b8 15. ♔h1 0–0 16. e4 f6 17. e×d5 f×e5 18. d×e5 e×d5 19. ♘×d5 ♕e6 20. ♕e4± I. Zaitsev – Laine, Jyväskylä 1994;

13. ♘c3 ♗h6 (13...♗g7 14. ♘a4 ♕d8 15. ♘c5 ♖c7 16. ♖c1 0–0 17. ♖f2 ♕e7 18. ♖fc2 ♘d8□ 19. ♘×d7 ♖×c2 20. ♘f6+! ♗×f6 21. ♖×c2 ♗g5 22. ♕c1± Kharlov – Gleizerov, Bled 1990) 14. ♕e1 0–0 15. ♘d1! (15. ♘a4 Sveshnikov – Piskov, Bled 1990) 15...f6 16. e×f6 ♖×f6 17. ♘f2 e5 18. b5 ♘×d4 19. ♘×e5 ♗×b5 20. e×d4±.

241   14. ♕e2 (14. ♕e1!?) 14...♘e7 (14...0–0 15. ♘b3 ♕d8 16. ♘c5 ♖c7 17. h4 ♘b8 18. g4 b6 19. ♘×d7 ♕×d7 20. g5 ♗g7 21. ♘h2± Ibragimov – Volzhin, Katowice 1992) 15. g4 ♖c3 (15...♗a4 16. h4 ♖c3 17. ♘e1 0–0 18. ♖a2 ♖c1 19. ♘df3 ♗g7 20. ♕h2↑ Gafner – Snatenkov, Orsk 2000) 16. ♖fc1 ♖×c1+ (16...♕c7 17. ♘b3 b6 18. ♕d2 ♖×c1+ 19. ♖×c1 ♕b8 20. g5 ♗g7 21. ♕c3 ♗a4 22. ♘bd2 ♔d7 23. ♕b2 ♖c8 24. ♘b1 ♖×c1+ 25. ♕×c1 ♕c8 26. ♕×c8+ ♘×c8 27. ♘c3± Heberla – Moskalik, Poland 1999) 17. ♖×c1 ♗a4!±; 17...0–0 18. ♘b3 ♖c8 19. ♘c5± Najer – Totsky, Capelle la Grande 2004.

Table 7

1. e4 e6 2. d4 d5 3. e5 c5 4. c3 ♘c6 5. ♘f3
♛b6 6. a3 ♘h6 7. b4 c×d4 8. c×d4[242] ♘f5

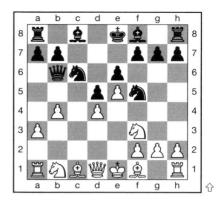

	9	10	11	12	13	14	15	16	
35	♗e3?!	♗d3[244]	f×e3	b5[245]	e×d4	♗×e4	♘e5		
	f6![243]	♘×e3	f×e5	♘×d4	e4	d×e4	♗d7[246]		∞
36	♗b2	♗d3!?[248]	♛a4[250]	b5	♗×f5	0–0	♘c3	♛b3	
	♗e7!?[247]	a5[249]	0–0	f6[251]	e×f5[252]	♗e6	♘a7	♖fd8[253]	±
37	...	h4	♗d3	♗×f5	♘c3	b5	♛d3	0–0	
	...	h5[254]	a5[255]	e×f5	♗e6[256]	a4!	♘a7	♖c8[257]	±
38	...	g4!?[258]	♖g1[259]	e×f6	♘c3	♘a4	♖c1	♘c5[262]	
	♗d7	♘h6	f6	g×f6	♘f7	♛c7[260]	♛f4[261]	♗×c5[263]	±
39	...	...	♘c3	g5[265]	♘a4	♗d3	♖c1	♖g1	
	...	♘fe7	h5[264]	♘f5[266]	♛d8	h4?!	♗e7	g6[267]	±
40	...	...	...	♛c2[268]	♗×c4	♘d2	♘ce4	♘×c4	
	...	...	♘a5	♘c4	d×c4	♛c6	♘d5[269]	♘b6!?[270]	±

242 8. ♗xh6 gxh6 9. cxd4

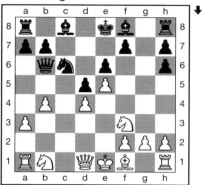

9…♗g7 10. ♘c3 0–0 11. ♗d3 f6 12. b5!? ♘xe5 (12…fxe5!? 13. bxc6 e4 14. ♘xe4 dxe4 15. ♗xe4) 13. dxe5 fxe5 14. 0–0 e4 15. ♘xe4 dxe4 16. ♗xe4 ♕xb5 (16…♗xa1!? 17. ♕xa1 ♕xb5∞) 17. ♖b1 ♕h5 18. ♕d3⯐ Sveshnikov – Yanovsky, Moscow (Rapidplay) 1990;

9…♗d7 10. ♗e2 a5!? [10…♖c8 11. 0–0 ♗g7 (11…♘e7 12. ♗d3 ♗g7 13. ♕d2 ♕c7 14. a4 a6 15. ♖a3 0–0 16. ♘c3 f6 17. exf6 ♖xf6 18. ♘e2± Motylev – San Segundo Carrillo, Úbeda 2000) 12. ♕d2 0–0 13. ♖a2 a6 14. ♕e3 f6 15. exf6 ♖xf6 16. ♘bd2 e5⇄ Polovnikova – Matveeva, Krasnoturinsk 2004] 11. b5 ♘e7 12. ♘c3 a4 13. 0–0 ♕a5 14. ♕d2 ♘c8 15. ♖fc1 ♘b6 16. h3!± Rogers – Velimirović, Vršac 1987.

243 9…g6 10. ♗d3 ♘xe3 11. fxe3 ♗h6 12. ♕d2 ♗d7 13. ♘c3 ♘e7 14. g4 ♗g7 15. 0–0 ♖c8 16. a4± Morozevich – Milos, FIDE World Championship, New Delhi/Teheran 2000.

244 **10. exf6** gxf6 11. ♗d3 (11. ♕d2? ♘xb4! 12. ♘c3 ♕a5 13. ♗b5+ ♗d7?! Sveshnikov – Doroshkevich, Anapa 1991; 13…♘c6∓) 11…♘xe3 12. fxe3 ♗h6 13. ♕e2 ♗d7 14. ♘c3 ♘e7 15. 0–0 0–0 16. ♔h1 ♖ac8⇄ Morozevich – Bareev, Monaco (blind) 2002;

10. b5 ♘xe5!? 11. dxe5 ♘xe3 12. fxe3 ♕xe3+ 13. ♗e2 (13. ♕e2 ♕c1+ 14. ♕d1 ♕e3+=) 13…♗c5∞.

245 12. 0–0 e4 13. ♘h4 exd3 14. ♕h5+ ♔d7 15. ♘g6 hxg6 16. ♕xh8 ♗e7 17. ♕xg7 a5∓.

246 Potkin – Filippov, Russian League, Togliatti 2003.

247 9…a5 10. b5 a4 11. g4 ♘fe7 12. ♘c3 ♘b8 13. ♗d3 ♘d7 14. 0–0 ♘g6 15. ♖c1 ♗e7 16. ♘xa4 ♕a5 17. ♘c5± Sveshnikov – Bareev, PCA, Moscow 1995.

248 10. ♗e2 0–0 11. 0–0 a5 12. b5 a4 13. g4 ♘h4 14. ♘xh4 ♗xh4 15. ♗d3 (15. ♕d2 ♘a5 16. g5 ♕d8 17. f4 ♘b3 18. ♕e3 ♘xa1 19. ♗xa1 f6∓ Sveshnikov – Slochevsky, Moscow (Rapidplay) 1989) 15…♘a5 16. ♘c3 ♘c4 17. ♗xc4 dxc4 18. ♗c1 f6 19. ♗e3∞ Sveshnikov – Bareev, Moscow (Rapidplay) 1989.

249

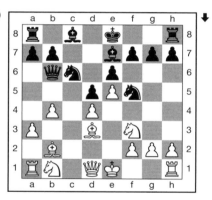

10…♗d7

a) 11. ♗xf5 exf5 12. ♘c3 ♗e6 13. 0–0 0–0 (13…♕d8 14. ♕d2 g5 15. ♘b5 h6⇄ Kamsky – Dokhoian, Pavlodar 1987) 14. ♕d3 ♖ac8 15. ♖ac1 a6 16. ♘a4 ♕a7 17. ♘c5± Gorelov – Yudasin, Minsk 1985;

b) 11. 0–0 ♖c8 [11…g5 12. ♗xf5 exf5 13. ♘c3 ♗e6 14. ♘a4 ♕d8 (14…♕b5 15. ♘c5 g4 16. ♘e1 ♗xc5 17. dxc5 a5 18. ♘c2 a4 19. ♘d4± Fedorowicz – Dokhoian, Wijk aan Zee 1989) 15. ♘c5 g4 16. ♘e1 b6 17. ♘xe6 fxe6 18. ♘d3± Fressinet – Salaun, French League, 1998] 12. ♘bd2 g5 13. ♘b3 h5 14. ♖c1 g4 15. ♘e1 a5 16. ♗xf5 exf5

17. ♘d3 axb4 18. ♘bc5 ♗e6 19. axb4 ♕b5 20. ♘f4 ♖h6 21. ♗c3± Khalifman – Dolmatov, Rethymnon 2003;

10...0–0 11. 0–0 f6?! 12. ♗xf5 exf5 13. ♘c3 ♗e6 14. ♘a4 ♕d8 15. ♘c5 ♗xc5 16. dxc5± Sveshnikov – Paramos Dominguez, Oviedo (Rapidplay) 1993.

250 11. ♗xf5 exf5 12. ♘c3 ♗e6 13. b5 a4 14. ♕d3 (14. bxc6 ♕xb2 15. 0–0 bxc6⇄ Shirov – Khalifman, Linares 2000; 14. 0–0 ♘a5 15. ♗c1 ♘c4 16. ♘xa4 ♕xb5 17. ♘c3 ♕c6 18. ♖b1 ♗xa3 19. ♗xa3 ♘xa3 20. ♖b3 0–0 21. ♕d3 ♘c4 22. h3 ♖fc8∓ Vasyukov – Moskalenko, Belgorod 1990) 14...♘b8 15. ♗c1 h6 16. ♘g1?! Sveshnikov – Moskalenko, Norilsk 1987; 16. 0–0±.

251 **12...♗d7** 13. 0–0 ♘h4 14. ♘xh4 ♗xh4 15. ♕c2 ♘a7 16. ♗xh7+ ♔h8 17. a4± Mukhametov – Rechel, Berlin 1997;

12...♘h4 13. ♘xh4 ♗xh4 14. g3 ♗d8 15. 0–0 ♗d7 16. ♖a2 ♘a7 17. ♘c3 f6 18. ♗a1 f5 19. f4 ♖f7∞ Kiik – Korchnoi, Stockholm 2003.

252 13...fxe5 14. ♗xh7+! (14. ♗h3 Vysochin – Sambuev, St. Petersburg 2003) 14...♔xh7 15. ♕c2+ e4 16. bxc6+–.

253 17. ♖fe1 fxe5 18. ♘xe5 ♗f6 19. a4 ♕xd4?! 20. ♘e4!± Lastin – Ivanov, Moscow 2004.

254

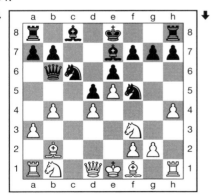

10...a5!? 11. b5 a4 (11...f6 12. ♕d2! ♘d8? 13. g4! ♘h6 14. exf6 ♗f8 15. g5± Sveshnikov – Starostits, Riga 1998) 12. g4 ♘h6 13. ♖g1 ♘a5 14. ♘c3 ♘b3 15. ♖a2 ♕a5

16. ♗d3 ♗d7∓ Yemelin – Dolmatov, 56th Russian Championship, Krasnoyarsk 2003;

10...♗d7 11. g4 ♘h6 12. ♖g1 a6 13. ♘c3 ♘a5 14. ♗c1 ♘c4 15. ♗xc4 dxc4 16. d5 exd5 17. ♘xd5 ♕c6 18. ♗xh6 gxh6 19. ♘xe7 ♔xe7 20. ♕e2± Sveshnikov – Doroshkevich, St. Petersburg 2000;

10...0–0 11. g4 ♘h6 12. ♖g1 ♗d7 13. ♘c3±.

255 **11...g6** 12. ♗xf5 gxf5 13. ♘c3 ♖g8 14. ♘g5 (14. 0–0 ♖g4 15. ♘e2 ♗d7 16. g3 0–0–0 17. ♗c1± Grischuk – Zhang Pengxiang, Shanghai 2001) 14...♕xd4 15. ♕xd4 ♘xd4 16. ♘xd5 ♘c2+ 17. ♔d2 exd5 18. ♔xc2 ♗xg5 19. hxg5 ♖xg5 20. ♗d4 ♗e6 21. g3⩱ Grischuk – Sakaev, Russian League, Tomsk 2001;

11...♗d7 12. ♗xf5 exf5 13. ♘c3 ♗e6±.

256 13...axb4 14. ♘xd5 ♕a5 15. ♘xe7 b3+ 16. ♘d2 ♘xe7 17. ♕xb3 ♖h6 18. ♗c3 ♕d5 19. 0–0 ♕xb3 20. ♘xb3± Sveshnikov – Bareev, Russian Championship, Elista 1996.

257 17. ♗c1 ♖c4 18. ♘e2!? (18. ♖d1?! ♘xb5 19. ♘e2 ♕c6 20. ♗g5 ♗xg5 21. ♘xg5 ♘c3 22. ♘xc3 ♖xc3 23. ♕e2 g6 24. ♖d3 0–0 25. ♖ad1 ♖c8∓ Grischuk – Lputian, 35th Olympiad, Bled 2002) 18...♕xb5 (18...0–0!?⇄ 19. ♗g5 ♗xg5 20. ♘xg5 ♖fc8 21. ♕f3 g6 22. ♘f4 ♕xd4 23. ♘gxe6 fxe6 24. ♕g3 ♕xf4 25. ♕xg6+=) 19. ♗g5 ♕b3 20. ♕xb3 axb3 21. ♗xe7 ♔xe7 22. ♖fb1 ♖hc8 23. ♖xb3 b5 24. ♘f4 g6± Vysochin – Polivanov, St. Petersburg 2002.

258

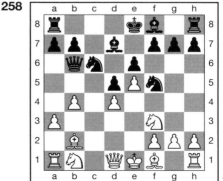

10. h4 ♗e7 11. g4 ♘h6 12. ♖g1 f6 13. exf6 gxf6 14. ♗d3 ♘f7 15. ♕e2 0–0–0 16. ♘c3 ♔b8 17. ♖c1 ♖c8∞ Svidler–Beliavsky, Novosibirsk 1995;

10. ♗e2 ♗e7 (10…h5 11. h4 ♗e7 12. ♕d2 ♖c8 13. g3 0–0 14. 0–0 f6⇄ Landa–Danielian, Yurmala 1991) 11. 0–0 0–0 12. ♕d2 (12. ♗d3!?) 12…f6 (12…a6 13. ♖d1 f6 14. ♘c3 fxe5 15. dxe5 ♖ad8 16. ♖ac1 ♕a7= Grosar–Jelen, Bled 1992) 13. g4 ♘h6 14. exf6 ♖xf6 15. g5 ♖xf3 (15…♖g6) 16. ♗xf3 ♘f5 17. ♖d1 ♕d8 Sveshnikov–Bareev, Moscow (Rapidplay) 1990; 17…♖f8!?∞.

259   11. h3 f6 (11…♗e7 12. ♗d3 ♖c8 13. ♘bd2 ♘b8 14. ♕e2 a6 15. ♘b1 ♘c6 16. 0–0 0–0 17. ♘c3 ♘xd4 18. ♘xd4 ♕xd4 19. ♘e4 ♕b6 20. ♘f6+→ Timman–Hansen, Malmö 2003) 12. ♘c3 [12. ♗d3 ♘f7 13. ♘bd2 fxe5 (13…♗e7 14. 0–0 ♘g5 15. ♔g2 0–0 16. exf6 ♗xf6 17. h4 ♘xf3 18. ♘xf3 g6⇄ Sveshnikov–Lputian, Training match, Sochi 1993) 14. dxe5 ♗e7 15. ♖c1 ♘g5 16. h4 ♘xf3+ 17. ♕xf3 ♘d4 18. ♕e3 ♘b5⇄ Sveshnikov–Lputian, Tilburg (Rapidplay) 1992] 12…fxe5 13. dxe5 ♗e7 14. ♘a4 ♕d8 15. ♖c1 0–0 16. ♘c5 ♗xc5 17. ♖xc5 ♘f7⇄ Sveshnikov–Lputian, Training match, Sochi 1993.

260   14…♕d8 15. ♘c5 b6 16. ♘xd7 ♕xd7 17. ♖c1 ♘cd8 18. h4! ♗d6 19. ♖c3± Vasyukov–Bukhman, St. Petersburg 1994.

261   15…♕d6?! 16. ♘c5 ♗c8 17. h4 ♗e7 18. g5± Sveshnikov–Dvoiris, Cheliabinsk 2004.

262   16. ♖c3 ♘g5 17. b5 ♘a5 18. ♘xg5 fxg5∞ Savić–Lputian, Bosnian League, Neum 2002.

263   17. dxc5 ♘ce5 18. ♘xe5 ♘xe5 19. ♖g3!± Short–Lputian, Batumi 1999.

264

11…♘g6 12. h4 (12. ♘a4 ♕d8 13. ♘c5 ♗xc5 14. dxc5 ♕c7 15. ♕e2± Vysochin–Prezerakos, Corinth 2004) 12…h5 13. g5 a5 14. b5 ♘ce7 15. ♘a4 ♕d8 16. ♘c5 ♘f5 17. ♖c1 b6 18. ♘xd7 ♕xd7 19. ♖c6 ♖b8 20. ♕c2± Sveshnikov–Miljanić, Tivat 1995;

11…♕d8!? 12. h4 (12. ♖c1 ♘g6 13. h4 h5 14. g5 ♗e7 15. ♘a4±; 12. ♗d3 ♘c8 13. h4 ♘b6 14. h5 h6⇄ Khairullin–Matlakov, Kirishi 2004) 12…h5 13. ♘b5 ♘c8 14. ♘g5 hxg4 15. ♕xg4 ♗e7 16. ♗c1 a6 17. ♖g1 f5 18. exf6 ♗xf6 19. ♘h7!?∞ Lastin–Malakhatko, St. Petersburg 2003.

265   12. ♘a4 ♕d8 13. ♘c5 ♗c8 14. g5 b6 15. ♘a6 ♘b8 16. ♖c1 ♗xa6 17. ♗xa6 ♘xa6 18. ♕a4+ ♕d7 19. ♕xa6 ♘g6= Flores–Vallejo Pons, Oropesa del Mar 1999.

266   12…♘g6 13. ♘a4 ♕d8 14. ♖c1 ♗e7 15. ♖g1 0–0∞ Peng Xiaomin–Korchnoi, Calcutta 2000.

267   17. ♗xf5 exf5 18. ♘c5 ♖b8 19. ♕e2 ♗e6 20. ♕e3± Shirov–Kramnik, Monte Carlo (blind) 1997.

268   12. ♘d2 ♖c8 13. ♖c1 [13…♘g6 14. h4 (14. ♕e2!? ♗e7 15. ♕e3 0–0 16. h4! f6 17. h5 ♘h8 18. ♖c2 ♘c6 (18… ♘c4 ♖f4 23. ♘g5!+–) 19. ♘a4 ♕d8=, Motylev–Ponomariov, World Cup, Khanty-Mansiysk 2005) 14…♗e7 (14…h5!? 15. gxh5 ♘f4 16. ♘a4 ♖xc1∓) 15. h5 [15. g5 h6 (15…0–0 16. ♘e2 ♖fd8 17. h5 ♘f8

18. ♖g1 ♖×c1 19. ♘×c1 ♘c6 20. ♖g4 ♖c8 21. ♘cb3 ♘d8!= Shirov–Gurevich, World Cup, Khanty-Mansiysk 2005) 16. g×h6 ♖×h6 17. h5 ♘h4 18. ♕g4 ♘f5 19. ♗d3 ♗f8 20. ♘e2 ♘c4⇄ Grischuk–Radjabov, Wijk aan Zee 2003] 15...♘f4 16. ♕f3 ♗g5 17. ♘e2 (17. ♖c2±) 17...♖×c1+ 18. ♘×c1 0–0 19. h6 g6⇄ Grischuk–Kruppa, Elista 2000] 13...h5 14. ♖c2 ♘c4 15. ♗×c4 d×c4 16. ♘ce4 ♘d5 17. ♘×c4 ♖×c4 18. ♖×c4 a5⊒ Ivanchuk–Bareev, Dubai (Rapidplay) 2002.

269 **15...c3!?** 16. ♘d6+ [16. ♕×c3 ♘d5 17. ♕b3 (17. ♕×c6 ♗×c6⊒) 17...♗e7 18. ♖c1 ♕b5 19. ♘c4 0–0 20. ♘ed6 ♗×d6 21. ♘×d6 ♕b6 22. g5□ a5 23. b5 (23. ♘c4 ♕b5 24. ♘d6 ♕b6=) 23...a4 24. ♕d3 ♖fd8 25. 0–0 ♗e8 26. ♖c5 ♖×d6 27. e×d6 ♕×d6⊒, Hába–Kosić, 36th Chess Olympiad, Calvià 2004] 16...♔d8 17. ♘×f7+ ♔e8 18. ♘d6+ ♔d8 19. ♘f7+ (19. ♘2e4 c×b2 20. ♕×b2⊒) 19...♔e8 20. ♘d6+ ♔d8= Sveshnikov–Radjabov, Tallinn (Rapidplay) 2004;

15...♘c8!? 16. ♕×c4 ♘b6 17. ♕×c6 ♗×c6 18. ♔e2 ♘a4 19. ♖hb1±.

270 17. ♘cd6+ ♗×d6 18. ♘×d6+ ♔e7 19. ♕×c6 ♗×c6 20. ♖g1± Sveshnikov–Potkin, Russian Championship, Krasnoyarsk 2003; 20. 0–0 h5±.

Notes

Table 8

1. e4 e6 2. d4 d5 3. e5 c5 4. c3 ♞c6 5. ♞f3
♛b6 6. a3 c4

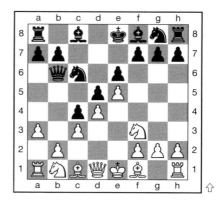

	7	8	9	10	11	12	13	14	
41	g3?![271]	♗h3[273]	♞×e5[274]	d×e5	♛h5+	♛e2	♞d2	♞f3	
	f6![272]	f×e5	♞×e5	♗c5[275]	g6	♗d7	♞e7[276]	h6[277]	∞
42	♞bd2!?	b3![279]	♞×b3	♞×a5	♗d2	♛b1	♗d3	0–0	
	♗d7?![278]	c×b3	♞a5	♛×a5	♛a4[280]	♗c6[281]	♞e7	h6[282]	±
43	...	♗e2[283]	♞×e5	d×e5	0–0	b4[287]	♞×b3	♞×c5	
	f6?!	f×e5!?[284]	♞×e5[285]	♗c5[286]	♞e7	c×b3	0–0	♛×c5[288]	±
44	...	g3[289]	♗h3!?	0–0[292]	♛e2[293]	♞e1	f4	♞df3	
	♞a5!	♗d7[290]	♗e7[291]	h5	0–0–0[294]	g6[295]	♞h6	♞b3[296]	⇄
45	...	...	h4	e×f6	♞e5	♗h3	d×e5	♛g4	
	...	...	f5[297]	♞×f6[298]	♗d6	♗×e5[299]	♞g8	g6[300]	±
46	...	♗e2	0–0	♖b1	g3[302]	♞h4[304]	e×f6	♗g4	
	...	♗d7	h6[301]	♞e7	0–0–0[303]	f5[305]	g×f6	e5[306]	±

271 7. ♗e2 ♗d7 8. ♘bd2 ♘a5 9. 0–0 see Note 301.

272 7...♗d7 [8. ♘bd2 ♘a5 9. ♗h3 0–0–0 10. 0–0 ♗e7 11. ♘e1?! (11. ♖e1⇄) 11...h5 12. f4?! g6 13. ♘df3 ♘b3 14. ♖b1 ♘h6 15. ♗e3 ♔b8 16. ♘g2∞ Sveshnikov – Kalinin, Cheliabinsk 1977] 8. h4!? ♘a5 9. ♘bd2

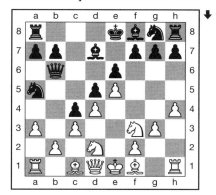

9...0–0–0 10. ♗h3 f5 11. ♗g2 (11. 0–0 ♘h6 12. ♘e1 ♘f7 13. ♘g2 g5 14. h×g5 ♘×g5 15. ♘f4 ♘×h3+ 16. ♘×h3 ♗e7 17. ♖b1 ♖dg8∓ Klinger – Portisch, Olympiad, Dubai 1986) 11...♔b8 12. ♘g5 ♘h6 13. ♘f1 ♘b3 14. ♖b1 ♘×c1 15. ♕×c1 ♗e7 16. ♘d2 ♗a4 17. 0–0 ♖df8 18. b3 c×b3 19. c4⇄ Reefat – Pelletier, 35th Olympiad, Bled 2002;

9...h5 10. ♗h3 (10. ♘g5!? ♘e7 11. ♕f3 ♘f5 12. ♗h3 g6 13. ♗×f5! g×f5 14. ♕e2 ♗a4 15. ♘df3 ♘b3 16. ♖b1 ♘×c1 17. ♖×c1± Degraeve – Sokolov, Baguio 1987) 10...♘h6 (10...f6?! 11. e×f6 g×f6 12. 0–0 0–0–0 13. ♖e1 ♘h6 14. ♘h2!± Sax – Kuligowski, Zonal Tournament, Warsaw 1979) 11. 0–0 ♗e7 12. ♘e1 g6 13. ♘g2 0–0–0 14. ♖b1 ♔b8 15. ♘f3! ♕b3 16. ♕e2 ♗a4 17. ♗g5± Sax – Ree, Amsterdam 1979;

9...h6 10. ♗h3 0–0–0 11. 0–0 ♘e7 12. ♖b1 (12. ♖e1 ♘ec6 13. ♖b1 ♗e7 14. ♕c2 ♔b8 15. ♘f1 ♕b3 16. ♕e2 ♕b6 17. ♗e3 ♘b3 18. h5 ♔a8 19. ♘3h2 ♖dg8∞ Vysochin – Rustemov, Polanica Zdrój 1997) 12...♔b8

13. ♘e1 ♘f5 14. ♘g2 ♗e7 15. ♕f3 ♗c8 16. h5 ♖hf8 17. ♘f4± Sax – Knaak, Szirák 1985;

9...♕c6 10. ♘g5 h6 11. ♘h3 ♕a4 12. ♕f3 ♕c2 13. ♘f4 ♘e7 14. ♘g2!? ♕h7?! (14...♘b3 15. ♘×b3 ♕×b3 16. ♘e3±) 15. b4! c×b3☐ 16. ♗d3 ♕g8 17. ♖b1 ♗a4 18. ♘e3 ♖c8 19. c4↑ Sveshnikov – Eingorn, Sochi 1986.

273 8. e×f6 ♘×f6

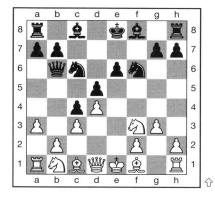

9. ♗h3 ♗d6 10. ♕e2 0–0 11. ♗×e6+ ♔h8 12. ♗×c8 ♖a×c8 (12...♖e8 13. ♗e6 ♘d8 14. ♘e5 ♘×e6⇄) 13. 0–0 ♖ce8 14. ♕c2 ♘e4 ⯒;

9. ♗g2 ♗d6 10. 0–0 0–0

a) 11. ♖e1 ♗d7 (11...♘e4 12. ♘bd2 ♘×d2 13. ♕×d2 ♗d7 14. ♕c2 ♖ae8⇄) 12. ♕c2 ♖ae8∓;

b) 11. ♘bd2?! e5! 12. d×e5 ♗×e5! 13. ♘×e5 ♘×e5 14. ♕e2?! ♖e8! 15. ♘f3 ♗g4∓ Przewoźnik – Uhlmann, Poland – GDR, Zakopane 1980;

c) 11. ♕e2 ♗d7 [11...♔h8 12. ♘e5 ♘d7 (12...♗×e5?! 13. d×e5 ♘d7 14. ♗e3 ♕a5 15. f4 ♘c5 16. ♘d2± Sax – Uhlmann, Sarajevo 1982) 13. ♘×c6 (13. f4 ♘d×e5 14. f×e5 ♖×f1+ 15. ♔×f1 ♗e7∓) 13...♕×c6 14. f4 (14. ♕×e6 ♘f6⯒) 14...♘f6 15. ♘d2 ♗d7 16. ♘f3 ♘e4= Gertler – Polgar, New York 1985] 12. ♘e5 ♖ae8 13. ♘d2 (13. ♗f4 ♗×e5 14. d×e5 ♘e4! 15. ♗×e4 d×e4∞) 13...♗c8 14. f4±.

274 9. dxe5 &c5 10. 0–0 ♘ge7 11. ♘bd2 0–0 12. b4 cxb3 13. ♖b1 (13. ♘xb3 ♖xf3! 14. ♘xc5 ♘xe5 15. &g2 ♖f8 16. &e3 ♛c7∓) 13...♘a5∓.

275 10...&d7 11. 0–0 ♘e7⇄.

276 13...0–0–0!?.

277 14...0–0–0 15. &g5 h6 16. &xe7 &xe7 17. ♘d4⇄;

14...h6 15. 0–0 0–0–0∞ Malaniuk–Uhlmann, Tallinn 1987.

278 7...♘ge7? 8. &xc4! dxc4 9. ♘xc4 ♛a6 10. ♘d6+ ♚d7 11. ♘xf7 ♖g8 12. ♛c2 h6 13. ♘d6± Sveshnikov–Milos, Budapest 1988.

279 8. &e2 ♘ge7? 9. &xc4!± Panarin–Nepomniashchy, Vladimir 2002.

280

11...&a4 12. ♛b1 ♛c7 13. &d3 ♘e7 14. 0–0 ♛d7 15. ♖c1 h6 16. ♖a2 ♘c8 17. c4 dxc4 18. ♖xc4 &c6 19. ♖xc6!! bxc6 20. d5!→ Prashnik–Yakimenko, corr. 1994/96;

11...♘e7 12. &d3 ♛c7 13. 0–0 h6

a) 14. ♘h4!? ♘c6 (14...♘f5? 15. ♘xf5 exf5 16. ♛f3±; 14...g6 15. g3 ♘c8?! 16. &xg6!?↑ Motylev–Hort, Hoogeveen 2003) 15. f4 &e7 16. ♛g4 g6 17. ♘xg6 ♖g8 18. ♛h5 fxg6 19. &xg6+ ♚d8 20. f5⩱;

b) 14. ♘e1 ♘c6 15. f4 g6 16. g4 0–0–0 17. f5 gxf5 18. gxf5 exf5 19. &xf5 &e6 20. ♛h5

♚b8 21. ♘d3 &e7⇄ Vlassov–Ilyushin, St. Petersburg 1995;

c) 14. ♛e2!? ♘c8 15. &e3 ♘b6 16. ♘d2 &c6 17. f4 g6 18. ♖fc1 ♛d7 19. a4 ♘xa4 20. c4⩲ Charbonneau–Bluvshtein, Montréal 2003.

281 12...♛c6 13. &d3 h6 14. 0–0 ♘e7 15. ♖c1± Sveshnikov–Kiselev, Moscow (Rapidplay) 1994.

282 15. ♖c1 ♘c8 (15...b5 16. ♖c2 ♖b8 17. ♖b2±) 16. c4± Sveshnikov–Timman, Tilburg 1992.

283 8. exf6 ♘xf6 9. b3 cxb3 10. ♖b1 &d6 11. &d3 0–0 12. 0–0 e5↑;

8. g3 fxe5 9. ♘xe5 ♘xe5 10. dxe5 &c5 11. ♛h5+ g6 12. ♛e2 ♘e7 13. &g2 &d7 14. 0–0 0–0–0 15. ♘f3⇄ Honfi–Uhlmann, Solingen 1974;

8. b3!? fxe5 (8...cxb3 9. ♘xb3 ♛c7 10. c4!?±)

a) 9. bxc4?! e4 10. ♘g5 (10. ♘h4? ♘f6 11. g3 &e7 12. ♖b1 ♛c7 13. &e2 0–0 14. 0–0 ♘a5!∓ Enders–Uhlmann, GDR Championship, Eggesin 1978; 10. ♖b1 ♛a5 11. ♘b3 ♛c7 12. ♘g5 ♘f6 13. cxd5 exd5 14. c4 &f5∓) 10...♘f6 (10...&e7 11. ♖b1 ♛d8 12. ♖xb7!? &xg5 13. ♖xg7 ♚f8□ 14. ♖xg5 ♛xg5 15. ♘xe4⩲) 11. f3?! (11. ♖b1 ♛c7 12. g3 h6 13. ♘h3 g5↑; 11. &e2 ♛a5 12. &b2 &d6 13. &h5+ ♚e7!∓) 11...♛a5?! Cherniaev–Korniushin, Vladivostok 1995; 11...e3∓;

b) 9. ♘xe5!? (Bronstein) 9...♘xe5 10. dxe5 &c5?! (10...♘h6!? 11. bxc4 &c5 12. ♛h5+ ♘f7 13. ♛e2 0–0 14. f4±) 11. ♛h5+ [11. ♛f3 cxb3 (11...♘e7?? 12. b4+– Hansen–Lovik, Copenhagen 2004) 12. ♖b1 ♛c7 13. ♛h5+ g6 14. &b5+ &d7 15. &xd7+ ♚xd7 16. ♛e2 ♘e7 17. ♘xb3± Buchnicek–Sebenik, Bled 2003] 11...g6 12. ♛h4 ♛c7 13. ♘f3 ♘e7 14. b4 ♘f5 15. ♛h3 &e7 16. &e2 0–0 17. g4 ♘g7 18. ♛g3± Bronstein–Roos, Hastings 1993/94.

284

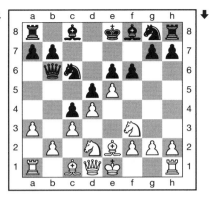

8...♗d7 9. 0–0 0–0–0 10. b3 c×b3 11. ♘×b3 ♛c7 12. ♖b1 ♗e8 13. ♗f4 h6 14. c4 g5 15. ♗d2 ♗g6 16. c×d5 ♖×d5 17. ♗c4 ♗×b1 18. ♗×d5 e×d5 19. ♕×b1± Sveshnikov – Meshkov, Russian League, Podolsk 1990;

8...♛c7?! 9. 0–0!? f×e5 (9...♗d7 10. b3!?↑) 10. ♘×e5 ♘×e5 11. d×e5 ♘e7 [11...♕×e5 12. ♖e1 ♕f6 (12...♕d6 13. b3 c×b3 14. c4 ♘f6 15. ♕×b3 ♗e7 16. c×d5 e×d5 17. ♗b5+± Casper – Knaak, GDR Championship, Fürstenwalde 1981) 13. ♘f3 ♗d7 14. ♗g5 ♕f5 15. ♗h4 ♗e7 16. ♗×e7 ♘×e7 17. ♘e5 ♖f8 18. ♔h1 ♖f6 19. ♗×c4 0–0–0 20. ♗d3± Baklan – Florath, Groningen 1996] 12. b3! c×b3 13. c4! ♕×e5 14. ♖b1→ ♘g6 (14...♗d7 15. ♗b2±△ ♗h5+) 15. c×d5± Casper – Uhlmann, Berlin 1982.

285 9...♘f6 10. f4! (10. 0–0 ♗d6 11. ♘df3 0–0 12. ♕c2 ♕c7 13. ♗f4 ♘h5 14. ♘×c6 ♘×f4 15. ♘ce5 ♗d7 16. ♖fe1 ♖f5 17. ♗f1 ♘g6∓ Teske – Uhlmann, GDR Championship, Nordhausen 1986) 10...♗d6 11. ♗h5+! (11. ♘df3± △0–0, ♕c2, ♔h1, ♗e3) 11...g6 12. ♗f3 0–0 13. ♕e2 ♕c7 14. g3 ♗d7 15. ♘×d7!± Pähtz – Uhlmann, GDR Championship, Nordhausen 1986.

286 10...♘h6 11. ♘×c4! d×c4 12. ♗×h6 ♗d7□ 13. ♗g5 ♕×b2 14. 0–0 ♕×c3 15. ♗h5+ g6 16. ♕b1!!± Pähtz – Uhlmann, Erfurt 1985.

287 12. ♗h5+ g6 13. ♗g4 h5 14. ♗e2 ♗d7 15. ♖b1 0–0 16. ♘×c4 d×c4 17. ♕×d7 ♖ad8 18. ♕a4 ♖×f2 19. ♖×f2 ♗×f2+ 20. ♔h1 ♕c6⇄ Vallejo Pons – Pelletier, Biel 2002.

288 **15. a4?!** ♕×c3 16. ♗a3 ♖f7 17. ♗d6 ♘f5 18. ♖c1 ♕a5∓;

15. ♕d4 ♕×d4 16. c×d4 ♗d7 17. ♖b1 ♖ab8 18. a4 ♖fc8= Prié – Lautier, Paris 1988;

15. ♕d3 ♕c7 (15...♖f7 16. ♖b1 b6 17. ♕h3 ♕c7 18. ♗d3 g6 19. ♖e1 ♕×c3 20. ♗b2 ♕c6 21. ♖bc1 ♕d7 22. ♖c2 ⯦ Conquest – Pelletier, French League, 2002) 16. ♗g5 (16. f4 ♗d7 17. a4 ♖ac8 18. ♗a3 ♖f7 19. ♗×e7 ♖×e7 ⇄) 16...♖f7 17. f4 ♗d7 18. ♗h5 ♕c5+ 19. ♔h1 ♖ff8 20. ♖ab1 (20. c4±) 20...b6 (20...b5 21. ♗×e7 ♕×e7 22. f5↑) 21. c4± Grischuk – Pelletier, Biel 2001.

289

8. h4!? ♗d7 9. h5 h6 10. g3 ♘e7 11. ♗h3 ♘b3 12. ♘×b3 ♗a4 13. ♘fd2 ♘c6 14. 0–0± (Bronstein – Mestel, London 1976) 14...♘a5 15. f4 ♘×b3 16. ♘×b3 ♗×b3 17. ♕e2 0–0–0 18. f5±;

8. ♖b1!? ♗d7 9. ♗e2 ♘e7 10. ♘f1 ♕b3 (10...f6 11. h4 0–0–0 12. h5 ♘ec6 13. ♗f4 f×e5 14. ♘×e5 ♘×e5 15. ♗×e5 ♘c6 16. ♗g3± Hába – Knaak, Halle 1987) 11. ♗f4 ♗a4 12. ♕×b3 ♗×b3 13. ♘e3 ♘g6 14. ♗g3 f5 15. e×f6 g×f6 16. ♘h4± Hába – Faragó, Wattens 1996;

8. b4!? (Keres) 8...c×b3 9. ♗b2 ♗d7 [10. ♖c1 ♗b5! 11. c4 d×c4 12. ♗×c4 ♘×c4 13. ♘×c4 ♗×c4 14. ♖×c4 ♘e7 15. ♖b4 ♕a6? (15...♕c6!∓) 16. ♕×b3 b6 17. ♘g5! ♘d5 18. ♖a4 ♕b7 19. ♕b5+ ♕d7 20. ♕×d7+ ♔×d7 21. ♘×f7 ♖g8 ⯦ Remizov – Ilinsky,

USSR 1975] 10. c4 ♗a4 (10…♘e7!) 11. ♖c1 ♘e7 12. c5 ♕d8 13. ♗d3 ♘g6 14. g3 ♗e7 15. ♕e2 a6 16. h4 h6 17. h5 ♘f8 18. ♘h4 ♕d7 19. f4 ⯒ Circenis–Katishonok, Latvia 2001.

290

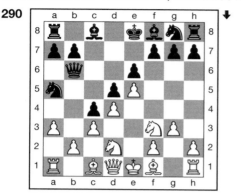

8…♗e7 9. h4 ♗d7 10. ♗h3 f5 11. e×f6 (11. 0–0 ♘h6 12. ♘e1 ♘f7 13. ♘g2 g5 14. h×g5 ♘×g5 15. ♕h5+ ♔d8 16. ♘f4 ♘×h3+ 17. ♕×h3 ♔c7 ∓) 11…g×f6 12. 0–0 h5 13. ♖e1 ♘h6 14. ♖b1!? (14. ♕e2 ♘g4 15. ♘h2 f5⇄; 14. ♘h2 0–0–0 15. ♕×h5 ♖dg8 ⯒ Grischuk–Korchnoi, Biel 2001) 14…0–0–0 (14…♘g4 15. ♘h2 f5 16. ♘df3 0–0–0 17. ♗f4!?±) 15. b4 c×b3 16. ♘×b3 ♘g4 (16…♘×b3 17. ♖×b3 ♕c6 18. ♗f4 ♘g4 19. ♕e2±);

8…f5 9. e×f6 g×f6 10. ♗g2 ♘h6 11. ♘h4 ♘f7 12. 0–0 ♗g7 13. f4↑ Kristjánsson–Thorsteinsson, Reykjavík 2004.

291

9…0–0–0 10. 0–0 ♘h6 (10…h6 11. ♘h4 g5 12. ♘g2 h5⇄) 11. ♖b1 ♗b5 12. ♖e1 ♕c6

13. b3 c×b3 14. ♘×b3 ♘×b3 15. ♕×b3 ♗d3 16. ♖a1∞ I. Zaitsev–Lunev, Orel 1994;

9…f6?! 10. e×f6! g×f6 11. 0–0 0–0–0 12. ♖e1 ♗g7 (12…♖e8 13. ♖b1 ♕c7 14. b3 c×b3 15. ♘×b3 ♘c4 16. ♗f4±) 13. ♖b1 ♔b8 14. b4± I. Zaitsev–Pokojowczyk, Sochi 1976;

9…♘e7 10. 0–0 h6 11. ♘h4

a) 11…g5!? 12. ♘g2 h5 13. g4 h×g4 14. ♗×g4 0–0–0 15. ♕f3 ♗e8 16. ♘e3⇄;

b) 11…0–0–0 12. ♘g2 ♔b8 13. ♖b1 ♕c7 14. ♘e3 ♘c8 15. f4 g6 16. f5!? (16. ♘g4 ♗e7 17. ♗g2 ♘b6 18. ♕e2 ♗a4 19. ♘f3 ♘d7⇄) 16…g×f5 17. g4 f×g4 18. ♘×g4 ♗e8 19. ♘f6± I. Zaitsev–Savon, Dubna 1976;

c) 11…♘ec6 12. f4 0–0–0 (12…g6 13. ♘g2 0–0–0 14. ♘e3 ♔b8 15. ♗g2 ♘e7 16. ♖f2 ♘b3 17. ♘d×c4!? d×c4 18. ♘×c4 ♕b5 19. ♘d6 ♕a4 20. ♘×f7 ♘×a1 21. ♕×a4 ♗×a4 22. ♘×d8± Sveshnikov–Riazantsev, St. Petersburg, 2000) 13. ♖b1 ♗e7 14. ♘g2 ♖dg8 15. ♔h1 g6 16. ♘e3 ♘b3 17. ♕f3 ♕c7 18. ♘×b3 c×b3 19. ♗d2± Psakhis–Faragó, Banja Luka 1985;

9…h6!? 10. 0–0 0–0–0 11. ♘e1 g5 (11…h5 12. ♘df3 ♘b3 13. ♖b1 ♘×c1 14. ♕×c1 ♗a4 15. ♘g5 ♘h6 16. f4 g6 17. ♘g2 ♗e7 18. ♕d2∞ Motylev–Balashov, Ekaterinburg 2002) 12. ♗g2 ♗e7 13. ♖b1 h5∞ Pintér–Schmidt, Budapest 1977.

292 10. ♖b1 h5!? 11. 0–0 ♗b5!? (11…g5!? 12. ♘e1 0–0–0 13. ♗g2 ♘h6 14. ♕e2 ♗a4 15. b4 c×b3 16. ♘d3 g4 17. ♖e1 ♔b8⇄ Stilling–van Manen, corr. 1990) 12. a4 ♗c6 13. ♖e1 g5!? 14. ♗f1 g4 15. ♘h4 ♗×h4 16. g×h4 ♘e7 17. b4 c×b3 18. ♗d3 ⯒ Minasian–Korchnoi, Ohrid 2001; 18. ♘×b3? ♗×a4 19. ♘×a5 ♗×d1 20. ♖×b6 a×b6 21. ♘×b7 ♗f3–+.

293 11. ♘e1!? g5! 12. ♗g2 0–0–0 13. ♘df3 (13. f4 g×f4 14. g×f4 ♘h6 15. ♕×h5?! ♘f5∓ Moroz–Glek, Kemerovo 1985) 13…g4 (13…♘b3?! 14. ♗×g5!⯒ Hennings–Hausner, GDR 1979) 14. ♘g5 ♘h6= Glek, ∓ *Fritz*.

294   11...g5!? 12. ♗g2 0-0-0 13. ♕e3 g4 14. ♘g5 ♘h6 15. ♕f4 ♖dg8 16. ♘xf7 ♖f8 (16...♘xf7 17. ♕xf7 ♗g5∓) 17. ♘xh8 ♖xf4 18. gxf4 ♗e8∓.

295   12...g5∓; 12...h4!?.

296   15. ♖b1 ♘xc1 16. ♖xc1 ♖dg8 17. ♘g5 ♕d8 18. ♕d2 b5⇄ Movsesian – Radjabov, Sarajevo 2002.

297

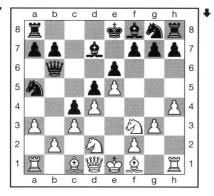

9...0-0-0!? – See 7. g3; **9...♗e7** – See 8...♗e7;

9...h6 10. ♗h3 0-0-0 11. ♔f1 (11. 0-0 ♘e7 12. ♘e1 f5 13. exf6 gxf6 14. ♖b1 e5 15. ♗xd7+ ♖xd7 16. b3 cxb3 17. ♘xb3 ♘xb3 18. ♘g2 ♕e6 19. ♕xb3 ♘c6⇄ Svesh-nikov – Levitt, Amantea 1995) 11...g6 12. ♔g2 ♗g7 13. ♖b1 ♘e7 14. ♘f1 ♖dg8 15. ♘1h2 ♘f5 16. ♘g4 ♕d8 17. ♗f4 ♘c6 18. ♕d2 b6 19. ♖he1 ♔b7 20. ♔g1 ♕e7 21. ♗g2± Tseitlin – Tregubov, Groningen 1994;

9...h5 10. ♗h3 ♘h6 (10...0-0-0 11. 0-0 ♘h6 12. ♖e1 ♔b8 13. ♖b1 ♗e7 14. ♘f1 ♔a8 15. ♕e2 ♗a4 16. ♗g5± Erenburg – Sangma, Goa 2002) 11. ♘f1 ♘b3 12. ♖b1 ♘xc1 13. ♕xc1 0-0-0 14. ♘e3 ♔b8 15. 0-0 ♗e7 16. ♘g2 g6 17. ♘f4± Sveshnikov – Balashov, Novgorod 1995;

9...f6 10. ♗h3 ♘h6 11. 0-0 0-0-0 12. ♖e1 ♘f7 13. ♖b1 f5 14. ♘f1 ♗e7 15. ♕e2 g6 16. g4± Popov – Novak, Nałęczów 1986;

9...♘e7 10. ♗h3 (10. ♘g5 h6 11. ♘h3 0-0-0 12. ♘f4 ♔b8 13. ♗e2 ♕c7 14. ♔f1

♘c8 15. ♗h5 g6 16. ♗e2 ♘b6⇄ Ivanchuk – Bareev, Monte Carlo (blind) 2003) 10...f5 (10...♘ec6 11. 0-0 ♗e7 12. ♖e1 h6 13. ♖b1 0-0-0 14. b4 cxb3 15. ♘xb3 ♘xb3 16. ♖xb3 ♕c7 17. ♖b1 ♘a5⇄ Gobet – Faragó, Lucerne 1985) 11. 0-0 h6 12. ♖b1 ♖g8 13. ♗g2 g5 14. hxg5 hxg5 15. b3 cxb3 16. ♘xb3 ♗a4 17. ♘fd2 0-0-0 18. ♕c2 ♕c6 19. ♕d1 ♗xb3 20. ♘xb3= Potkin – Vysochin, Cappelle la Grande 2004.

298   10...gxf6 11. ♗h3 (11. ♘e5? fxe5 12. ♕h5+ ♔e7 13. ♕g5+ ♔f7 14. ♘f3 ♗g7 15. ♘xe5+ ♗xe5 16. ♕xe5 ♘f6–+ Korbut – Novikova, Vladimir 2002) 11...0-0-0 12. 0-0 ♘h6 13. ♖e1 ♖g8 14. ♘f1 ♘b3 15. ♗xh6 ♗xh6 16. ♖b1∓ Cherniaev – Harestad, Gausdal 1993.

299   12...♗c7 13. ♕e2 ♖f8 14. 0-0 0-0-0 15. ♘xd7 ♔xd7 16. ♖b1 ♖de8 17. b3 ♘xb3 18. ♘xb3 cxb3 19. c4↑ García Fernán-dez – Rayo Gutiérrez, Spanish Champion-ship, Almeria 1989.

300   15. 0-0 ♘e7 16. ♘f3 ♘b3 17. ♗e3!± Grischuk – Apicella, French League, Bordeaux 2003.

301

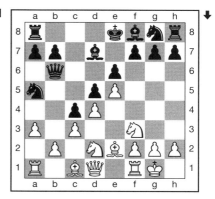

9...♘e7

a) 10. ♖e1

a1) 10...♕c6 11. ♕c2 ♘c8 12. ♘g5 h6 13. ♘h3 ♘b6 14. ♘f4 0-0-0! 15. ♘h5 ♕c7 16. a4! ♗c6 17. ♗d1 ♔b8 18. ♖e3!± Svesh-nikov – Eingorn, Palma de Mallorca 1989;

a2) 10...♘g6!? 11. g3 (11. h4!? Glek) 11...♗e7 12. h4 f5 13. h5 ♘f8 14. ♖b1 g5∞ Motwani – Gurevich, Hastings 1991/92;

a3) 10...h6 11. ♖b1 (11. ♕c2?! 0–0–0 12. ♖b1 ♔b8 13. ♘f1 ♕b3 14. ♕×b3 ♘×b3 15. ♗f4 ♘c8 16. ♘g3∞ Sveshnikov – Nikolenko, 58th USSR Championship, Moscow 1991)

a31) 11...0–0–0 12. ♕c2 ♔b8 13. ♗d1 ♖c8 14. ♘f1 ♘b3 15. ♗f4± Sveshnikov – Casper, Moscow 1987;

a32) 11...♕c7 12. ♗f1 ♘c8 13. ♖e3 ♘b6 14. ♘e1 0–0–0 15. f4 g6 16. ♖h3 ♗e7 17. ♘df3 ♗a4 18. ♕e2 h5 19. ♗e3 ♗b3 20. ♗f2± Kharlov – Ilyushin, Tula 2002;

a33) 11...g5 12. ♘f1 ♘g6 13. ♗e3 ♗e7 14. ♘3d2 0–0–0 15. ♘g3 ♔b8 16. ♘h5 ♖df8 17. ♕c2 ♘h4 18. ♗d1 ± Sherwin – Evans, New York 1954;

a34) 11...♘c8 12. ♘f1 ♕b3 13. ♕×b3 ♘×b3 14. ♗f4 ♗a4 15. ♘g3 b5 16. ♘h5 ♘b6 17. g4! ♘a5 18. ♖ec1 ♘b3 19. ♖f1! ♘a5 20. ♘e1 ♘c6 21. ♗e3 0–0–0 22. f4± Sveshnikov – Lutz, Berlin 1989;

b) 10. ♖b1 (I. Zaitsev)

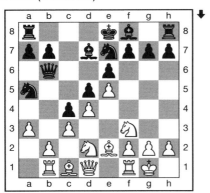

b1) 10...♘b3 11. ♗×c4!±;

b2) 10...♘ec6 11. ♖e1 [11. ♕e1!? f5 12. e×f6 g×f6 13. b4 c×b3 14. c4 ⯑ (Gdański – Owczarzak, Warsaw 2002) 14...d×c4 15. ♘×c4 ♘×c4 16. ♗×c4 ♘a5 17. ♗×e6 ♗×e6 18. d5 ♘c5 19. d×e6±) 11...♗e7 12. ♕c2 ♖c8 13. ♘f1 ♕b3 14. ♗d1 ♕×c2

15. ♗×c2 ♘b3 16. ♗f4 ♘ca5 17. ♘g3 ♗a4 18. ♖e2 b5 19. ♘h5± Sveshnikov – Donchev, Lvov 1983;

b3) 10...♗b5!? 11. ♘e1 ♘b3 12. ♘×b3 ♗a4 13. ♗f4 ♗×b3 14. ♕d2 ♘c6 15. g3 (15. g4!? ♗e7 16. ♗g3 0–0–0 17. ♘g2±) 15...♘a5 16. ♘g2 ♗a4 17. ♗h5± Sveshnikov – Ivkov, Sochi 1983;

b4) 10...♕c7 11. ♘g5 (11. ♖e1 ♘c8 12. ♘f1 ♘b6 13. ♗f4 (13. ♗g5! h6 14. ♗h4 ♗a4 15. ♕c1 ♔d7 16. ♕e3! ♗c2 17. ♖bc1 ♗h7 18. ♘3d1! ♖e8 19. ♗d1 =, Predojević – Wang Hao, Istanbul 2005) 13...♘b3 14. ♘3d2 ♘a5 15. ♘g3 ♗a4 16. ♕c1 0–0–0∞, Ni Hua – Bareev, Beijing 2003) 11...h6 12. ♘h3 0–0–0 13. ♘f4 ♔b8 14. ♘h5 ♔a8 15. g4 ♘c8 16. f4 ♘b6 17. ♕e1±, I. Zaitsev – Vasyukov, 37th USSR Championship, Moscow 1969;

b5) 10...♖c8 11. g3 h6 12. ♘h4 ♗b5 13. ♖a1 ♘b3 14. ♘×b3 ♗a4 15. ♗e3 ♕×b3! 16. ♕d2 ♖c6! (16...♕c2? 17. ♗d1 +−) 17. ♗d1 ♕b5 18. ♗g4± Sveshnikov – Gofshtein, Rostov on Don 1976;

b6) 10...h6 11. ♖e1 (11. ♕c2 ♕c7 12. b3 c×b3 13. ♘×b3 ♗a4 14. ♘fd2 ♘ec6 15. ♕b2⇄ Tal – Petrosian, Tbilisi 1956) 11...♗c6 12. ♘f1 ♕b3 13. ♗f4 ♗a4 14. ♕c1 ♕b6 15. ♘3d2 ♘g6 16. ♗e3 ♘h4 17. f4 h5 18. ♗f2 ♘f5⇄ Sveshnikov – Eingorn, 52nd USSR Championship, Riga 1985;

9...♗e7 10. ♖e1 (10. g3; 10. ♖b1 ♘h6 11. ♖e1 ♘f5 12. ♘f1 0–0–0 13. ♗f4 ♖df8 14. ♘g3 ♘×g3 15. ♗×g3 h5 16. h4± Prié – Apicella, French Championship, Auxerre 1996) 10...♘h6! 11. ♕c2 ♘f5 12. ♗d1!? h5 13. ♖b1 ♕c7 14. ♘f1 0–0–0 15. ♗g5! f6 16. ♗f4 ♕b6 17. ♘g3⇄ Kholmov – Naumkin, Moscow 1991;

9...f6 10. ♖b1 ♘e7 11. b3 c×b3 12. c4 ♗a4 13. e×f6 g×f6 14. c×d5 ♘×d5 15. ♘e4 ♗e7 16. ♗d2 ♖c8 17. ♕e1 ⯑ Hába – Schmittdiel, Böblingen 1999.

302 **11. ♕c2!?** 0–0–0 (11...♘b3 12. ♘×b3 ♗a4 13. ♘fd2 ♗×b3 14. ♘×b3 c×b3 15. ♕d3 ♖c8 16. ♕f3±) 12. b3 c×b3 13. ♘×b3 ♗a4 14. ♘fd2 ♘ec6 15. ♕a2± I. Zaitsev– Naumkin, Moscow 1995; **11. ♖e1!?**.

303 11...♘ec6 12. ♘h4 ♗e7 13. ♘g2 0–0–0 14. ♔h1 ♗e8 15. f4 f5 16. e×f6 ♗×f6 17. ♗h5 ♘e7 18. ♗×e8 ♖d×e8 19. g4 g6 20. ♘f3 ½–½ Sveshnikov–Faragó, Novi Sad 1979.

304 12. b4 c×b3 13. c4 ♗a4 14. ♗b2⇄.

305 12...♔b8 13. ♗h5 g6 14. ♗e2 ♕c7 15. ♘g2 ♗c6 16. h4 ♕d7 17. h5 ♗a4 18. ♕e1 ♗c2 19. ♖a1 ♗g7 20. ♘e3 ♗a4∞ Timman– Liberzon, Venice 1974.

306 15. b3! c×b3 16. ♘×b3 f5 (16...♘×b3 17. ♖×b3 ♕c7 18. ♗×d7+ ♕×d7 19. ♕h5±) 17. ♗h3!± I. Zaitsev–Faragó, Szolnok 1975.

Notes

Chapter 3

A summary of the 3. e5 system

It is time to draw some conclusions. Briefly they are as follows:

1. e4 e6?

An error – 1...c5! is better, or failing that 1...e5!? although in the latter case Black has serious problems with the defence of the e5 pawn after 2. ♘f3 ♘c6 3. ♗b5!.

2. d4 d5

Otherwise White has a strong pawn pair in the centre and a winning position.

3. e5!?

Objectively 3. ♘c3! is stronger, after which Black has a bad position. But White also has a big advantage after 3. e5!?, greater than he has after 1. e4! in the initial position.

3...c5!

The correct move, beginning immediate counterplay against White's pawn centre. The alternative plan to exchange the light-squared bishops with 3...b6 4. c3 or 3...♘e7 4. ♘f3 b6 5. c3 ♕d7 6. a4 does not offer Black any prospect of equality.

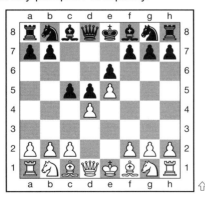

4. c3

The gambits introduced by Nimzowitsch bring White no advantage. In fact 4. ♕g4?! is not even sufficient for equality (see the annotations to the game Sveshnikov–Komarov, Vrnjačka Banja 1999 (Volume 1, game 28 on page 57). The line 4. ♘f3?! c×d4! 5. ♗d3 is somewhat better. However, I advise all players below the level of candidate master to include these gambits in their repertoire and learn how to handle them by studying the games of Nimzowitsch and Keres. Mastering the methods of gambit play is an important stage in the development of a chessplayer. The move 4. d×c5?! – suggested by Louis Paulsen – was later tried a few times by Steinitz but gives Black easy equality. He has several playable plans, such as that demonstrated by Emanuel Lasker in his game against Tarrasch (St. Petersburg 1914; Volume 1, game 7 on page 18). Also playable is 4...♗×c5 5. ♗d3 ♘c6 6. ♘f3 ♘ge7 with equal chances.

4...♘c6!

The best move, obeying all the principles of the opening. Furthermore it is consistent with Black's plan of counterattack against the d4 pawn. Transferring the other knight to c6 does not equalise, since it loses time and weakens the kingside. The plan with 4...♗d7 and 5...a6 is also too slow.

5. ♘f3

White has nothing better than this move, since after 5. ♗e3?! c×d4 6. c×d4 Black can turn his fire on the e5 pawn with 6...♘h6, 7...♘f5 and 8...f6!?. The move 5. f4 is not in harmony with the spirit of this opening, since it incarcerates the c1 bishop, weakens the light squares and simply wastes time.

5...♕b6!

We know from the annotated games and the Encyclopaedia that the variations 5...♘h6?! 6. dxc5! and 5...♘ge7 6. ♘a3! are not sufficient for equality.

An interesting possibility for Black is the move 5...♗d7!? recommended by Botvinnik, which we call the "flexible defence". However, this line also offers White a greater choice than he has after the more active 5...♕b6, since he has the additional possibility 6. ♗e3!?. After the insertion of the move ...♗d7, the immediate development of the bishop at e3 is more favourable than on the 5th move, since after an exchange on f5 (♗d3×♘f5) White will gain a tempo, because Black will have to move the bishop again (to e6) to defend the d5 pawn (in reply to ♘c3). If instead Black sends the knight to g4 via h6 and then exchanges on e3, he is liable to come under attack on the kingside. Alternatively White can withdraw the bishop from e3, leaving the g4 knight out on a limb in the danger zone.

The strongest reply to 5...♗d7 is definitely 6. ♗e2! after which a counter-attack directed at d4 comes too late and Black must switch to attacking the e5 pawn with 6...f6!?. But experience has shown that he does not equalise in this case. The plan used several times by Korchnoi comes into consideration: 5...♗d7 6. ♗e2 ♘ge7 7. 0–0 ♘g6!?.

6. a3!

An attentive reading of this book will have persuaded you that 6. ♗e2?! brings no advantage after 6...cxd4! 7. cxd4 ♘h6!, the move order used against me by Portisch near the end of the 1993 Biel Interzonal 1993 (game 51 on page 43). Portisch is well known for his expertise in the openings; his games constitute a whole openings manual in themselves! Now 8. ♗×h6?! ♕×b2! is bad, since White does not get enough compensation for the pawn. But if Black plays 6...♘h6?! instead of 6...cxd4! then the variation 7. ♗×h6!

g×h6 (7...♕×b2? loses to 8. ♗e3!) 8. ♕d2 ♗g7 9. ♘a3 is better for White.

The move 6. ♗d3?! is inadequate because of 6...cxd4! 7. cxd4 ♗d7 8. ♘c3 ♘xd4 9. ♘×d4 ♕×d4, and White has serious worries about equalising.

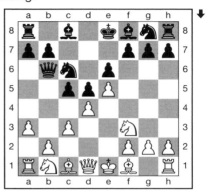

6...♘h6!?

Only at this point does Black have a choice of reasonable continuations.

a) 6...c4!? closing the position. Now after 7. ♘bd2! Black cannot ignore the threat of 8. b3 since if 7...♗d7?! White can gain the advantage by 8.b3! cxb3 9. ♘xb3 ♘a5 10. ♘×a5 ♕×a5 11. ♗d2 ♕a4 12. ♕b1 as shown in the game Sveshnikov–Timman, Tilburg 1992 (Volume 1, game 29 on page 60). But even after the better move 7...♘a5 White still has an advantage, as both theory and practice testify.

b) 6...♗d7 7. b4 cxd4 8. cxd4 ♖c8 9. ♗b2 ♘a5 10. ♘bd2 ♘c4, and here too theory promises White the better game by 11. ♘×c4 dxc4 12. ♖c1 a5 13. ♘d2!.

c) 6...a5. White now has three playable continuations – 7. ♗d3!?, 7. ♗e2 and 7. b3!?.

The move 7. ♗d3!? entails a pawn sacrifice: 7...cxd4 8. cxd4 ♗d7 9. ♘c3 ♘×d4 10. ♘×d4 ♕×d4. For White to gain any advantage, improvements need to be found for him in the games I. Zaitsev–Lempert, Moscow 1994 (game 26 on page 26) and Shirov–Anand, Teheran 2000 (Volume 1, game 22 on page 44). If no white advantage can be found in that line, White can play 7. &e2 instead, since now the plan for Black shown in the game Sveshnikov – Portisch (game 51 on page 43) does not work (there is no check on a5 available, the b5 square is weakened, and White does not lose castling rights). On the other hand Black can develop an initiative on the queenside with 7...a4. Finally White can play 7. b3!? as in the game Sveshnikov – Volkov, Togliatti 2003 (Volume 1, page 55) and this should be sufficient for some advantage.

7. b4 c×d4 8. c×d4 &f5 9. &b2!

The alternative 9. &e3?! brings White no advantage in view of 9...f6! 10. e×f6 (10. b5 leads to a draw after 10. &×e5, as in Romanishin – Lputian, Yerevan 1988 (Volume 1, page 77); if 10. &d3?! Black even gains the advantage; see Potkin – Filippov, Togliatti 2003; Volume 1, game 40 on page 77) 10...g×f6 with chances for both sides (Morozevich – Bareev, Monte Carlo 2002, game 42 on page 36).

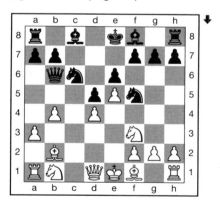

Now Black is again presented with a choice. The main options are 9...&d7 and 9...&e7. Instead 9...a5 10. b5 gives White the advantage, as in Sveshnikov – Bareev, Moscow 1995 (Note 247 on page 100 and game [1] on page 116). Incidentally, 9...a5 was Korchnoi's choice in a rapid game against Erenburg

(See Volume 1, Test position 65 on page 145; Solution on page 155).

These six positions (the four black options at move six and the two at move nine) are the main bastions of Black's defence against 3. e5. They also represent the directions in which I expect the theory to develop in the coming years.

A.

9...&d7 10. g4

Black has fewer problems after 10. &e2 &e7 11. 0–0 0–0 with chances for both sides, Sveshnikov – Bareev, Moscow 1990 (game [2] on page 116).

10...&fe7

Black fails to solve his problems with 10...&h6 11. &g1! f6 12. e×f6 g×f6 13. &c3 &f7 14. &a4 &c7 15. &c1 &f4 (15...&d6?! is weaker, see Sveshnikov – Dvoiris, Cheliabinsk 2004 (game 59 on page 52) 16. &c5 and White had the better chances in the game Short – Lputian, Batumi 1999 (Volume 1, game 52 on page 103), which is the most important game played with this variation. However, on this theme I also recommend detailed study of the games Vasyukov – Bukhman, St. Petersburg 1994 (Volume 1, page 104), Savić – Lputian, Neum 2002 (game [3] on page 117), Lautier – Bauer, French Championship, Val d'Isère 2002 (page 50) and Vallejo Pons – Hillarp Persson, Benidorm 2003 (game [4] on page 117).

11. &c3 &a5

The earliest known game with this variation is Rellstab – Unzicker, West German Championship, Bad Pyrmont 1950 (game [5] on page 117). Other important games include: Shirov – Kramnik, Monte Carlo 1997 (Volume 1, game 48 on page 95) and Nevednichy – Lputian, Ohrid 2001 (game [6] on page 118).

12. &c2!?

An unclear position results from 12. ♘d2 ♖c8 13. ♖c1.

12...♘c4 13. ♘×c4 d×c4 14. ♘d2 ♘d5 15. ♘×c4 ♕c6 16. ♘e4 ♘b6 17. ♘cd6+ ♗×d6 18. ♘×d6+ ♔e7 19. ♕×c6 ♗×c6 20. ♖g1, and Black had to struggle for a draw (Sveshnikov – Potkin, Russian Championship, Krasnoyarsk 2003; Volume 1, page 95). You should also study the games Alekseev – S. Ivanov, Tomsk 2001 (game [7] on page 118) and Sveshnikov – Radjabov, Tallinn 2004 (game 61 on page 53).

B.

9...♗e7 10. ♗d3

Another interesting idea here is 10. h4!? with the plan of capturing later on f5 (♗×♘) and then exchanging the dark-squared bishops; this plan was used in a game of Mark Tseitlin's. With the help of this move I was able to defeat Bareev in the 1996 Russian Championship (Volume 1, game 34 on page 65) and Doroshkevich in St. Petersburg 2000 (Volume 1, page 65). See also the games Grischuk – Lputian, 35th Olympiad, Bled 2002 (Volume 1, game 51 on page 101) and Vysochin – Polivanov, St. Petersburg 2002 (Volume 1, page 102).

10...h5 (10...♗d7 is weaker: 11. g4 ♘h6 12. ♖g1 with advantage for White) 11. ♗d3 a5 12. ♗×f5 e×f5 13. ♘c3 ♗e6 14. b5 a4 15. ♕d3 ♘a7 16. 0–0 ♖c8 17. ♗c1 ♖c4 18. ♘e2!? ♕×b5 19. ♗g5 ⯢.

10...a5!?

Or 10...♗d7 11. 0–0 ♖c8 12. ♘bd2 g5!? 13. ♘b3 h5 (13...g4 14. ♘fd2 h5 15. ♗×f5 e×f5 16. ♘c5 ♗e6 17. ♘db3±) 14. ♖c1 g4 15. ♘e1 a5 16. ♗×f5 e×f5 17. ♘d3±, Khalifman – Dolmatov, Rethymnon 2003 (game 20 on page 22).

11. ♕a4!

This move restrains Black's queenside initiative, allowing White to complete his development and then start active operations on the kingside.

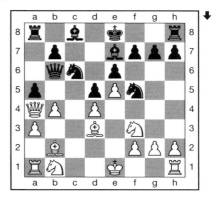

11...0–0 12. b5 ♗d7

The order of moves used in the game Kiik – Korchnoi, Rilton Cup, Stockholm 2003 (Volume 1, page 95) deserves attention: 12...♘h4!? 13. ♘×h4 ♗×h4 14. g3?! (14. 0–0± is better).

13. 0–0 ♘a7 14. ♘c3 ♘h4 15. ♘×h4 ♗×h4 16. ♕d1 f5 17. ♘a4 ♕d8.

In the game Motylev – Alavkin, Sochi 2004 (Game [8] on page 118) White also gained an advantage with 18. ♕b3.

18. ♕e2±

Finally I should like to stress that if you want to keep up to date with developments in a particular opening variation, do not confine your interest to the games of players with a high ELO rating: look at the games of players who specialise in that variation, since they are always on the lookout for new ideas.

Chapter 4

Games for further study

In his final chapter of this Advanced Course the author picked out the following eight games as being especially significant. The Publisher has therefore agreed to include these in an extra chapter for further study. Diagrams have been placed at significant points, suggested by Sveshnikov's comments in Chapter 3.

Game [1]
Sveshnikov – Bareev
Moscow (Rapidplay) 1995

1. e4 e6 2. d4 d5 3. e5 c5 4. c3 ♘c6 5. ♘f3 ♛b6 6. a3 ♘h6 7. b4 c×d4 8. c×d4 ♘f5 9. ♗b2 a5 10. b5 a4 11. g4 ♘fe7 12. ♘c3 ♘b8 13. ♗d3 ♘d7 14. 0–0 ♘g6 15. ♖c1 ♗e7 16. ♘×a4 ♛a5 17. ♘c5

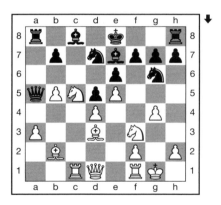

17...0–0 18. ♗×g6 h×g6 19. ♛d3 ♛b6 20. a4 ♗×c5 21. d×c5 ♘×c5 22. ♛e3 ♘×a4 23. ♗d4 ♛d8 24. ♖a1 ♗d7 25. ♖fb1 ♛e7 26. h4 b6 27. ♗×b6 ♘×b6 28. ♛×b6 ♖×a1 29. ♖×a1 ♛b4 30. ♛d4 ♛×b5 31. ♖a7 ♖c8 32. ♛f4 ♗e8 33. ♔g2 ♛b6 34. ♖e7 ♔f8 35. ♖×e8+ ♔×e8 36. h5 ♖c4 37. ♛g5 ♛d8 38. ♛×d8+ ♔×d8 39. ♔g3 g×h5 40. g×h5 ♔e7 41. ♘g5 ♖c1 42. f4 ♖f1 43. ♘f3 ♖×f3+ 44. ♔×f3 f5 45. ♔g3 ♔d7 46. ♔h4 d4 47. ♔g5 ♔e7 48. ♔g6 ♔f8 0–1

Game [2]
Sveshnikov – Bareev
Moscow 1990

1. e4 e6 2. d4 d5 3. e5 c5 4. c3 ♘c6 5. ♘f3 ♛b6 6. a3 ♘h6 7. b4 c×d4 8. c×d4 ♘f5 9. ♗b2 ♗d7 10. ♗e2 ♗e7 11. 0–0 0–0

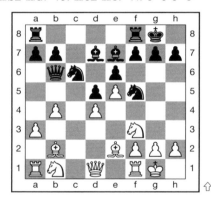

12. ♛d2 [12. ♗d3!?] 12...f6 13. g4 ♘h6 14. e×f6 ♖×f6 15. g5 ♖×f3 [15...♖g6] 16. ♗×f3 ♘f5 17. ♖d1 ♛d8 [17...♘f8!? ∞] 18. ♗g4 ♗×g5 19. ♛d3 ♗f4 20. ♗×f5 e×f5 21. ♘d2 ♛g5+ 22. ♔h1 ♛h4 23. ♘f3 ♛×f2 24. ♗c1 ♗×c1 25. ♖a×c1 f4 26. ♖c2 ♛e3 27. ♛×e3 f×e3 28. ♔g2 ♗g4 29. ♖e2 ♖e8 30. ♖d3 ♖e4 31. ♖e×e3 h6 32. b5 ♗×f3+ 33. ♔f2!!± ♘a5 34. ♔×f3 ♖h4 35. ♔g3 ♖h5 36. ♖e5 ♖×e5 37. d×e5 ♔f7 38. ♖×d5 ♔e6 39. ♖c5 ♔f5 40. h4 g6 41. a4 b6 42. ♖c7 ♔×e5 43. ♖×a7 ♘c4 44. ♖g7 g5 45. h5+– ♘d6 46. ♖g6 ♘e4+ 47. ♔f3 ♘c5 48. ♖×b6 ♘×a4 49. ♖×h6 1–0

Game [3]
Savić – Lputian
Neum 2002

1. e4 e6 2. d4 d5 3. e5 c5 4. c3 ᐁc6 5. ᐁf3
Wb6 6. a3 ᐁh6 7. b4 c×d4 8. c×d4 ᐁf5
9. ᐃb2 ᐃd7 10. g4

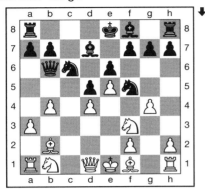

10...ᐁh6 11. ᐄg1 f6 12. e×f6 g×f6 13. ᐁc3
ᐁf7 14. ᐁa4 Wc7 15. ᐄc1 Wf4 16. ᐄc3 ᐁg5
17. b5 ᐁa5 18. ᐁ×g5 f×g5 19. ᐃc1 W×h2
20. ᐄgg3 ᐃd6 21. ᐄh3 Wg1 22. We2 0–0
23. ᐃe3 ᐁc4 24. ᐄ×c4 ᐃ×b5 25. f3 ᐃ×c4
26. ᐃ×g1 ᐃ×e2 27. ᐃ×e2 ᐃ×a3 28. ᐃe3 e5
29. d×e5 ᐄae8 30. ᐃc5 ᐃ×c5 ½–½

Game [4]
Vallejo Pons – Hillarp Persson
Benidorm 2003

1. e4 e6 2. d4 d5 3. e5 c5 4. c3 Wb6 5. ᐁf3
ᐁc6 6. a3 ᐁh6 7. b4 c×d4 8. c×d4 ᐁf5
9. ᐃb2 ᐃd7 10. g4 ᐁh6 11. ᐄg1 f6 12. e×f6
g×f6 13. ᐁc3 ᐁf7 14. ᐁa4

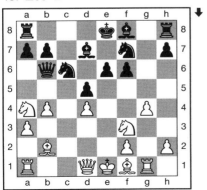

14...Wd8 15. ᐁc5 ᐃc8 16. ᐄc1 ᐁd6 17. ᐃd3
We7 18. g5 f5 19. ᐁe5 ᐁ×e5 20. d×e5
ᐁe4 21. Wh5+ ᐃd8 22. ᐁb3 ᐄg8 23. h4
ᐃd7 24. ᐃd4 b6 25. ᐃe2 ᐃe8 26. Wf3 h6
27. g×h6 ᐄ×g1 28. ᐄ×g1 ᐃ×h6 29. ᐃe3 ᐃ×e3
30. ᐃ×e3 W×h4 31. ᐁd4 ᐃf7 32. ᐄh1 Wg5+
33. Wf4 Wg7 34. f3 ᐄc8 35. f×e4 d×e4
36. Wh4+ ᐃc7 37. ᐄc1+ ᐃb8 38. ᐄ×c8+
ᐃ×c8 39. ᐃa6+ ᐃd7 40. ᐃb5+ ᐃc8
41. ᐃa6+ ᐃd7 42. ᐃb5+ ᐃc8 43. ᐃa6+ ᐃd7
44. Wh2 Wg5+ 45. Wf4 Wg1+ 46. Wf2 f4+
0–1

Game [5]
Rellstab – Unzicker
West German Championship,
Bad Pyrmont 1950

1. e4 e6 2. d4 d5 3. e5 c5 4. c3 ᐁc6 5. ᐁf3
Wb6 6. a3 c×d4 7. c×d4 ᐁge7 8. b4 ᐁf5
9. ᐃb2 ᐃd7 10. g4 ᐁfe7 11. ᐁc3

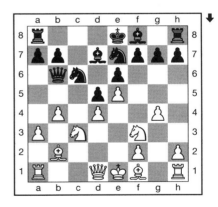

11...ᐁg6 12. h4 h5 13. g5 ᐄc8 14. ᐁa4 Wd8
15. ᐁc5 ᐃ×c5 16. d×c5 Wc7 17. We2 0–0
18. We3 d4 19. ᐁ×d4 ᐁc×e5 20. ᐃe2 ᐁf4
21. 0–0–0 ᐁ×e2+ 22. W×e2 ᐁg6 23. ᐃb1
b6 24. c×b6 W×b6 25. ᐄd2 a5 26. b×a5
W×a5 27. ᐁb3 Wa4 28. We3 e5 29. ᐃa1
ᐃc6 30. ᐁc5 Wc4 31. ᐄc1 W×h4 32. ᐃ×e5
ᐁ×e5 33. W×e5 ᐄa8 34. ᐄd3 ᐄfe8 35. Wd6
Wb4 36. ᐁb7 Wb5 37. g6 f×g6 38. ᐁc5 ᐄeb8
39. ᐄd2 ᐄ×a3+ 0–1

Game [6]
Nevednichy – Lputian
Ohrid 2001

1. e4 e6 2. d4 d5 3. e5 c5 4. c3 ♘c6
5. ♘f3 ♕b6 6. a3 ♘h6 7. b4 cxd4 8. cxd4
♘f5 9. ♗b2 ♗d7 10. g4 ♘fe7 11. ♘c3 ♘g6
12. ♘a4

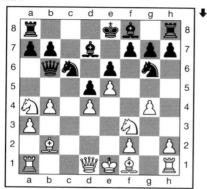

12...♕d8 13. h4 h5 14. g5 b6 15. ♗d3 ♘f4
16. ♗a6 ♘e7 17. ♘c3 ♘f5 18. ♘e2 ♘g2+
19. ♔d2 b5 20. ♕g1 g6 21. ♕xg2 ♕b6
22. ♘g3 ♘e7 23. ♘e1 ♕xa6 24. ♘d3 ♘c8
25. ♘c5 ♕c6 26. ♖hc1 ♘b6 27. ♔e1 ♘c4
28. ♗c3 ♗e7 29. ♘f1 0–0 30. ♘d2 ♗xc5
31. dxc5 ♘xd2 32. ♗xd2 d4 33. ♕xc6 ♗xc6
34. ♔e2 ♖fd8 35. ♔d3 ♔f8 36. f4 ♖d7 ½–½

game [7]
Alekseev – S. Ivanov
Tomsk 2001

1. e4 e6 2. d4 d5 3. e5 c5 4. c3 ♕b6 5. ♘f3
♘c6 6. a3 ♘h6 7. b4 cxd4 8. cxd4 ♘f5
9. ♗b2 ♗d7 10. g4 ♘fe7 11. ♘c3 ♘a5

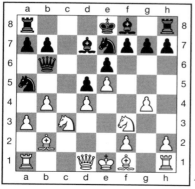

12. ♕c2 ♘c4 13. ♗xc4 dxc4 14. ♘d2 ♘d5
15. ♘xc4 ♕c6 16. ♘e4 ♘b6 17. ♘cd6+ ♗xd6
18. ♘xd6+ ♔e7 19. ♕xc6 ♗xc6 20. ♖g1 ♘c8
21. b5 ♗d5 22. ♖c1 ♘xd6 23. ♖c7+ ♔d8
24. exd6 ♖c8 25. ♖xc8+ ♔xc8 26. ♗c3 ♔d7
27. ♗b4 ♖c8 28. ♔d2 ½–½

Game [8]
Motylev – Alavkin
Sochi 2004

1. e4 e6 2. d4 d5 3. e5 c5 4. c3 ♘c6 5. ♘f3
♕b6 6. a3 ♘h6 7. b4 cxd4 8. cxd4 ♘f5
9. ♗b2 ♗e7 10. ♗d3 a5 11. ♕a4 ♗d7 12. b5
0–0 13. 0–0 ♘a7 14. ♘c3 ♘h4 15. ♘xh4
♗xh4 16. ♕d1 f5 17. ♘a4 ♕d8 18. ♕b3

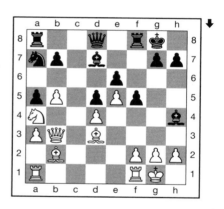

18...b6 19. ♘c3 ♗e8 20. a4 ♗e7 21. ♘e2
♗f7 22. h3 ♗b4 23. ♗a3 ♗xa3 24. ♕xa3
♖c8 25. ♖ac1 ♕d7 26. g4 fxg4 27. hxg4
♖xc1 28. ♖xc1 ♖c8 29. ♔g2 ♖xc1 30. ♕xc1
♘c8 31. ♕c2 g6 32. ♕c1 ♔g7 33. ♘g3 ♘e7
34. ♕g5 ♘g8 35. ♘h5+ ♔h8 36. ♘f6 ♕e7
37. ♕h4 h6 38. g5 ♔g7 39. gxh6+ ♘xh6
40. ♘h5+ ♔f8 41. ♕f4 gxh5 42. ♕xh6+ ♔e8
43. ♗g6 ♕h4 44. ♗xf7+ ♔xf7 45. f3 ♕xd4
46. ♕xh5+ ♔e7 47. ♕h7+ ♔d8 48. ♕g8+
♔e7 49. ♕g7+ ♔e8 50. ♕g6+ ♔e7 51. ♕f6+
♔d7 52. ♕f7+ ♔d8 53. ♕xe6 ♕d2+ 54. ♔h3
♕d4 55. ♕g8+ ♔e7 56. ♕g7+ ♔e8 57. ♕h8+
♔e7 58. ♕h4+ 1–0

Chapter 5

The latest theoretical developments

The publication date of the German edition of this book was in July 2006. Since the research for that edition was completed, literally thousands of games have been played in national and international tournaments – 6,500 alone in the 36th Chess Olympiad in Turin (20th May to 4th June 2006). Naturally the Advance Variation of the French Defence has been subjected to further tests. To reflect these developments, for the English edition of the book Evgeny Sveshnikov has specially selected what, in his opinion, are the twenty-four theoretically most important recent games for further study material.

Game 62
Sveshnikov – Yashtylov
Russian League, Cheliabinsk 2005

1. e4 e6 2. d4 d5 3. e5 c5 4. c3 ♘c6 5. ♘f3 ♕b6 6. a3 f6!? 7. b4

7. ♗d3!? c4 (7...fxe5 8. ♘xe5±; 7...♗d7 8. b4 cxd4 9. cxd4±) 8. ♗c2 fxe5 (8...♗d7 9. ♘bd2 0-0-0 10. b3 cxb3 11. ♘xb3±) 9. ♘xe5 ♘xe5 10. dxe5 ♘e7 11. ♘d2 g6 12. ♘f3±.

7...fxe5

7...c4!?⇄; 7...cxd4 8. cxd4±.

8. bxc5

8. dxc5!? ♕c7 9. c4 ♘f6 10. ♘c3↑ (10. ♘c3 d4∞); 8. ♘xe5±.

8...♕a5!

8...♕c7?! 9. ♗b5±.

9. dxe5

9. ♘xe5 ♘xe5 10. dxe5 ♗xc5 11. ♕g4 g6 (11...♕c7?! 12. ♗b5+±) 12. ♗d3⇄ ♘e7 13. ♗g5 ♕c7 14. ♗f6 ♖f8 15. 0-0 ♘g8!? (15...♘c6) 16. ♗b5+ ♔f7 17. ♗h8 ♘h6

18. ♕f4+ (18. ♕h4 ♖xh8∓) 18...♔g8 19. ♗f6 ♘f5∓.

9...♗xc5 10. ♗d3 ♘h6?!

10...♘ge7 11. 0-0 (11. ♕c2 ♕c7∞) 11...0-0⇄.

11. ♗xh6 gxh6 12. 0-0±

12. ♕c1!? ♕c7 (12...♗f8!? 13. 0-0 ♗g7 14. ♖e1±) 13. ♕xh6 ♘xe5 14. ♗b5+ ♘c6 15. 0-0↑.

12...♕c7 13. ♕e2

13. ♘bd2!? ♘xe5 (13...0-0 14. ♘b3 ♗e7 15. ♖e1±) 14. ♘xe5 ♕xe5 15. ♘b3∓ (15. ♖e1∓).

13...♕g7 14. ♘bd2

14. ♔h1!? ♖g8 15. ♖g1±.

14...♗d7 15. ♘b3 ♗b6 16. ♖ae1

16. ♔h1; 16. c4.

16...♖g8 17. g3 ♕e7 18. ♘fd4 0-0-0

18...♕xa3 19. ♕h5+ ♔d8 20. ♕xh6↑.

19. ♕h5?!

19. a4!? ♘xd4 20. cxd4 ♗xa4 21. ♖c1+ ♔b8 22. ♘c5 ♗e8 23. ♖c3∓.

19...♕xa3! 20. ♕xh6?

20. ♖a1 ♕f8 21. f4∓.

20...♔b8?

20...♗xd4! 21. ♘xd4 ♘xd4 22. ♖a1 ♘f3+
23. ♔g2 ♕f8 24. ♕h5 ♘d2−+.

21. ♖a1⇄ ½–½

Game 63
Sveshnikov – Alavkin
Russian League, Cheliabinsk 2005

**1. e4 e6 2. d4 d5 3. e5 c5 4. c3 ♕b6
5. ♘f3 ♗d7 6. a3 cxd4 7. cxd4 ♗b5
8. ♗xb5+ ♕xb5 9. ♘c3 ♕a6 10. b4!?**

10. ♘e2 ♘e7 11. 0–0 ♘d7 12. ♘f4±
(12. ♘g3±; 12. b4±).

10...♘d7

10...♗xb4?! 11. axb4 ♕xa1 12. ♘b5±.

11. ♗d2 ♘e7 12. b5?

12. a4!? ♕b6 (12...♖c8 13. ♘b5 ♘c6
14. ♘d6+ ♗xd6 15. b5 ♕b6 16. bxc6 ♖xc6
17. exd6+−; 12...♘f5 13. g4 ♘h6 14. ♘b5
♖c8 15. ♖c1 ♖xc1 16. ♕xc1 ♕c6 17. ♕xc6
bxc6 18. ♘xa7+−) 13. a5 ♕d8 14. a6±,
Belov−Lisy, Vladimir 2002.

12...♕b6 13. a4 a5! 14. bxa6

14. 0–0±.

14...bxa6 15. a5

15. 0–0 ♘c6 16. ♘e2 ♗e7 17. ♖b1 ♕c7
18. ♕c2 ♖c8 19. ♕d3 ♕a7 20. ♖b3 0–0
21. ♗g5↑.

**15...♕c7! 16. 0–0 ♘c6 17. ♕a4 ♗e7
18. ♖fc1 ♖c8 19. ♘a2 0–0 20. ♘b4 ♗xb4**

20...♘db8 21. ♘xc6 ♘xc6 22. ♖ab1± ♕d7
23. ♖b6 ♘xe5 24. ♕xd7 ♖xc1+ (24...♘xd7
25. ♖xc8 ♖xc8 26. ♖xa6±) 25. ♗xc1 ♘xd7
26. ♖xa6 (26. ♖b7 ♖d8 27. ♖a7 ♗f6 28. ♗f4
♘b8 29. ♗c7 ♖f8 30. ♘e5±) 26...♘b8
27. ♖a8 ♘c6 28. ♖xf8+ ♔xf8 29. a6 ♔e8
30. ♘e5 ♘a7 31. ♗f4±.

21. ♗xb4 ♖fe8! 22. h3?!

a) 22. ♕c2 ♕b7 23. ♗c3±;

b) 22. ♖ab1! ♕b7 23. ♗d2 ♕a8 24. ♖b2
♘db8 25. ♖bc2±;

c) 22. ♗d6 ♕xa5 23. ♕xa5 ♘xa5 24. ♖xc8
♖xc8 25. ♔f1 ♘c4 26. ♖xa6=.

**22...♕b7! 23. ♗c5 ♘xc5 24. ♖xc5 ♘a7=
25. ♖ac1 h6 26. g4?!**

26. ♘e1 ♘b5 27. ♘d3±.

26...♘b5 27. ♕c2?!

27. g5∞; 27. ♕b4 ♖ed8 28. ♔g2 ♖xc5
29. ♕xc5±.

27...♘a3! 28. ♕c3?!

a) 28. ♖xc8 ♘xc2 29. ♖xe8+ ♔h7 30. ♖f8
(30. ♖f8⇄) 30...♕b2 31. ♖d1 ♕b7 (31...♕b3
32. ♖xf7 ♔g6 33. ♖f8⇄) 32. ♔g2=;

b) 28. ♕c3?! ♖xc5 29. dxc5 (29. ♕xc5?
♘c4∓) 29...♘c4 30. ♕d2 ♖c8 31. ♖b1 ♕a7
32. ♘xc4 ♕xc5 33. ♖b6 ♕xc4∓.

½–½

Game 64
Brunello – Luther
Verona 2005

**1. e4 e6 2. d4 d5 3. e5 c5 4. c3 ♘c6
5. ♘f3 ♗d7 6. a3?! f6 7. ♗d3 ♘h6?**

7...c4!⇄.

8. 0–0

⌂8. exf6 ♕xf6 9. ♗g5 ♕f7 10. b4↑.

**8...♘f7 9. ♖e1 fxe5 10. ♘xe5 ♘cxe5
11. dxe5 ♕c7 12. ♘d2 0–0–0**

12...c4 13. ♗c2 ♗e7 14. ♘f3 0–0⇄.

13. ♘f3 ♗e7 14. b4! c4

14...g5!?.

**15. ♗c2 g5 16. ♕e2 g4 17. ♘d4 ♖dg8
18. a4 h5 19. ♘f5!?**

19. ♗f4 ♗g5 20. ♕e3 h4⇄.

19...♗d8

a) 19...exf5 20. e6 ♗d6 (20...♗f6 21. ♗xf5
♗xc3 22. exd7+ ♔b8 23. ♗b2±) 21. ♗xf5
♗xe6 22. ♗xe6+ ♔b8 23. ♗xd5 ♗xh2+
24. ♔h1±;

b) 19...♗g5!? 20. ♗xg5 ♖xg5 21. ♘d6+
♘xd6 22. exd6 ♕xd6 23. ♕e3 ♖gg8
24. ♕xa7 h4 25. a5 g3 26. fxg3 hxg3 27. h3
♔c7 28. ♕e3±.

20. a5

20. ♘d4 h4 21. ♗f4 ♛b8!? (21…♗g5?! 22. ♛×g4 h3 23. g3 ♘h6 24. ♛f3 ♖f8 25. ♘e2±) 22. a5 ♗c7 23. ♗a4 ♗×a4 24. ♖×a4 ♔d7⇄.

20…e×f5 21. e6 ♘d6

21…♗c6!?∞ 22. e×f7 ♛×f7 23. ♗f4 ⯒.

22. e×d7+ ♛×d7 23. ♗a4.

23. ♗f4!? ♖e8 24. ♛d2 ♘e4 25. ♛d4±.

23…♛f7 24. ♗f4 ♘e4 25. ♛e3 ♗c7

25…b6 26. ♗c6±.

26. ♗×c7 ♛×c7 27. ♛×a7± ♘×c3.

27…♖g6 28. ♗c2±.

28. a6 b5□

28…b6 29. ♛a8+ ♛b8 30. ♛c6+ ♛c7 31. ♖e7 ♛×c6 32. ♗×c6+−.

29. ♛d4 ♘×a4 30. a7+− 1–0.

Game 65
Shirov – Del Rio Angelis
Gibraltar Masters, Caleta 2005

1. e4 e6 2. d4 d5 3. e5 c5 4. c3 ♘c6 5. ♘f3 ♗d7 6. ♗e2!

6. ♗e3!?.

6…♘ge7 7. ♘a3.

a) 7. 0–0 c×d4 8. c×d4 ♛b6 9. ♘c3 ♘f5 10. ♘a4±;

b) 7. d×c5 ♘g6 8. ♗e3 ♘g×e5 9. ♘×e5 ♘×e5 10. f4 ♘c6 11. ♘d2 ♗e7⇄.

7…c×d4 8. c×d4 ♘f5 9. ♘c2 ♛b6

9…♘b4 10. 0–0 ♘×c2 11. ♛×c2 ♛b6 12. ♛d3±.

10. 0–0 ♘a5!? .

10…♖c8!?⇄.

11. g4

11. b3!? ♗b5 12. ♗×b5+ ♛×b5 13. ♘e3 ♘×e3 14. f×e3 ♗e7 15. ♗d2±.

11…♘e7 12. ♘fe1

12. b3 ♗b5 13. ♗a3 ♘g6 14. ♗×b5+ ♛×b5 15. ♗×f8 ♖×f8 16. ♛d2 ♘c6 17. ♖fe1 (17. ♖ac1 f6⇄) 17…f6 (17…♖c8 18. ♖ac1±) 18. e×f6 ♖×f6 19. ♘g5 ♘f8 20. ♖e3 h6 21. ♘f3±.

12…h5

12…♗b5 13. ♘d3 h5 14. b4 ♘ac6 15. a4 ♗c4 16. a5 ♛c7⇄.

13. g×h5.

13. g5 ♗b5 14. ♗×b5+ ♛×b5 15. b3⇄.

13…♗b5 14. ♗×b5+

14. ♘g2 ♗×e2 15. ♛×e2 ♖c8↑.

14…♛×b5 15. ♘e3.

15. b4 ♘c4 16. a4 ♛b6 (16…♛d7 17. ♘e3 ♖c8 18. ♘d3±) 17. ♘d3 ♘f5 18. a5 (18. ♗g5∞) 18…♛b5 19. ♗g5⇄.

15…♘ac6 16. b3

16. ♘1c2!?

a) 16…g6 17. ♘g4 (17. b4 ♖×h5 18. a4 ♛b6⇄) 17…0–0–0∞;

b) 16…♖c8 17. a4 ♛b6 18. b4!? ♘×b4 19. a5! ♛b5 20. ♘×b4 ♛×b4 21. ♗a3 ♛b5 22. ♛g4 ♖c3 (22…g6!?∞) 23. ♖fb1 ♖b3 24. ♛d1 ♖×b1 25. ♖×b1 ♛×a5 26. ♗×e7 ♗×e7 27. ♖×b7↑.

16…g6!? 17. ♘g4

17. h×g6 ♘×g6 18. ♘g4 ♗e7 ⯒.

17…0–0–0 18. h6.

18. h×g6 ♘×g6 19. ♗g5 ♗e7 20. ♗×e7 ♘g×e7 ⯒.

18…♘f5 19. ♗g5 ♖d7 =

19…♗e7 20. ♗×e7 ♘c×e7 21. ♖c1+ ♔b8 22. ♘f3 ♘×h6 23. ♖c5 ♛b4 24. ♘×h6 ♖×h6 25. ♛d3⇄.

20. ♘f6 ♖c7 21. ♘e8 ♖d7 22. ♘f6 ♖c7 23. ♘e8 ½–½

Game 66
Volkov – Vaganian
Aeroflot Open, Moscow 2005

1. e4 e6 2. d4 d5 3. e5 b6?! 4. ♘f3 ♕d7 5. c4

5. a4 ♗a6 6. ♗xa6 ♘xa6 7. 0–0±.

5...♘e7.

5...dxc4 6. ♗xc4 ♗a6 7. ♗xa6 ♘xa6 8. ♘c3 ♘b4⇄.

6. ♘c3 ♗b7 7. ♗e3 h6

7...♘bc6 8. ♖c1 dxc4 9. ♗xc4 ♘b4⇄ (9... a6!?).

8. ♖c1 ♘bc6 9. a3 dxc4 10. ♗xc4 ♘f5 11. ♕e2.

11. 0–0.

11...♘xe3 12. fxe3± ♘a5 13. ♗b5 c6 14. ♗a4 b5 15. ♗c2 ♘c4 16. ♗d3± ♗e7

16...♘b6? 17. ♘xb5+–; 16...♖d8 17. 0–0 c5 18. ♘xb5+–.

17. 0–0 .

⌂17. ♗xc4 bxc4 18. ♕xc4 0–0 19. ♘e4+–.

17...0–0 18. ♘e4 a5 19. ♖f2

19. ♗xc4 bxc4 20. ♘fd2 (20. ♘ed2 c5 21. ♘xc4±) 20...c5 21. ♘f6+ ♗xf6 22. exf6 cxd4 23. ♘xc4 dxe3 24. ♕g4 (24. ♘b6 ♕d2 25. ♕g4 g6 26. ♘xa8 ♖xa8=) 24...g5 (24...g6 25. ♘e5+–) 25. ♘xe3 (25. ♘b6 ♕d2 26. ♘xa8 ♖xa8 27. h4 ♔h7!⇄ or 27...♖d8 28. hxg5 h5 29. ♕g3+–) 25...♕d3 26. ♖c3 ♕g6 27. ♘c4±.

19...♗a6□ 20. h3

20. ♗b1 ♖fc8 21. ♕d3 g6 22. b4↑.

20...a4 21. ♘h2 f5.

21...c5!? 22. ♗xc4 bxc4 23. ♘f6+ ♗xf6 24. exf6 cxd4 25. fxg7 ♔xg7 26. ♕g4+ ♔h7 27. ♖f6 ♕d5 28. ♖cf1 ♕g5 29. ♕xd4 c3 30. h4 ♕g7 31. ♕e4+ ♔h8 32. ♖xf7+–.

22. exf6 ♗xf6 23. ♘xf6+ ♖xf6 24. ♖xf6 gxf6 25. ♘g4!

25. ♕g4+ ♔h8 26. ♗xc4 bxc4 27. ♕h4 ♕g7 28. ♘g4 ♕g5 29. ♕xh6+ ♕xh6 30. ♘xh6 c5 31. dxc5 ♔g7 32. ♘g4 ♖c8 33. ♘f2 ♖xc5 34. ♘e4 ♖e5 35. ♘c3 ♖xe3 36. ♔f2 ♖d3 37. ♖c2±.

25...♔g7 26. ♘xf6!?

26. ♕f3+–.

26...♔xf6 27. ♖f1+ ♔e7 28. ♕h5+– ♕d5 29. ♖f7+ ♔d6 30. ♕xh6 ♖e8 31. ♕f4+

31. ♕g7+–.

31...e5 32. ♕h6+ ♕e6□ .

32...♖e6 33. ♕f8+ ♖e7 34. ♕xe7#.

33. ♖f6 exd4 34. exd4 ♗c8 35. ♗f5 ♘xb2 36. ♗xe6 ♗xe6 37. ♖f8 1–0

Game 67
Shabalov – S. Ivanov
Aeroflot Open, Moscow 2005

1. e4 e6 2. d4 d5 3. e5 c5 4. c3 ♕b6 5. ♘f3 ♘c6 6. a3 ♘h6 7. b4 cxd4 8. cxd4 ♘f5 9. ♗b2 ♗e7

9...♗d7.

10. h4.

10. ♗d3!?.

10...a5 11. b5 a4!?

11...h5.

12. g4 ♘h6 13. ♖g1.

13. ♗c1 ♘a5 14. ♗xh6 ♘b3 15. ♗xg7 ♖g8 16. ♖a2 ♖xg7 17. g5 ♕a5+ 18. ♘bd2 ♗d7⇄;

13. ♘c3 Sandipan–Dolmatov, Moscow 2002.

13...♘a5.

13...♘d8 14. ♘c3 ♕a5 15. ♗d3±.

14. ♕xa4 ♗d7 15. ♘bd2N

15. ♗c1!? 0–0± (15...♘g8±);

15. ♘c3 Lavrov–Sambuev, Russian Cup, Tomsk 2003 and Yemelin–Dolmatov, Russian Championship, Krasnoyarsk 2003 (Volume 1, game 125 on page 102);

15. ♗d3 Leuw–Witt, Büssum Open 2004.

15...0–0 16. ♖c1 ♘c4?! .

16...♔h8.

17. ♘xc4 dxc4 18. ♕xc4 ♗xa3

18...♖fc8 19. ♕b3 ♖xc1+ 20. ♗xc1 ♕a5+ 21. ♔d1!? (21. ♗d2 ♕xa3 22. ♕xa3 ♖xa3 23. ♗xh6 gxh6 24. ♗e2 ♗xb5 25. ♗xb5 ♖xf3 26. ♔e2 ♖b3 27. ♗d3 ♗xh4⇄) 21...♗xa3 22. ♗d2 ♕b6 23. ♗d3 ♗c6 24. ♘g5 ♗e7 25. ♔e2±.

19. ♗xa3 ♖xa3 20. ♘d2

20. ♕c7 ♕a7! (20...♕xc7 21. ♖xc7 ♖d8 22. ♗e2 ♗xb5 23. ♗xb5 ♖xf3 24. ♖xb7 ♖f4 25. ♗e2 ♖fxd4 26. f3=) 21. ♕xd7 (21. ♖g3) 21...♖xf3 22. ♖c8 (22. ♗e2 ♖f4⇄) 22...g6 23. ♔e2 ♖b3∓.

20...g6

20...♕a5 21. ♗d3 ♖a2 22. ♕c3 ♕xc3 23. ♖xc3 ♗xb5 24. ♔e2 ♗xd3+ 25. ♔xd3±.

21. ♕b4.

21. ♖b1 ♖fa8 22. ♕c5 ♕a5∓.

21...♖fa8 22. ♘e4

22. ♕d6!? ♕xd6 23. exd6 ♖a1 24. ♔d1

a) 24...♖xc1+ 25. ♔xc1±;

b) 24...f5?! 25. ♘b3 ♖xc1+ 26. ♔xc1 fxg4 27. ♘c5?! (27. ♔b2) 27...♗xb5 28. ♗xb5 ♖a1+ 29. ♔d2 ♖xg1 30. d7 ♘f7 31. ♘xe6 g3 (31...♖g2 32. ♔e3 g3 33. ♗c4+−) 32. fxg3 ♖xg3 33. ♗c4±.

22...♖a1 23. ♖xa1 ♖xa1+ 24. ♔d2 ♔g7 25. ♘c3

25. ♔e3↑.

25...♕d8.

25...♘xg4 26. ♖xg4 ♖xf1⇄.

26. ♕b2! ♕a5 27. ♔c2

27. f3 ♘g8∓.

27...♘xg4! 28. ♖xg4 ♖xf1 29. ♖f4?! .

△29. ♔d3 ♖h1∓.

29...♖a1 30. ♖e4 ♖a3∓ 31. d5 exd5?

31...♗xb5!

a) 32. dxe6 ♗c6! 33. ♖c4 fxe6∓;

b) 32. ♖b4 exd5

b1) 33. e6 d4 34. ♖xd4 fxe6 35. ♖b4 ♔g8∓;

b2) 33. ♖xb5 ♖xc3+ 34. ♔d2 (34. ♕xc3 ♕xb5 35. e6+ ♔f8 36. ♕h8+ ♔e7 37. exf7 ♕e2+ 38. ♔c3 ♕f3+ 39. ♔d4 ♕xf2+ 40. ♔xd5 ♕xf7+−+).

32. e6! d4 33. exd7 dxc3 34. ♕b4□ ♖a2+ 35. ♔xc3 ♕c7+ 36. ♕c4 ♕a5+ 37. ♕b4 ♕c7+ 38. ♕c4 ♕a5+ ½−½

Game 68
Cherniaev – Mason
Coventry Open 2005

1. e4 e6 2. d4 d5 3. e5 c5 4. c3 ♕b6 5. ♘f3 ♘c6 6. a3 ♘h6 7. b4 cxd4 8. cxd4 ♘f5 9. ♗b2 ♗d7 10. g4 ♘fe7 11. ♘c3 ♘a5 12. ♘a4

a) 12. ♘d2!? ♖c8!? (12...♘g6 13. ♘a4±) 13. ♘a4 ♗xa4 14. ♕xa4+ ♘ac6 15. ♖c1 a6 16. ♘b3 h5 17. g5 ♘f5±;

b) 12. ♕c2!? ♘c4 13. ♗xc4 dxc4 14. ♘d2 ♖c8 15. ♘ce4 ♘d5 16. ♘xc4±.

12...♕c6 13. b5

13. ♘c5 ♘c4⇄.

13...♕c7 14. ♖c1?! .

14. ♘c5 ♘c4 15. ♕b3⇄.

14...♘c4∓ 15. ♘d2□

15. ♗xc4 dxc4 16. ♘c5 (16. ♘c3 ♘d5∓) 16...♗xb5∓.

15...♗xb5 16. ♘c3 ♗c6?! .

△16...a6∓.

17. ♗xc4 dxc4 18. ♘xc4?

18. ♘ce4 ♘g6 19. ♖xc4 ♕d7∓.

18...♘g6.

18...♗xh1 19. ♘b5 ♕b8! 20. ♘cd6+ ♔d7 21. ♖c7+ (21. f3 ♘d5∓) 21...♕xc7 22. ♘xc7 ♔xc7 23. ♘xf7 ♖g8 24. f3! ♘d5∓.

19. 0−0 ♘f4 20. f3 ♖d8?

a) 20...b5 21. ♘d6+ (21. ♘e3 ♕b7∓) 21...♗xd6 22. exd6 ♕xd6 23. ♘e4 ♗xe4 24. fxe4 g5 25. d5∞;

b) 20...h5 21. g5 ♕d8 22. h4 ♘g6∓ 23. ♘e4 ♘xh4 24. ♘cd6+ ♗xd6 25. ♘xd6+ ♔f8∓.

21. ♘e4∞ h5 22. g5 ♗e7

22...h4.

23. h4 f6?.

23...0–0 24. ♕d2 ♘g6∓.

24. g×f6 g×f6 25. e×f6 ♗×e4

25...♗f8 26. ♘e5 ♗d6 27. f7+ ♔f8 28. ♘×d6 ♕×d6 29. ♕c2+– or 29. d5!? ♗b5 (29...♗×d5 30. ♗c3+–) 30. ♖e1+–.

26. f×e4 ♗×f6 27. ♔h1

◔27. ♕a4+! b5 28. ♕×b5+ ♔f8 29. ♔h1+–.

27...♖g8?.

27...0–0□ 28. ♘e5 ♕h7 29. ♖×f4 ♗×e5 30. ♖×f8+ ♖×f8 31. ♕c2 (31. ♕e2 ♖f4 32. ♕g2+ ♖g4 33. ♖c8+ ♔g7 34. d×e5 ♖×g2 35. ♖c7+ ♔g6 36. ♖×h7 ♖×b2 37. ♖e7 ♖b6=) 31...♕e7 (31...♖f4? 32. ♕c8++–) 32. ♖g1+ ♗g7 33. ♕h2 ♔h7⇄.

28. ♘e3+– ♕b8 29. ♕f3 ♘d3?

29...♗×d4 30. ♗×d4 ♖×d4 31. ♕×f4 ♕×f4 32. ♖×f4+–.

30. ♕×f6 1–0.

Game 69
Motylev – Anastasian
Dubai Open 2005

1. e4 e6 2. d4 d5 3. e5 c5 4. c3 ♕b6 5. ♘f3 ♗d7 6. a3 c×d4 7. c×d4 ♗b5 8. ♗×b5+ ♕×b5 9. ♘c3 ♕a6 10. b4 ♘d7 11. ♗d2 ♘e7 12. a4 ♕b6! 13. 0–0

13. a5 ♕d8 14. a6 ♖b8 15. a×b7 ♖×b7 16. b5±.

13...a6.

13...♕d8 14. a5 ♘f5 15. ♕b1±.

14. a5 ♕d8 15. b5±

15. ♘a4 ♘c6 16. ♘c5 ♖b8 17. ♕e2 ♗e7 18. ♖fc1±.

15...a×b5 16. ♘×b5.

16. ♕b3!? ♘c6 17. ♕×b5 ♕c8 (17...♖×a5 18. ♕×b7 ♖×a1 19. ♖×a1 ♘a5 20. ♖×a5+–) 18. ♖fc1 ♖a6 19. ♘a4↑.

16...♘c6 17. ♗g5 ♕b8

17...♕c8.

18. ♕c2 h6 19. a6!? .

19. ♗d2 ♗e7 20. a6 ♖×a6 21. ♖×a6 b×a6 22. ♘d6+ ♗×d6 23. ♕×c6 ♗c7 24. ♕×a6 0–0 25. ♖c1 ♘b6⇄.

19...h×g5 20. a×b7 ♖×a1 21. ♕×c6! ♖×f1+ 22. ♔×f1 ♗b4 23. ♘c7+ ♔e7 24. ♘a6□ ♕d8□ 25. ♘×b4 ♘b8 26. ♘×g5 ♔f8 27. ♕c8

27. ♕c5+!

a) 27...♕e7 28. ♕c8+ ♕e8 29. h3 (29. ♘f3 f6 30. ♔e2 ♔f7 31. ♕c7+ ♕e7 32. ♕×e7+ ♔×e7) 29...g6 30. ♘d3 ♔g7 31. ♕c5 ♕d7 32. ♕b4 ♘a6 33. ♕b6 ♕a4 34. ♔e2±;

b) 27...♔e8 28. h3 g6 (28...♕×g5 29. ♕c8+ ♕d8 30. ♘c6 ♘×c6 31. ♕×c6+ ♔e7 32. ♕c5+ ♔e8 33. ♕b5+ ♔e7 34. ♕b4++–) 29. f4 ♖h4 30. ♕c8+–.

27...♕e8 28. ♕c5+

28. ♔g1 g6 29. f4 ♔g7 30. ♕c7 ♕d7 31. ♕×d7 ♘×d7 32. ♘c6 ♘b8 33. ♘a7 ♖e8 34. ♘c8 f6 35. ♘d6 ♖e7 36. ♘f3±.

28...♔g8 29. ♕c8 ♔f8 30. ♘d3 g6

30...♖×h2 31. ♕c7 ♖h1+ 32. ♔e2 ♔g8 33. ♘×f7±.

31. ♘c5 ♔g7 32. ♕×e8?.

32. ♕c7! ♕b5+□ 33. ♔e1 ♕b4+ 34. ♔e2 ♕c4+ 35. ♔f3 ♕c3+ 36. ♔g4 ♕×d4+ 37. ♘ce4!+–.

32...♖×e8 33. h4 ♘c6 34. ♘a6 ♘b8 35. ♘c5= ½–½

Game 70
Fressinet – Halkias
6th European Championship,
Warsaw 2005

1. e4 e6 2. d4 d5 3. e5 c5 4. c3 ♕b6 5. ♘f3 ♗d7 6. a3 a5 7. c4!? c×d4

7...♗c6!?.

8. cxd5 exd5 9. ♕xd4 ♝c5 10. ♕d2 ♘e7 11. ♘c3 a4 12. ♗d3 ♘a6?!

12...♘bc6 13. 0–0 ♝g4⇄.

13. 0–0 ♘c7 14. ♕d1 0–0 15. ♗c2 ♕a6 16. ♗g5 ♝c6?! .

16...♖fe8.

17. ♖c1± ♘e6 18. ♗xe7 ♝xe7 19. ♘d5 ♝c5 20. ♗xh7+

20. ♗d3 ♕a5∞.

20...♔xh7 21. ♖xc5.

21. ♘g5+ ♘xg5 22. ♕h5+ ♔g8 23. ♖xc5 ♝xd5 24. ♖xd5 ♘e6–+.

21...♖fd8??

21...♘xc5 22. ♘g5+ ♔h6□ 23. ♕d4!

a) 23...♕e2□ 24. f3! ♘e4□ 25. ♘xe4 ♝xd5 26. ♘c3 (26. ♕xd5 ♕xb2 27. ♘d6 ♕b3⇄) 26...♕c4 27. ♕d2+ ♔h7 28. ♕xd5 (28. ♘xd5 ♕c5+ 29. ♔h1 ♖fd8 30. ♖d1 ♔h8!–+) 28...♕xd5 29. ♘xd5 ♖a5 30. ♖d1 ♖c8⇄;

b) 23...♔h5? 24. ♕e3! ♘e6 25. ♘xe6 fxe6 26. h4 ♖f5 (26...♔xh4 27. ♕h3+ ♔g5 28. f4+ ♔g6 29. ♕g4+ ♔f7 30. ♕h5+ g6 31. ♕h7+ ♔e8 32. ♕e7#) 27. g4+ ♔g6 28. gxf5+ exf5 29. ♕g5+ ♔h7 30. ♕xf5+ ♔h8 31. ♕h5+ ♔g8 32. ♘e7+ ♔f8 33. ♘g6+ ♔e8 34. ♕g5+–.

22. ♘g5++– ♔g8

22...♔g6 23. ♕g4+–;

22...♔h6 23. ♘xf7+ ♔g6 24. ♕c2+ ♔xf7 25. ♕f5+ ♔g8 (25...♔e8 26. ♕xe6+ ♔f8 27. ♕f5+ ♔e8 28. ♕h5+ ♔f8 29. e6+–) 26. ♘e7+ ♔h8 27. ♕h3#.

23. ♕h5

23. ♘xe6!? ♖xd5 24. ♖xd5 ♝xd5 25. ♘c7+–.

23...♝xd5.

23...♘xg5 24. ♘e7+ ♔f8 25. ♘f5 ♘f3+ 26. gxf3 ♔g8 27. ♕g5 g6 28. ♘e7+ ♔f8 29. e6+–.

24. ♕xf7+ ♔h8 25. ♕h5+ ♔g8 26. ♖xd5 ♘xg5 27. ♖xd8+ ♖xd8 28. ♕xg5 ♕b6 29. ♖e1 ♖f8 30. ♕d2 ♖d8 31. ♕c3 1–0

Game 71
Movsesian – Potkin
6th European Championship,
Warsaw 2005

1. e4 e6 2. d4 d5 3. e5 c5 4. c3 ♘c6 5. ♘f3 ♝d7 6. ♗e2 ♘ge7 7. ♘a3 cxd4 8. cxd4 ♘f5 9. ♘c2 ♕b6 10. h4!?

10. 0–0!.

10...♘b4 11. ♘xb4 ♕xb4+ 12. ♔f1 ♝b5 13. g4 ♝xe2+ 14. ♔xe2 ♘e7 15. h5 ♘c6

15...h6.

16. ♕d3.

16. h6 g6∓.

16...f6?!

16...h6!∓ 17. ♗d2 ♕b6 18. a4 a6!? (18...♝e7 19. a5 ♕d8 20. a6 ♕d7 21. ♖hc1↑) 19. a5 ♕d8 20. ♖hc1 ♝e7∓.

17. a3

17. exf6 gxf6 18. ♖e1±.

17...♕b6.

17...♕e7 18. ♗f4±.

18. exf6 gxf6 19. b4

19. ♖e1!?.

19...0–0–0 .

19...a5 20. b5 ♘a7 21. ♖b1±.

20. ♗e3± ♔b8 21. g5 e5

21...♝e7.

22. dxe5 d4 23. ♗d2 ♘xe5 24. ♘xe5 fxe5 25. f3 e4?! .

25...♕e6⇄.

26. fxe4 ♕e6 27. ♖af1 ♕g4+ 28. ♕f3

28. ♔e1 ♝d6 29. ♖fg1±.

28...d3+ 29. ♔f2 ♕e6 30. ♕f6 ♝c5+?.

30...♕d7! 31. ♗f4+ ♔a8 32. ♕f5 (32. ♕xh8 ♝c5+ 33. bxc5 ♖xh8 34. ♗d6⇄) 32...♕e8!?

(32...♕d4+ 33. ♔f3 ♗d6 34. ♕f6! ♗xf4
35. ♕xd4 ♖xd4 36. ♔xf4 ♖e8 37. g6!±)
33. ♗e5 ♖g8∓.

31. bxc5+– 1–0

Game 72
van Wely – Topalov
Dortmund 2005

**1. d4 e6 2. e4 d5 3. e5 c5 4. c3 ♘c6
5. ♘f3 ♗d7 6. a3?! f6! 7. ♗d3**

7. b4 c4⇄.

**7...♕c7 8. ♗f4 0–0–0 9. 0–0 c4 10. ♗c2
♕b6.**

10...g5!? 11. ♗g3 ♕b6 12. b3 cxb3 13. ♗xb3
g4 14. ♘fd2 fxe5∓.

**11. b3 cxb3 12. ♗xb3 g5 13. ♗e3 g4
14. ♘e1 ♘a5! 15. ♗c2 f5**

15...♘c4 16. exf6 ♘xf6 17. ♗g5 ♗e7
18. ♘d2⇄.

16. ♘d3 ♔b8 17. a4.

17. ♘d2!? ♖c8 18. ♗a4 ♕d8 19. ♗xd7 ♕xd7
20. ♕c2±.

17...♖c8 18. ♕e2

18. ♗c1!? ♘c4 19. ♘d2±.

**18...♕a6 19. ♕e1 b6 20. ♘a3 ♗xa3
21. ♖xa3 ♘e7 22. ♘b4 ♕b7 23. ♗d3
♘c4 24. ♗xc4 dxc4 25. a5 b5 26. a6
♕a8 27. ♕e2 ♘d5 28. ♘xd5 ♕xd5 29. f4
h5 30. ♖b1 h4 31. ♔f1 ♗c6 32. ♗g1 ♔a8
33. ♖b4 ♖b8 34. ♖a2 ♖b6 35. ♔e1 h3
36. g3 ♖c8 37. ♗e3 ♗d7 38. ♖a5 ♕h1+
39. ♔d2 ♗c6 40. ♕f2 ♗d5 41. ♕g1 ♕e4
42. ♔c1 ♖cc6 43. ♕f2 ♖xa6 44. ♖axb5
♖a1+ 45. ♖b1 ♖xb1+ 46. ♖xb1 ♖a6
47. ♕d2 ♕h1+ 0–1**

Game 73
Movsesian – Yusupov
Warsaw 2005

**1. e4 e6 2. d4 d5 3. e5 c5 4. c3 ♘c6
5. ♘f3 ♗d7 6. ♗e2 ♖c8 7. 0–0 ♘ge7**

**8. ♘a3 cxd4 9. cxd4 ♘g6 10. ♘c2 ♗e7
11. ♘fe1?!**

11. ♗d3.

11...f6! 12. f4.

12. exf6 ♗xf6.

12...0–0 13. ♘d3 fxe5 14. fxe5 ♕b6

⌒14...♖xf1+ 15. ♗xf1 ♕c7∓.

**15. ♗e3 ♘h4 16. ♔h1?! ♖xf1+ 17. ♗xf1
♘f5 18. ♗g1.**

18. ♗f2.

**18...a5⇄ 19. ♖c1 ♗g5 20. ♖b1 ♗e8
21. ♘c5 ♘ce7 22. b4!± a4 23. b5 ♗g6
24. ♗d3 ♗h6 25. ♘xa4 ♕a5 26. ♘c5 b6
27. g4**

27. ♘xe6 ♗f7 28. g4! ♗xe6 29. gxf5 ♗xf5
30. ♗xf5 ♘xf5 31. ♕d3 ♘e7 32. ♘b4±.

**27...♘xd4 28. ♘xd4 bxc5 29. ♗xg6
♘xg6 30. ♘xe6?!**

⌒30. g5 cxd4 31. gxh6 ♕xa2 32. ♕g4!? ♖e8
(32...♕xb1 33. ♕xe6+ ♔f8 34. ♕xc8+ ♔f7
35. ♕g4 gxh6 36. ♕f3+ ♔e8 37. ♕xd5 ♘e7
38. ♕a8+ ♔f7 39. ♕f3+±) 33. ♖c1 gxh6
34. ♖c8! ♖xc8 35. ♕xe6+ ♔f8 36. ♕xc8+
♔f7 37. ♕f5+ ♔e8 38. b6±.

30...♕xa2! 31. ♕b3?!

31. ♖a1 ♕c4 32. ♖a4 ♕xb5 33. ♕xd5 ♘e7
34. ♘c7+ ♘xd5 35. ♘xb5 ♗f4! 36. ♖e4 ♖c6
37. ♘d6 ♗xe5 38. ♖xe5 ♖xd6 39. ♗xc5
♖d8=.

31...♕a8?

31...♕xb3 32. ♖xb3 c4 33. ♖a3 ♔f7

a) 34. ♖a6 c3 35. g5 c2 36. ♗e3 c1♕+
37. ♗xc1 ♖xc1+ 38. ♔g2 ♘xe5 39. gxh6
gxh6=;

b) 34. ♘d4 ♘xe5 35. ♖a7+ ♔f6 36. ♖a6+
♔f7= (36...♔g5 37. h3).

32. b6.

32. ♘xc5!±.

32...♕b7

32...c4 33. ♕h3 ♕c6 34. b7 ♕xe6
35. bxc8♕+ ♕xc8 36. ♕f3±.

33. ♘xc5+– ♕f7 34. b7 ♖b8 35. e6 ♕f4 36. ♕xd5 ♘e7 37. ♕e4 1–0

Game 74
Sveshnikov – Berend
37th Olympiad, Turin 2006

1. e4 e6 2. d4 d5 3. e5 c5 4. c3 ♘c6 5. ♘f3 ♕b6 6. a3 ♘h6 7. b4 cxd4 8. cxd4 ♘f5 9. ♗b2 ♗d7 10. g4 ♘h6 11. ♖g1 f6 12. exf6 gxf6 13. ♘c3 ♘f7 14. ♘a4 ♕c7 15. ♖c1 ♕f4 16. ♘c5 ♗xc5 17. dxc5

17. ♖xc5∞.

17...♘fe5 18. ♘xe5.

18. ♖g3!? ♖f8 19. ♗e2∞.

18...fxe5!?

18...♘xe5 19. ♖g3 a5!?∞.

19. ♕d2.

19. b5 ♘d4 20. ♗xd4 exd4 21. c6 bxc6 22. bxc6 ♗c8⇄.

19...♕xd2+ 20. ♔xd2 0–0

20...♘d4!?⇄.

21. ♔e1 ♖f4?! .

a) 21...♘d4 22. ♗xd4 exd4⇄;

b) 21...a6

b1) 22. ♖g3 ♘d4 23. ♗g2 ♖f4⇄;

b2) 22. g5 ♘d4 23. ♗xd4 exd4∓ 24. ♖g3 (24. ♗h3 ♖ad8 25. ♖g3 e5 26. ♗g2 ♗b5 27. h4) 24...e5 25. ♗g2 ♗e6 26. h4⇄.

22. b5 ♘d4

22...♖e4+ 23. ♗e2 ♘d4 24. ♗xd4 exd4 25. ♔d2 (25. c6 bxc6 26. bxc6 ♗xc6 27. ♖xc6 d3 28. ♔d2 dxe2 29. f3 ♖a4 30. ♖a1∓) 25...♖f8 26. ♖g2⇄.

23. ♗xd4 exd4

23...♖xd4 24. ♖g3±.

24. c6 bxc6 25. bxc6 ♗c8 26. c7 a5!? .

26...e5!? 27. ♖b1 ♗e6 28. ♖b8+ ♖f8 29. ♖xa8 ♖xa8 30. f4± (30. ♗a6 ♗c8 31. ♗e2±).

27. ♖g3 a4 28. ♖d3

28. g5 ♖f7 29. g6 hxg6 30. ♖xg6+ ♔h8 31. ♖g4 ♖a7 32. ♖xd4 ♖fxc7 33. ♖xc7 ♖xc7 34. ♗b5±.

28...♖a7 29. ♖d2

29. h3±.

29...♖f3.

29...♖f7 30. ♖xd4 ♖axc7 31. ♖xc7 ♖xc7 32. ♗b5 ♖c5 33. ♖b4 ♖c3 34. ♖xa4 e5 35. h4±.

30. ♗d3!?

30. ♖xd4 ♖xa3 31. ♖b4 ♖f3!⇄.

30...e5 31. ♖b2!± e4 32. ♖b8 ♖f8 33. ♗b5 ♔g7 34. f4!?

34. h3!?±.

34...d3.

34...♗xg4 35. ♖xf8 ♔xf8 36. c8♕+ ♗xc8 37. ♖xc8+ ♔e7 38. ♖c6 ♖a5 (38...h5 39. h4±).

35. ♖c5

35. h3±.

35...♗xg4 36. ♖xd5.

36. ♖xf8 ♔xf8 37. c8♕+ ♗xc8 38. ♖xc8+ ♔e7 39. ♔d2 ♖b7 40. ♗xa4 ♖b2+ 41. ♔e3 (41. ♔c3 ♖a2 42. ♔d4 ♖xa3⇄) 41...♖xh2 42. ♔d4±.

36...♖xc7 37. ♖g5+ ♔f7 38. ♖xf8+ ♔xf8 39. ♖xg4+– ♖c3?!

39...♖c2 40. ♖g3 ♖e2+ 41. ♔f1! ♔f7 42. ♖g2 ♖c2 43. ♗xa4 ♖c3 (43...♖c1+ 44. ♔f2 d2 45. ♔e2 e3 46. ♗d1+–) 44. ♖a2 e3 45. ♖a1 ♔f6 46. ♗b5 ♔f5 47. a4 ♔xf4 48. a5 d2 49. ♖a4+ ♔e5 50. ♗e2 ♖c1+ 51. ♔g2 d1♕ 52. ♗xd1 ♖xd1 53. ♔f3+–.

40. ♔d2 ♖xa3 41. ♗c4 ♖a1 42. f5 a3 43. f6 ♔e8 44. f7+ ♔e7 45. ♖xe4+ 1–0

Game 75
Shabalov – Abrahamyan
34th World Open, Philadelphia 2006

1. e4 e6 2. d4 d5 3. e5 c5 4. c3 ♘c6 5. ♘f3 ♕b6 6. a3 ♘h6 7. b4 cxd4 8. cxd4

♘f5 9. ♗b2 ♗d7 10. ♖a2!? ♖c8 11. ♗a1 ♗e7 12. ♗e2 h5 13. 0–0 g5 14. ♖d2?!

14. b5 ♘a5 15. a4 g4 16. ♘e1 ⇄.

14...g4 15. ♘e1 ♗g5 16. b5.

16. ♖d3 ♘cxd4 17. ♗xd4 ♘xd4 18. ♖xd4 ♖c1 19. ♕d3 ♖xb1 20. ♘c2 ♖xf1+ 21. ♗xf1 ♕c7!∓.

16...♘a5

16...♘ce7∓.

17. ♖c2 ♖xc2 18. ♘xc2 ♗xb5∓ 19. ♘c3 ♗d7?! .

19...♗xe2 20. ♕xe2 ♘c4 21. ♖b1 ♕c6∓.

20. ♗d3 ⩱ ♘h4 21. ♕e2 a6 22. ♖b1 ♕d8 23. ♘e3 ♖g8 24. ♔h1 b5 25. a4 bxa4 26. ♗xa6 ♘b3 27. ♕d3?!

27. ♘xa4! ♗xa4 28. ♗b5+ ♗xb5 29. ♕xb5+ ♔f8 30. ♕xb3 (30. ♖xb3 ♗xe3 31. fxe3 ♘f5 32. ♕f1 ⇄) 30...♔g7 31. ♕d3 ♘g6 32. ♗c3 ⇄.

27...♕a5∓ 28. ♘e2 ♘xa1 29. ♖xa1 ♗xe3 30. fxe3 ♘f5 31. ♘c3 ♔e7 32. e4 dxe4 33. ♘xe4 ♗c6 34. ♖c1?

34. ♕a3+! ♔d8 35. ♘f6 ♖h8 36. ♗d3†.

34...♗xe4–+ 35. ♕xe4 ♕xa6 36. d5 ♖c8 37. d6+ ♔d8 38. ♖d1 ♕c4 39. ♕e1 ♕c3 0–1

Game 76
Sveshnikov – Ghane Gardeh
36th Olympiad, Calvià 2004

1. e4 e6 2. d4 d5 3. e5 c5 4. c3 ♗d7 5. ♘f3 ♘c6 6. ♗e3 ♘ge7 7. ♗d3

7. dxc5!?.

7...♕b6 8. dxc5!? ♕xb2 9. 0–0 ♘f5.

9...g5!?∞; 9...♕xa1 10. ♕d2±.

10. ♗xf5 exf5

10...♕xa1 11. ♕d2 exf5 12. ♘a3 ♕xf1+ 13. ♔xf1±.

11. ♘bd2.

11. ♕b3 ♕xb3 12. axb3 a6⇄.

11...♕xc3 12. ♖b1 d4

12...♖b8.

13. ♖xb7 ♗xc5□ .

13...♕xc5 14. ♘xd4 ♘xd4 15. ♖xd7 ♔xd7 16. ♘b3+–.

14. ♘b3 ♗b6 15. ♘bxd4?

15. ♘fxd4! ♘xd4 16. ♖xd7!

a) 16...♘xb3 17. ♕d6 ♗c5 18. ♗xc5 ♕xc5 19. ♖e7+ ♔f8 20. ♖xa7+! ♕xd6 21. ♖xa8+ ♔e7 22. exd6+ ♔xd6 23. ♖xh8+–;

b) 16...♘e2+ 17. ♕xe2 ♔xd7 18. ♕b5+ ♔e7 19. ♖c1 ♕xe3 20. fxe3 ♗xe3+ 21. ♔f1 ♗xc1 22. ♕c5++–;

c) 16...♔xd7 17. ♗xd4 ♗xd4 18. ♘xd4+– ♔e8 (18...♔c8 19. ♘b5 ♕c5 20. ♘d6+ ♔c7 21. ♕d2+–) 19. ♘xf5 ♖d8 20. ♕a4+ ♔f8 21. ♕xa7 ♕xe5 22. ♕a3+ ♔g8 23. ♘e7+ ♔f8 24. ♘g6+ ♔g8 25. ♘xe5+–.

15...♘xd4 16. ♖xd7 ♘xf3+

16...♔xd7 17. ♗xd4 ♗xd4 18. ♘xd4.

17. ♕xf3 0–0□ .

17...♔xd7 18. ♖d1+ ♔e7 19. ♗g5+ f6 20. exf6+ gxf6 21. ♕xc3+–.

18. ♕xf5 ♖ae8!

18...♗xe3 19. fxe3 ♕c4! 20. a4 ♖ae8 21. ♖xa7±.

19. ♗xb6.

⌒19. ♗f4!?±.

19...axb6 20. f4± ♖a8 21. ♕b1 ♕e3+ 22. ♔h1 ♕e2 23. ♖g1 ♕xa2 24. ♕xb6 ♖ab8 25. ♕d4± h6 26. h3 ♕e6 27. ♖f1 ♖b3 28. f5 ♕a6 29. ♖a1 ♕c6 30. ♔h2 ♖b2 31. ♖g1 ♖b4 32. ♕xb4 ♕xd7 33. ♕e4 ♕c7 34. ♔h1 ♖e8 35. ♖e1 ♕c3± 1–0

Game 77
Sveshnikov – Bochkarev
Riga (Rapidplay) 2005

1. e4 e6 2. d4 d5 3. e5 c5 4. c3 ♘c6 5. ♘f3 ♕b6 6. a3 a5 7. b3 f6

7...♗d7 8. ♗e2 (8. ♗e3 ♘h6 9. ♗d3 ♘g4 10. 0–0 ♗e7 11. ♘bd2 ♘xe3 12. fxe3 0–0⇄) 8... cxd4 9. cxd4 ♘ge7⇄.

8. ♗d3 ♗d7 9. 0–0 cxd4 10. cxd4± f5?! 11. ♗e2 h6 12. h4 ♗e7 13. h5 ♗f8

13...♔d8!?.

14. ♘c3 ♘ge7 15. ♘a4 ♕c7 16. ♖a2 g5 17. hxg6 ♘xg6 18. ♘e1 ♗e7 19. ♗h5 ♔f7 20. ♖c2 ♕d8 21. ♘d3 ♔g7 22. ♗xg6 ♔xg6 23. ♘ac5+– ♘xd4 24. ♘f4+ ♔h7 25. ♕xd4 ♗xc5 26. ♖xc5 ♖g8 27. ♗e3 ♖g4 28. f3 ♖g5 29. ♖fc1 h5 30. ♖c7+– 1–0

Game 78
Sveshnikov – Galstian
Aeroflot Open, Moscow 2005

1. e4 e6 2. d4 d5 3. e5 c5 4. c3 ♕b6 5. ♘f3 ♗d7 6. a3 a5 7. b3

a) 7. a4!? ♘c6 8. ♗b5 cxd4 9. cxd4 ♖c8 10. ♘c3 ♘ge7 11. 0–0 ♘f5⇄;

b) 7. ♗e2 ♘c6 8. 0–0 a4 9. ♗d3

b1) 9...♘a5 10. ♗c2 ♘c4 11. ♖a2!?±;

b2) 9...cxd4 10. cxd4 ♘xd4 11. ♘xd4 ♕xd4 12. ♘c3⩱ (12. ♕e2⩱).

7...♘c6!? 8. ♗e3

8. ♗e2!? cxd4 (8...♘ge7 9. dxc5 ♕c7 10. 0–0±) 9. cxd4 ♘ge7 10. ♖a2 (10. ♘c3 ♘f5 11. ♘a4 ♕a7 12. ♗b2 b5! 13. ♗xb5 ♘xe5 14. ♗xd7+ ♘xd7 15. ♖c1⇄) 10...♘f5 11. ♖d2 ♗e7 12. 0–0 ♖c8 13. ♗b2 h5 14. ♘c3 g5 15. ♘a4 ♕a7 16. ♘e1 g4 17. ♘c2⇄.

8...♘h6 9. ♗d3 ♘g4 10. 0–0 ♗e7 11. ♘bd2

11. dxc5

a) 11...♘xe3 12. cxb6 ♘xd1 13. ♖xd1 ♗c5 14. c4 ♘d4⇄ 15. cxd5 ♘xb3 16. ♖a2 exd5 17. ♘c3 d4 18. ♘d5 ♖d8 19. ♗c4±;

b) 11...♕c7 12. ♕e2 (12. ♗d4 ♘gxe5 13. ♘xe5 ♘xe5 14. ♖e1 ♘xd3 15. ♕xd3

♗xc5 16. ♗xg7 ♕f4⇄) 12...♘gxe5 13. ♘xe5 ♕xe5;

If 13...♘xe5 then 14. ♗f4 f6 15. b4 0–0 16. ♘d2 b6 17. ♘f3 ♘xf3+ 18. ♕xf3 ♕c6 19. cxb6 ♕xb6 (19...e5 20. ♖fe1 (20. ♕h5!? g6 21. ♗xg6 hxg6 22. ♕xg6+ ♔h8 23. ♕h5+ ♔g8 24. ♗h6 f5 25. ♗xf8 ♗xf8 26. bxa5 ♖xa5 27. ♖fb1±) 20...♗e6 21. bxa5±) 20. ♖fe1± (20. ♖fb1 ♖ac8⇄).

11...♘xe3 12. fxe3 0–0 13. ♕b1 g6 14. h4

14. ♕e1⇄.

14...cxd4 15. cxd4.

15. exd4 f5∞ (15...f6 16. ♗xg6 hxg6 17. ♕xg6+ ♔h8=).

15...♔g7 16. ♕e1 f5 17. exf6+ ♗xf6 18. ♕g3 ♖ac8!

18...e5.

19. ♘g5?! .

19. ♖ac1⇄.

19...♕c7! 20. ♕g4?!

20. ♕xc7 ♖xc7 21. ♖ac1 h6∓.

20...e5 21. ♘e6+ ♗xe6 22. ♕xe6 e4∓ .

22...exd4–+.

23. ♗b5 ♘xd4 24. exd4 ♗xd4+ 25. ♔h1 ♗xa1–+ 26. ♖xa1 ♕f4 27. ♖f1 ♕xh4+ 28. ♔g1 ♖xf1+ 29. ♘xf1 ♖d8 30. ♕b6 ♕e7 31. ♘g3 ♖d6 32. ♕xa5 b6 33. ♕b4

△33. ♕c3+.

33...♕e5 34. ♘f1 d4 35. ♘d2 ♖e6 36. ♗d7 ♖f6 37. ♗b5 h5 38. a4 h4 39. ♕c4

39. ♘c4 ♕f4–+.

39...h3 40. ♕e2 e3 41. ♘f3 ♕g3 42. ♗d3 ♖c6 43. ♗c4 ♖xc4! 44. bxc4 d3 45. ♕b2+ ♔h7 46. ♘e5 d2 0–1

Game 79
Sveshnikov – Monakhov
Miass 2005

1. e4 e6 2. d4 d5 3. e5 c5 4. c3 ♘c6 5. ♘f3 ♗d7 6. ♗e2 ♘h6 7. ♗xh6

7. ♘a3; 7. 0–0.

7...gxh6 8. 0–0 ♕b6 9. ♕d2 ♗g7 10. ♘a3 cxd4 11. cxd4 0–0 12. ♘c2 f6 13. exf6 ♖xf6 14. b4 ♖af8 15. a4

15. b5 ♘a5 (15...♘e7 16. ♘e5 ♗e8 17. a4±) 16. ♘e5 ♗e8 17. ♗d3±.

15...♖f4 16. a5 ♕d8 17. b5 ♘e7 18. ♖a3±

18. a6 b6 19. ♖a3±.

18...♕e8 19. ♖b1 ♘g6 20. g3?! .

20. b6! axb6 21. ♖xb6 ♗c6 22. a6 bxa6 23. ♖axa6 ♗d7 24. ♖a7 ♖4f7 25. ♘e3 ♘f4 (25...e5 26. ♘xd5 e4 27. ♘e5 ♘xe5 28. dxe5 ♕xe5 29. ♗c4 ♔h8 30. ♘e3 ♖xf2 31. ♕xd7+−) 26. ♗d1±.

20...♖4f5 21. ♕d1?!

21. b6±.

21...♕f7 22. ♔g2?! .

22. b6±.

22...e5 23. dxe5 ♘xe5 24. ♘cd4 ♔h8?

24...♖h5⇄.

25. ♖bb3?.

25. ♘xf5 ♗xf5 26. ♘xe5 ♗xe5 27. ♖bb3±.

25...♖h5 26. ♕e1 ♗c8 27. ♘xe5 ♖xe5 28. ♖e3?

28. ♖f3±.

28...♖xe3 29. fxe3 ♗xd4.

29...♕e7−+.

30. exd4 ♕e7 31. ♖f3 ♖e8∓ ½–½

Game 80
Sveshnikov – Rustemov
Russian League (Rapidplay),
Dagomys 2005

1. e4 e6 2. d4 d5 3. e5 ♘e7 4. ♘f3 b6 5. c3 ♕d7 6. a4 ♗a6 7. ♗xa6 ♘xa6 8. 0–0 c5 9. ♕e2 ♘c7 10. b3 ♘c6 11. ♗e3 ♗e7 12. ♖d1 cxd4 13. cxd4 0–0 14. ♗g5 ♘a5 15. ♕d3 ♖fc8 16. ♘bd2 ♗f8 17. ♘f1 h6 18. ♗d2 ♘e8 19. g4 ♗e7 20. h4 ♖c7 21. g5 hxg5 22. hxg5 ♖ac8

23. ♘1h2 ♘c6 24. g6 ♗d8 25. ♘g4 f5!? 26. ♘gh2?!

26. exf6! gxf6 (26...♗xf6 27. ♘fe5±) 27. ♘h6+ ♔g7 28. ♘f7 ♗e7 29. ♗h6+ ♔g8 30. ♗f4 ♘b4 31. ♕f1 e5 32. dxe5 ♕g4+ 33. ♕g2 ♕xg2+ (33...♕xf4 34. ♕h3+−) 34. ♔xg2±.

26...a5 27. ♘g5?!

27. ♘e1±; 27. ♕e2!± ♘e7 28. ♘h4+−.

27...♗xg5 28. ♗xg5 ♘e7□ 29. ♕h3 ♘xg6 30. ♘f3 ♖c3 31. ♔g2 ♖xb3 32. ♖ac1 ♖cc3 33. ♖xc3 ♖xc3 34. ♖b1 ♕xa4 35. ♖xb6 ♕d7! 36. ♗d2 ♖c6?

a) 36...a4?!⇄

a1) 37. ♕h5 ♖b3 38. ♖a6 ♘f8∓;

a2) 37. ♖b1!? ♖b3 38. ♖h1 ♔f8 (38...♘f8 39. ♕h8+ ♔f7 40. ♘g5+ ♔e7 41. ♕g8+−) 39. ♕h5→;

b) 36...♖a3! 37. ♖b8 ♘f8 38. ♕h5 g6 39. ♕h4∞.

37. ♖b1± ♖c8 38. ♘g5 ♔f8 39. ♕h5 ♖c2 40. ♕xg6 ♖xd2 41. ♘xe6+ ♔e7 42. ♘c5 1–0

Game 81
Sveshnikov – Filippov
Satka 2005

1. e4 e6 2. d4 d5 3. e5 c5 4. c3 ♘c6 5. ♘f3 ♘h6 6. dxc5 ♗xc5 7. b4 ♗e7 8. ♗xh6 gxh6 9. b5 ♘b8

9...♘a5 10. ♗d3±.

10. ♗d3 f5?.

10...♕c7.

11. 0–0

11. ♘d4!? 0–0 12. f4±.

11...0–0 .

⌒11...♕c7.

12. c4!± b6 13. ♘c3

13. cxd5 ♕xd5 14. ♘c3 ♕c5 15. ♘e2+−.

13...♗b7 14. cxd5 ♗xd5 15. ♘xd5 ♕xd5 16. ♕e2+− ♖c8 17. ♖fd1 ♕c5 18. ♕d2 ♔g7 19. ♖ac1 1–0

Game 82
Sveshnikov – Dizdar
Slovenian Championship, Bled 2005

1. e4 e6 2. d4 d5 3. e5 c5 4. c3 ♘c6 5. ♘f3 ♕b6 6. a3 ♘h6 7. b4 c×d4 8. c×d4 ♘f5 9. ♗b2 ♗d7 10. g4 ♘h6 11. ♖g1 ♖c8!?

11...f6?! 12. e×f6 g×f6 13. ♘c3±.

12. ♘c3 ♘a5 13. ♘a4.

13. ♘d2.

13...♕c6 14. ♘c5

14. b×a5 ♕×a4 15. ♕×a4 ♗×a4 16. ♗d3⇄.

14...♘c4□ 15. ♗c1.

15. ♗c3 b6 16. ♘×d7 ♕×d7 17. ♗d3∞.

15...♘g8!? 16. ♗d3

16. ♖g3∞.

16...♗×c5 17. d×c5.

17. b×c5 b6∓.

17...b6! 18. ♗×c4∓ ½–½

Game 83
Sveshnikov – Topi-Hulmi
Keres Memorial (Rapidplay),
Tallinn 2006

1. e4 c5 2. c3 e6 3. d4 d5 4. e5 ♘c6 5. ♘f3 ♗d7 6. ♗e2 ♕b6 7. 0–0 c×d4 8. c×d4 ♘ge7 9. ♘a3 ♘f5 10. ♘c2 ♗e7 11. ♗d3

11. b4; 11. b3; 11. g4.

11...g6 12. g4!? .

12. b3.

12...♘h4

12...♘g7?!.

13. ♘×h4 ♗×h4 14. g5 h6 15. g×h6 0–0–0 .

15...♗e7.

16. b4! ♗e7

16...f5 17. e×f6 ♗×f6 18. ♗e3 ♘e7 19. a4±.

17. ♗e3.

17. a4.

17...♗f8 18. ♕d2 ♘e7 19. a4 ♖e8 20. a5 ♕d8 21. ♗g5 ♔b8 22. b5 ♔a8 23. ♖fc1 +– ♕b8 24. b6 a6 25. ♘b4 ♘f5 26. ♘×a6 b×a6 27. ♗×f5

27. ♗×a6+–.

27...g×f5 28. ♖c7 ♗b5 29. ♖ac1 ♗c4.

29...♗a3.

30. ♖1×c4 d×c4 31. ♕e2 ♕×c7 32. b×c7 ♔b7 33. ♕b2+ ♔×c7 34. ♕b6+ ♔d7 35. ♕b7# 1–0

Game 84
Sveshnikov – Bareev
37th Olympiad, Turin 2006

1. e4 e6 2. d4 d5 3. e5 c5 4. c3 ♘c6 5. ♘f3 ♗d7 6. ♗e2 ♖c8 7. 0–0 a6 8. ♘a3!?

8. d×c5; 8. b3.

8...c×d4.

8...♘ge7 Sveshnikov – Razuvaev, Moscow (Rapidplay) 1992 (game 98 on page 79).

9. c×d4 ♗×a3

9...♘ge7.

10. b×a3 ♘ge7 11. ♖b1 ♘a5 12. a4.

12. ♗d3.

12...♗c6 13. ♗d3± h6

13...♘c4 14. ♘d2 (14. ♘g5 h6 15. ♕h5 g6 16. ♕h3↑) 14...♘f5 (14...0–0 15. ♕h5↑) 15. ♗×f5 e×f5 16. ♕f3±.

14. ♗c2

14. ♘d2!? ♘c4 15. ♕g4↑.

14...♘c4 15. ♘e1 a5?! 16. h4!? .

16. ♕g4 g6±.

16...♘f5 17. g3 0–0

17...♕d7 18. ♘g2⇄.

18. ♘g2 ♕e7 19. ♘f4.

19. ♕d3 h5 (19...f6 20. g4 f×e5 21. g×f5 e4 22. ♕g3 ♖×f5 23. ♗×h6 ♘a3 24. ♖bc1 ♘×c2

25. ♖xc2 ♕f6 26. ♗e3±) 20. ♘f4 g6 21. ♕c3 ♘g7 22. ♘d3±.

19...♘a3 20. ♗xf5 exf5 21. ♗xa3

21. ♖b2 ♘c4 22. ♖e2 ♕d7 23. ♕d3 ♗xa4 24. e6 fxe6 25. ♘xe6 ♗b5∓.

21...♕xa3 22. ♕h5?! .

22. ♕b3 ♕e7 23. ♘xd5 ♗xd5 24. ♕xd5 ♖fd8 25. ♕xb7 ♕xb7 26. ♖xb7 ♖xd4 27. ♖fb1±.

22...♕xa4 23. ♖fd1 ♕c2 24. ♖e1 ♖ce8 25. ♖bc1 ♕b2 26. ♖cd1

26. ♕xf5 ♕xd4 27. ♖cd1 ♕c4 28. ♖d2∞.

26...♗a4 27. ♖c1 ♕xd4 28. ♕xf5 ♗c6 29. ♖cd1 ♕b4 30. ♕d3 ♕c4 31. ♕d2 a4 32. ♖c1

32. ♘xd5 ♕g4∓.

32...♕b5 33. ♕d4 a3 34. ♖c2 ♖e7 35. ♖c3 ♖a8 36. ♖b3 ♕c4 37. ♕d2 d4 38. ♖c1?!

38. ♖b4 ♕c5∓ 39. ♕xd4 ♖xe5!−+.

38...♕a4!∓ 39. ♖b4 ♕a5 40. e6 fxe6 41. ♕xd4 ♖d8 42. ♕c4 ♕f5 43. ♖e1 g5 44. ♖xe6 ♖xe6 0−1

Game 85
Sveshnikov – Batchuluun
37th Olympiad, Turin 2006

1. e4 e6 2. d4 d5 3. e5 c5 4. c3 ♘c6 5. ♘f3 ♕b6 6. a3 c4 7. ♘bd2 ♘a5 8. g3 ♗d7 9. h4 0−0−0 10. ♗h3 f5 11. exf6 gxf6 12. 0−0 ♘h6

12...♘e7.

13. ♖e1?! .

13. ♖b1; 13. b4!? cxb3 14. ♖b1 ♘f5 15. ♘xb3 ♗a4 16. ♘fd2 ♔b8 17. ♖e1±.

13...♗g7

13...e5! 14. ♗xd7+ ♖xd7 15. dxe5 ♗c5→.

14. ♖b1 ♖he8 15. ♕c2 e5 16. ♗xd7+ ♖xd7 17. ♕h7?.

17. b3 cxb3 18. ♘xb3 ♘xb3 19. ♖xb3 ♕a6 20. ♗xh6 (20. ♕xh7 ♖h8 21. ♕g6 e4 22. ♘d2 ♕d3 23. ♘f1 ♕c4 24. ♖b1±) 20...♗xh6 21. dxe5 ♗g7 22. c4 dxc4 23. ♖c3 ♖c7 24. ♕xh7±.

17...f5

17...e4 18. ♕g6∞.

18. h5?! .

18. ♘xe5 ♗xe5 19. ♘xc4 ♘xc4 (19...♖xh7 20. ♘xb6+ axb6 21. ♗xh6 ♖xh6 22. dxe5∓).

18...e4!−+ 19. b4 cxb3 20. ♘xb3 ♖h8 21. ♘xa5 ♕xb1 22. ♕g6 ♕b6

22...exf3 23. ♘c6 bxc6 24. ♕xc6+ ♖c7 25. ♕e6+ ♔b7 26. ♗xh6 ♕b5 27. ♗f4⩱.

23. ♘e5 ♗xe5 24. dxe5 ♕xg6 25. hxg6 ♘g4 26. ♗f4 ♖e7 27. ♖b1 ♖g8 28. ♖b5

28. e6 ♖xg6 29. ♘c6 ♖gxe6 30. ♘xa7+ ♔d8 31. ♗g5 ♘f6 32. ♘b5 ♖g7 33. ♘d4 ♖a6 34. ♗xf6+ ♖xf6 35. ♖b5 ♖d7∓.

28...♖xg6 29. ♖xd5 ♖b6 30. ♘c4?

30. e6 ♖exe6 (30...♖b1+ 31. ♔g2 ♖xe6 32. ♖xf5 ♖b2 33. ♖c5+ ♔d8∓) 31. ♖xf5 ♖b1+ 32. ♔g2 ♖b2∓.

30...♖b1+ 31. ♔g2 ♖h7−+ 32. ♘d6+

32. ♖c5+ ♔d7 33. e6+ ♔xe6−+.

32...♔c7!.

32...♔b8 33. ♘xe4 fxe4 34. e6+ ♔c8 35. ♖c5+ ♔d8 36. ♗g5+ ♖e7 37. ♖c4 ♖b2 38. ♖xe4 ♘xf2 39. ♖d4+ ♔e8 40. ♗xe7 ♔xe7 41. ♔f3 ♔xe6∓.

33. ♘e8+ ♔c6 34. ♖d6+ ♔c5 35. ♗e3+ ♔c4 36. ♗h6 ♖xh6 0−1

Appendix

I- indicates page numbers in Volume 1
II- indicates page numbers in Volume 2

Index of themes

Index of names

Index of games

A page number in normal print means the first-named player had White; bold indicates that the player had Black; italic is used for games in the Encyclopaedia section. A page number between brackets means that a reference to this game can be found on the page indicated.

Index of variations